INTRODUCTION TO LITERATURE

Anna Faktorovich, PhD
EDITOR

ANAPHORA LITERARY PRESS

QUANAH, TEXAS

Anaphora Literary Press
1108 W 3rd Street
Quanah, TX 79252
https://anaphoraliterary.com

Book design by Anna Faktorovich, Ph.D.

Copyright © 2018 by Anna Faktorovich

All rights reserved. No part of this book may be reproduced in any form or by any electronic or mechanical means, including information storage and retrieval systems, without permission in writing from Anna Faktorovich. Writers are welcome to quote brief passages in their critical studies, as American copyright law dictates.

Printed in the United States of America, United Kingdom and in Australia on acid-free paper.

Edited by: Rebecca Baird

Published in 2018 by Anaphora Literary Press

Introduction to Literature
Anna Faktorovich—1st edition.

Library of Congress Control Number: 2018906964

Library Cataloging Information
Faktorovich, Anna, 1981-, author.
   Introduction to literature / Anna Faktorovich
   300 p. ; 9 in.
   ISBN 978-1-68114-442-9 (softcover : alk. paper)
   ISBN 978-1-68114-443-6 (hardcover : alk. paper)
   ISBN 978-1-68114-444-3 (e-book)
1. Language Arts & Disciplines—Reading Skills.
2. Literary Criticism—Comparative Literature.
3. Fiction—Literary.
PE1001-1693: Modern English
808: Rhetoric & collections of literature

INTRODUCTIOIN TO LITERATURE

ANNA FAKTOROVICH

CONTENTS

Introduction	7
Comprehending and Writing About Readings	9
Types of Literary Criticism	10
Short Stories and Novel Segments	**14**
Fiction Terms	14
Edgar Allan Poe	19
The Sphinx	22
Hop-Frog	31
How to Write a Blackwood Article	44
Miguel de Cervantes	58
Don Quixote	59
The Author's Preface	61
Dedication of Volume I	67
Volume I. Chapter I	68
Chapter II	72
Notes on the Text	78
Chapter III	84
Chapter IV	89
Chapter V	95
Notes on the Text	99
Jonathan Swift	105
Gulliver's Travels	107
The Publisher to the Reader	107
A Letter from Captain Gulliver	108
Part I. A Voyage to Lilliput: Chapter I	112
Chapter II	120
Notes on Text	128
Chapter III	136
Chapter IV	142
Chapter V	146
Notes on the Text	151
Play	**153**
Drama Terms	153
Aristophanes	158
Lysistrata	160
Notes on Text: First Half	183

Lysistrata Continued…	187
Questions for Discussion: Second Half	233

Poetry — 234

Poetic Terms	234
William Shakespeare	239
It Was a Lover and His Lass	240
To His Love	241
True Love	242
End of the Civil War: From King Richard III, Act I. Sc. I.	243
Sir Walter Scott	245
To a Lock of Hair	248
The Outlaw	249
Scotland: From "The Lay of the Last Minstrel", Canto VI	251
Beal' an Dhuine (1411): From "The Lady of The Lake", Canto VI	252
Lord George Gordon, 6th Baron Byron	258
All for Love	261
Oscar Wilde	262
Ave Imperatrix	263
Elizabeth Barrett Browning	267
A Court Lady	268
Robert Browning	271
Incident of the French Camp	272
Rudyard Kipling	274
Danny Deever	275
Edgar Allan Poe	278
Annabel Lee	279
Walt Whitman	282
To a Foiled Revolter or Revoltress	282
Henry W. Longfellow	284
The Song of Hiawatha	284

Assignments — 295

Comparison/Contrast	295
Close Reading of Lysistrata	297
6-Page Research Paper	298

INTRODUCTION

While there are some shorter books in the market, they typically fail to offer enough contextual and critical information to be the sole textbooks for a course. This book is perfectly suitable for the content that can fit into a single semester. The readings are obscure enough that students are not likely to have been exposed to them previously. At the same time, they are canonical enough to enrich their understanding of the major tropes of literary history. Each of the sections on fiction, drama and poetry provides the most essential definitions and concept related to these fields, without becoming repetitive. Succinct information allows students to consume the important bits of knowledge that will help them succeed in their essays and other components of the class.

Literary theory should be the focus of any Introductory Literature course because students have to understand what literary criticism is to apply it to their own essays about the literature they are reading. While the Introductory Literature books are more expensive than graduate textbooks on literary studies because they are much thicker, frequently running at over 1,000 pages, they are also more expensive because more students are required to take these introductory classes, so they cannot avoid the class simply because of the prohibitive cost of the books. In colleges with impoverished student populations there should be more Intro textbook alternatives at the lower price range. This brief textbook attempts a condensed alternative.

Over my years as a college instructor, I have taught from most of the Introduction to Literature textbooks available in the market. And I have read as part of my research into the field the remainder of the commonly used texts. From my study of these books, they all convey some of the same information in pretty much the same way. Thus, if a student took a literature course in high school, much of what is covered in even the most expensive books like Kennedy and Gioia's *Literature* is a repetition of something the students read before. I shake this formula up and bring in unique perspectives on literature that propose theories that have not even been published in scholarly journals before. For example, I examine the merchants' language that Swift uses to disguise his meaning. Swift combines several different languages together to give the appearance of it being an invented language, but clearly, he hid messages in this language only accessible to merchants with knowledge of several languages. Understanding Swift's seemingly made up words is easier today than ever before because translation programs like Google Translate instantly interpret words even if their spelling is slightly divergent from the standard. This explanation made my students curious to find additional clues and secrets in Swift's narrative, whereas without this analysis they might have simply skimmed the story. I tried to infuse all parts of this textbook with similar bits of unusual information that turns literary theory on its head.

Because of the complexity of some of the discussions in this textbook, it can be used for some introductory graduate literature classes, especially if an instructor adds additional books to supplement it. But, the primary audience is Introductory Literature undergraduate students to whom I taught this content.

Across this book "Readings", includes short stories, a play and poetry selections, and mixed with commentary on these readings. These fit the length of a 3-credit Introduction to Literature class at the college level. The readings have been edited slightly to fix typos and a few other glitches that were left in the original publications. These readings include three short stories from Edgar Allan Poe: "The Sphinx," "Hop-Frog" and "How to Write a Blackwood Article." The novel segments include Miguel de Cervantes' *Don Quixote*, which is considered to be the first novel by some, and represents Spanish-language literature in this collection. The final work of fiction included is Jonathan Swift's *Gulliver's Travels into Several Remote Nations of the World*. Swift represents the British Isles, whereas Poe is American. The uniting element in these stories is satire, sarcasm, and other forms of derisive humor. Who doesn't like humor? The political, social and cultural questions that this canonical criticism veiled under the guise of fiction should inspire students to want to write about them.

COMPREHENDING AND WRITING ABOUT READINGS

Each author is introduced at the start of a section with biographical and contextual details. After the original work is reproduced, a section is offered that explains its structure, linguistics, and other elements. The summaries are followed by sections that explain some of the unique vocabulary these authors from different countries and time periods are using. The vocabulary is not given with simple definitions, but rather is full of complex information that enriches the reading. There are also sections called "Comments on the Text," in which an in-depth analysis is offered of the genre, word choice, reference sources, and various other components that help to explain the fiction. Finally, there are "Questions for Discussion" that invite students to consider what is behind the surface meaning. These questions should stimulate classroom discussion, or can be used as prompts for additional essay assignments. An Essay 1 Assignment is included at the back of the book in case an instructor wants to use it, rather than creating a new assignment for his or her students. A possible Revision Workshop for this first essay is also proposed. Essay 1 is a comparison or contrast essay that asks students to concentrate on any two of the short stories or novel segments.

TYPES OF LITERARY CRITICISM

The essays you will be writing for this class should engage one of the common types of literary criticism. I will discuss three of these potential approaches in this section. These categories are derived from the three elements common to most fictional works. A fictional story must have a structure, female and/or male characters, and a socio-political background in which the characters exist. There are many different story structures, and many different fantastical and realistic socio-political environments, but the presence of each of these is necessary to make a dynamic fictional story. Because these elements are so common, critics frequently study them. A literary theory is a collection of related ideas or examination points. If you write an essay that touches on anything that comes to mind related to a story, it will be a very disjointed essay, and it will not be making a coherent argument. If you limit your analysis to one of the major literary theories, you are starting with a narrow field, and it should be easier to choose a specific argument from within its bounds.

Students might want to acquire copies of the three optional external books discussed in this section that I previously published. Each of these is relevant to one of the critical genres covered. My *Gender Bias in Mystery and Romance Novel Publishing* book is a great source of information on feminism and gender studies. *Radical Agrarian Economics* is an introduction to economic and political theory, as it reviews the history and writings of major economic and political shifts across world history. Finally, the chapter out of *Rebellion as Genre* focuses on Scott's *Scottish Nationalism*, thus it is also a socio-economic analysis. Without them, the summaries of these theories offer plenty of introductory information.

Structuralism

The structure of a story is similar to the architectural plan for a building. When you examine a story's structure, you are considering the plotline, types of characters presented, and the types of settings depicted. How does the story begin and end? Is it a tragedy or a comedy based on the shape of its plotline? Are the characters typical heroes and heroines, or are they atypical? Some structuralists go beyond these basic elements to examine how a given structure of a fictional story fits with typical structures of human behavior. They use anthropology, cultural studies and psychology to examine how marriages, murders, and other common plots play out in reality and how these are interpreted in fiction. But for an introductory literature essay, you should look at the basic structure of the text(s) you choose without complicating this analysis with cultural norms.

Feminism

In politics, feminism refers to the fight for equal rights for women. When the term is used in connection with literary theory, it typically means an examination of the biases against female characters in male-authored sexist texts. A feminist critic searches for stories that portray women in submissive or otherwise demeaning roles, and attempt to prevent similar fictional abuse by pointing out the injustice of such biased perspectives. Feminists can also applaud strong female leads and explain how some female fictional characters help to promote equal rights for women. Feminist critics also ask who has the agency in a story; agency means power. Who is in control? Who is the acting subject and who is the passive object in the narrative, the leading man or woman? There are various other approaches feminists can take as most arguments related to sex or gender fall into this domain.

Economics and Politics

If no ideas come to mind regarding the structure or gender dimensions of a story, you should consider writing about economic or political aspects. Economics is the study of the flow of money between individuals on the micro level, and within the economy as a whole on the macro level. How are goods and services sold and bought? Political science is the study of how a political system functions. In modern times, the main duality discussed in relation to politics is that between communism and capitalism. In its ideal form, communism is a system where workers pool their resources together for the benefit of all. Idealized capitalism is a system where small companies compete with each other for buyers by lowering prices to a level where they can profit from the sales, while consumers search for the best deals and support the cheapest and best competitors, who survive in this race. Literary theorists that examine political and economic aspects of a story work to explain the type of economic system that the characters in the story exist in.

Satires, such as Swift's *Gulliver's Travels*, ridicule or criticize the political and economic systems that the author experienced. Satire, by definition, is the process of ridiculing or pointing out problems in the system. Swift was ridiculing the two-party monarchy and the corruptions of the Church in his novel. If you take a political approach to examining Swift's novel, you might explain how Swift shows the weaknesses of monarchies in the details of the fantastic fictional world he has created.

Gender Bias in Mystery and Romance Novel Publishing

As an optional assignment, students might want to access versions (available for free for students through libraries via EBSCO and ProQuest) of my previously published books to help with understanding different literary theories. The first of these is *Gender Bias in Mystery and Romance Novel Publishing*. This book is a study of the fact that most mysteries are written and consumed by men while most romance novels are written and consumed by women. I don't believe this split is accidental, but is due to the innate biases that exist in modern societies. The section you are reading is called, "The Economics and Politics of Authorship and Gender." This was an introductory part that explained the statistics behind gender-based discrimination that has been and continues to be with us in the West. The approach taken is in the title of the book, "gender"; it is a feminist criticism. Reading this section might help you to understand why it's important to study the power (or lack of it) given to female characters. The fictions people read become engrained in their psyches and influence the choices they make across their lives, as seeing a strong female character can encourage a girl to fight for higher wages.

Radical Agrarian Economics: **Chapter 3**

This section is called, "Feudalism, Capitalism, Communism, and Agrarianism." If you want to take the political or economic approach to studying the story of your choice, you should closely read this section. It defines the key terms and theories that dominate these fields of study. You will find many quotes from the classical theorists that represent these ideologies, such as Karl Marx and Adam Smith. This is a condensed summary of the theories, whereas you would have to read several other books to find the same information on each of these separately. Reading this content will help you to figure out which theorists you might want to read more closely to make a strong, researched argument in your paper. This information might also help you to understand the political or economic system in the story you are studying, so that you can explain it, in turn, to your readers. This chapter is pretty long, so I recommend searching automatically for the political term(s) that matches your subject rather than also reading the irrelevant explanations.

Rebellion as Genre (McFarland): Scott's Scottish Nationalism: Chapter 7

This last chapter is an example of political literary criticism. It also touches some structuralist elements in the discussions of the rebellion genre, which is the primary topic of the rest of this book. I discuss Sir Walter Scott's Scottish nationalism, or his subversive support of the separation of Scotland from the United Kingdom, or, if that was not possible, for equal rights for the Scottish people. My examination of Scott's novels is done with the help of historical details about the political actions Scott took. It also touches on the political events that he wrote about in his novels, as well as the political turmoil that was raging during and before Scott's time that influenced his fiction. Reading how I approached this political criticism might help you to do a similar analysis in your own essay. You might also want to research the history surrounding the story you are analyzing. Were there political events that inspired the events in the story? These events might be specifically depicted in the fiction, or they might have merely inspired a satirical fantasy, as is the case in Swift's *Gulliver's Travels*.

SHORT STORIES AND NOVEL SEGMENTS

FICTION TERMS

Plot

The main events of a play, novel, film, or similar work, devised and presented by the writer as an interrelated sequence. —*Oxford Living Dictionaries*

This figure from my McFarland book, *Formulas of Popular Fiction*, shows the common movements in the plot of speculative fiction, including science fiction, fantasy and horror. These works typically have similar timeframes for the introduction of the villain, and the immediate introduction of death threats that force the hero (or infrequently, the heroine) into action. The hero's life remains under threat across the plotline, forcing readers to remain in a constant state of suspense as they worry if the hero will die on the following page.

The three short stories we read by Poe have anti-formulaic plots. The heroes and heroines are anti-heroic, but are not exactly antagonists either. If they are under the threat of death, as the narrator of "The Sphinx" perceives himself to be, their fears are frequently undermined and shown to be illusions rather than being realized in the predictable heroic resolutions of formulaic speculative fiction. "Hop-Frog's" plotline is more formulaic, as the king can be perceived as a villain that Hop-Frog and his sidekick fight against across the narrative before they successfully kill their enemies. The plot of "Blackwood Article" is completely removed from these schemes as in it, Zenobia describes going to Mr. Blackwood, the editor of a famous Scottish periodical, to listen to his speech about how Zenobia should go about writing an article he is

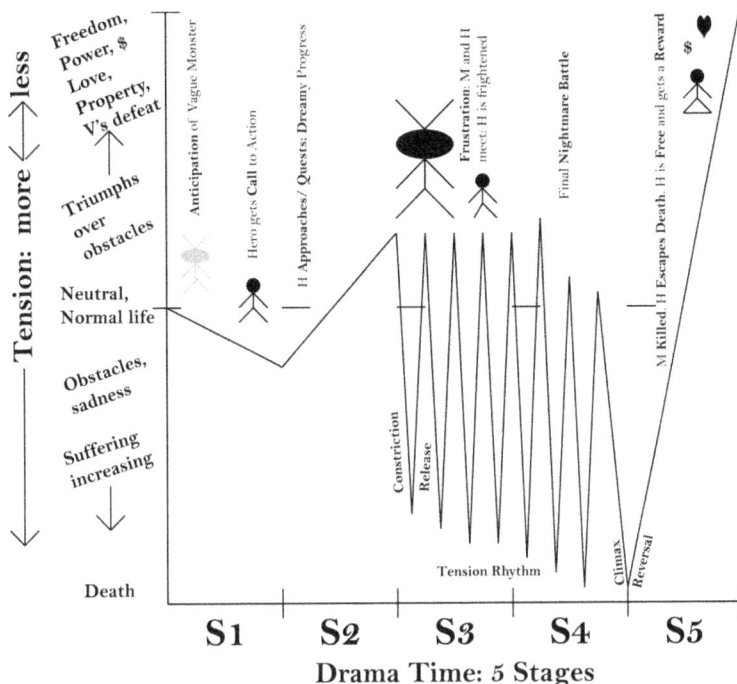

likely to accept. There isn't even much of a dialogue between them, as Zenobia agrees with everything Mr. Blackwood proposes, even so far that upon his instructions she proceeds to kill herself in the story that follows this piece. In formulaic stories, whenever there is a discussion between two characters, they typically disagree on most of the points they discuss, or otherwise there is no dramatic tension between them. Despite breaking all these rules, Poe creates extreme peaks of tension in all three of these stories. The tricks that Poe invents in these were later mimicked by the horror writers that followed him without his satirical intentions.

To summarize, a plotline is a series of events across a story's timeline. Sometimes these events are chronological, or presented in sequence, but at other times they jump around between different time periods because this order allows for a more interesting narrative. These events can be measured in terms of their intensity or tension, which is typically associated with the degree to which the main characters' lives are under threat by their foes. The moment when this death threat or tension is at its highest is known as the **climax**, at which the protagonist (hero/ heroine) typically kills or wins over the antagonist (villain) and is then rewarded in the resolution that follows, in which the tension gradually dissipates. The plotline of most canonical or classical fiction is anti-formulaic as it follows a different path, which is thus more surprising for readers. Any literary critic has to understand, and frequently summarize the plotline or the narrative depicted in a story before he or she can more closely explore other elements. The plotline shows the author's intention as, for example, a reward or victory at the end offered to a character that appeared as a villain, suggests the author's sympathy for this character.

Character

A person in a novel, play, or film. —*Oxford Living Dictionaries*
Critical readers have to step away from the illusion of reality that fiction creates. The people presented in fiction are characters, and not real people the author photographed and inserted in their full-detail into the story. Most formulaic fiction has stock characters that frequently appear, such as the ruler, the servant, or the beautiful girl in distress. Very realistic fiction includes people going about their daily lives, including the narrator of "The Sphinx." The destiny and decisions of characters in fiction are deliberately plotted by the author with a specific purpose in mind. The author might want to make a moral point about how good actions are rewarded, or how evil deeds are punished (as they are for the king in "Hop-Frog"). So, when you read fiction, consider what the characters represent, or what they signify beyond what they are doing and saying.

While Hop-Frog overcomes the king who is persecuting him, the anti-formulaic element is that Hop-Frog is grotesque in his deformity, as are the fat king and his ministers. Formulaic heroes are supposed to be beautiful. Formulaic villains are supposed to be grotesque and disfigured. Additionally, kings are traditionally the heroes, as they were in the original chivalry tales, which were written in the environment of European monarchies; Poe flips this on its head, and thus makes an anti-establishment, revolutionary statement.

Setting

The place and time at which a play, novel, or film is represented as happening. —*Oxford Living Dictionaries*

The time and place where the actions are taking place frequently change the genre of a formulaic novel. For example, modern romance novels are grouped by the period they depict into Regency, Victorian, and the like. In the nineteenth century, authors typically started their stories by describing the exact city or village, and the historical time period that would be portrayed. This habit is less popular in modern fiction because readers are too lazy to read through this backstory and expect to be shown the time and place in brisk, sweeping wide views of a city in a film scape, rather than in long, descriptive paragraphs. Despite this, time and place frequently changes the manners, linguistics, style, plotline, characters and other elements in a fictional work, so it is unlikely that they will ever fully disappear even from formulaic pop fiction.

You should be alert to hints about time and place an author is offering regardless of the genre we will be reading (prose, poetry or theater). Poe begins "The Sphinx" by placing the narrative in the "reign of the Cholera in New York," which critics have pinpointed to an actual outbreak some years before Poe wrote this story. If you know which period the author is depicting, you can research the historical context to make an argument about the author's intentions, allusions, implications, conclusions and the like. If the author deliberately refuses to name the time and place where the narrative takes place, as in "Hop-Frog," this is always deliberate and meant to make the problems shown more universal. If Poe specified the king's country and the country from which Hop-Frog originated, the narrative would be about the conflict between these two nationalities, but by leaving these out Poe allows any disenfranchised group to see themselves in Hop-Frog, and their enemies in the king and his ministers. On the other hand, Poe is very specific in the setting of the "Blackwood Article," as he specifically blames Mr. Blackwood and his magazine in Edinburgh for sponsoring the production of subpar gothic fiction.

Perspective

> A particular attitude towards or way of regarding something; a point of view... Origin: Late Middle English (in the sense optics): from medieval Latin *perspectiva* (ars) (science of) optics, from *perspect-* looked at closely, from the verb *perspicere*, from *per-* through + *specere* to look. —*Oxford Living Dictionaries*

All three of Poe's short stories begin from the first-person perspective. Even though the narrator is not one of the main characters in "Hop-Frog," the story begins from the perspective of somebody that was supposedly alive during the clash between Hop-Frog and the king. The **first-person** perspective puts the reader in the middle of the action, and makes everything that befalls the characters more immediate, threatening and engaging. Examples of first person sentences are: *I went to the mall... My ball ended up in the bucket...* Stories told from a **third-person** perspective typically have an **omniscient**, or all-knowing storyteller. Examples of this would be: *The frog lived in a soft, and mushy pond, which it liked very much...* If the narrator knows all sides of the story, it is harder for the author to hide behind the unreliability of a biased first-person narrator that can be blamed for lying occasionally. In a **second-person** narrative, the story is told as if the reader is participating in the related actions, as in: *You go up to the window, and find a corpse below...* As you draw conclusions from the plotline, dialogue and other elements in poetry, prose and drama, consider from whose perspective these are seen from. Are there conflicting perspectives in the same story, and if so, which perspective can readers trust? Are you more likely to sympathize with a first-person narrator even if his or her actions are immoral?

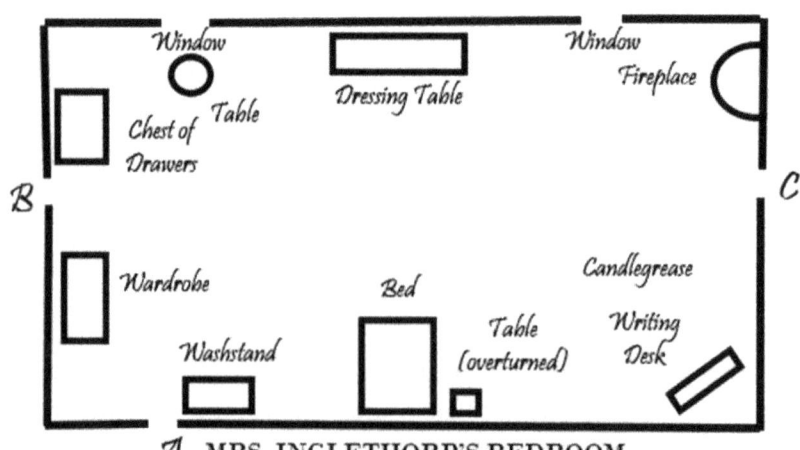

Setting: Diagram from Agatha Christie's *Mysterious Affair*

Edgar Allan Poe

Edgar Allan Poe is best known for his short horror stories because the one novel he published with Harper's, *The Narrative of Arthur Gordon Pym of Nantucket* (1838) was not a success, and they refused to sponsor a new release, and Poe was too poor to sponsor a publication. Meanwhile, Poe spent most of his career working as a professional writer and editor. He placed several of his stories in periodicals, and to compete for these he polished them to a very fine prose that rivaled any of his contemporaries. One of the stories of his that we are reading in this class, "Hop-Frog," was first printed in March of 1849 in *The Flag of Our Union*, which became very popular in Boston within years of its founding, so that it was equivalent in popularity to the *New York Times* today. Another story we are reading, "The Sphinx" was published in January of 1846 in *Arthur's Magazine* in Philadelphia. We will also read one of Poe's poems, as his poetry brought him more sales and critical acclaim than the bulk of his prose, with notable examples like "Annabel Lee" and "The Raven."

Poe's first editorial job started in August of 1835. He worked part-time for the *Southern Literary Messenger*, a periodical run by Thomas Willis White in Richmond. It became full-time in November of that year. While Poe was the *de facto* editor-in-chief, the December 1835 issue introduced him with, "the paper is now under the conduct of the Proprietor, assisted by a gentleman of distinguished literary talents…" Poe left this periodical at the end of 1836, and ran a retirement notice in the January 1837 issue. In 1839, Poe obtained a part-time editorial position for William Evans Burton's Philadelphia magazine at $10 a week for 10 hours of work. Burton had attained his wealth from acting, and this afforded him the publication of two plays and some sketches, and the acquisition of four theatres, in which he frequently acted himself. Thus, he was an actor-proprietor, and then also became an author-publisher when he started his *Burton's Gentleman's Magazine*. Burton exploited Poe to create a spike in circulation and then fired him. Poe later wound up back at *Burton's*, which soon merged with George Rex Graham's periodical, and became known as *Graham's Magazine*, after the purchase was finalized in October, and Graham was now in charge. Poe's young wife, Virginia, was diagnosed with tuberculosis in January of 1842, so his resignation might have coincided with this news. Virginia died five years later on January 30, 1847. Back in 1842, Poe's salary had risen by $300 from what he made at *Burton's* and he had an assistant editor to take care of some busy work, but this was still a tiny portion of what Graham was reaping and paying authors. After terminating his employment with *Graham's*, Poe contributed articles to the *New York Evening Mirror* newspaper for a couple of years before he convinced its owner, N. P. Willis, to give him an assistant editor position for $750 per year.

In 1845, Poe started contributing to the *Broadway Journal* and became its assistant editor under Charles F. Briggs. Only a month later, in February, Poe became a coeditor. Poe was paid a salary and a third of the profits: a three-way split between Briggs, the publisher and Poe. Poe bought out Briggs' share and became the sole editor in July. He borrowed the money for the purchase.

The events that led to Poe's death began in 1849, when Sarah Elmira Royster Shelton accepted Poe's marriage proposal on September 22. Poe had started a relationship with Sarah in their youth, in 1825, but her father disapproved, and she married a wealthy businessman instead. After her husband died, and she inherited his money, Poe came back into her life. One of the reasons critics have suggested that Poe's death was a suicide is because a letter survived that he sent to his sister Annie on November 16, 1848, when he felt that he would not succeed in winning Sarah's hand in marriage, and described how he had taken an ounce of laudanum from despair (Ostrom, Vol. 2 401-2). On September 27, 1849, Poe left Richmond for New York on a Baltimore steamer, with an added stop in Philadelphia, all to edit "poems of a Philadelphia piano manufacturer's wife for one hundred dollars." He supposedly arrived in Baltimore on the 28th. He was found at the Gunner's Hall tavern on October 3 by a "young printer named Joseph W. Walker." Poe's friend Joseph Evans Snodgrass received a note from Walker, and found Poe in the specified spot. He then took Poe to the Washington College hospital. Curiously, Gunner's Hall was being used as a "polling place for the Fourth Ward" on that day (Hutchison 244-5). Critics have suggested that Poe had been paid in assisting with election fraud, potentially in part with the liquor of which he had so much that it had put him in the stupor in which Snodgrass found him.

Hutchison states that other sources have concluded that Poe must have been the "victim of political violence" (244-6), perhaps because he attempted to intervene when he saw corruption, just as he did when he saw plagiarism.

THE SPHINX

DURING the dread reign of the Cholera in New York, I had accepted the invitation of a relative to spend a fortnight with him in the retirement of his *cottage ornee* on the banks of the Hudson. We had here around us all the ordinary means of summer amusement; and what with rambling in the woods, sketching, boating, fishing, bathing, music, and books, we should have passed the time pleasantly enough, but for the fearful intelligence which reached us every morning from the populous city. Not a day elapsed which did not bring us news of the decease of some acquaintance. Then as the fatality increased, we learned to expect daily the loss of some friend. At length we trembled at the approach of every messenger. The very air from the South seemed to us redolent with death. That palsying thought, indeed, took entire possession of my soul. I could neither speak, think, nor dream of anything else. My host was of a less excitable temperament, and, although greatly depressed in spirits, exerted himself to sustain my own. His richly philosophical intellect was not at any time affected by unrealities. To the substances of terror he was sufficiently alive, but of its shadows he had no apprehension.

His endeavors to arouse me from the condition of abnormal gloom into which I had fallen were frustrated, in great measure, by certain volumes which I had found in his library. These were of a character to force into germination whatever seeds of hereditary superstition lay latent in my bosom. I had been reading these books without his knowledge, and thus he was often at a loss to account for the forcible impressions which had been made upon my fancy.

A favorite topic with me was the popular belief in omens—a belief which, at this one epoch of my life, I was almost seriously disposed to defend. On this subject we had long and animated discussions—he maintaining the utter groundlessness of faith in such matters—I contending that a popular sentiment arising with absolute spontaneity—that is to say, without apparent traces of suggestion—had in itself the unmistakable elements of truth, and was entitled to as much respect as that intuition which is the idiosyncrasy of the individual man of genius.

The fact is that soon after my arrival at the cottage there had occurred to myself an incident so entirely inexplicable, and which had in it so much of the portentous character, that I might well have been excused for regarding it as an omen. It appalled, and at the same time so confounded and bewildered me, that many days elapsed before I could make up my mind to communicate the circumstances to my friend.

Near the close of exceedingly warm day, I was sitting, book in hand, at an open window, commanding, through a long vista of the river banks, a view of a distant hill, the face of which nearest my position had been denuded by what is termed a land-slide, of the principal portion of its trees. My thoughts had been long wandering from the volume before me to the gloom and desolation of the neighboring city. Uplifting my eyes from the page, they fell upon the naked face of the hill, and upon an object—upon some living monster of hideous conformation, which very rapidly made its way from the summit to the bottom, disappearing finally in the dense forest below. As this creature first came in sight, I doubted my own sanity—or at least the evidence of my own eyes; and many minutes passed before I succeeded in convincing myself that I was neither mad nor in a dream. Yet when I described the monster (which I distinctly saw, and calmly surveyed through the whole period of its progress), my readers, I fear, will feel more difficulty in being convinced of these points than even I did myself.

Estimating the size of the creature by comparison with the diameter of the large trees near which it passed—the few giants of the forest which had escaped the fury of the land-slide—I concluded it to be far larger than any ship of the line in existence. I say ship of the line, because the shape of the monster suggested the idea—the hull of one of our seventy-four might convey a very tolerable conception of the general outline. The mouth of the animal was situated at the extremity of a proboscis some sixty or seventy feet in length, and about as thick as the body of an ordinary elephant. Near the root of this trunk was an immense quantity of black shaggy hair—more than could have been supplied by the coats of a score of buffaloes; and projecting from this hair downwardly and laterally, sprang two gleaming tusks not unlike those of the wild boar, but of infinitely greater dimensions. Extending forward, parallel with the proboscis, and on each side of it, was a gigantic staff, thirty or forty feet in length, formed seemingly of pure crystal and in shape a perfect prism—it reflected in the most gorgeous manner the rays of the declining sun. The trunk was fashioned like a wedge with the apex to the earth. From it there were outspread two pairs of wings—each wing nearly one hundred yards in length—one pair being placed above the other, and all thickly covered with metal scales; each scale apparently some ten or twelve feet in diameter. I observed that the upper and lower tiers of wings were connected by a strong chain. But the chief peculiarity of this horrible thing was the representation of a Death's Head, which covered nearly the whole surface of its breast, and which was as accurately traced in glaring white, upon the dark ground of the body, as if it had been there carefully designed by an artist. While I regarded the terrific animal, and more especially the appearance on its breast, with a feeling or horror and awe—with a sentiment of forthcoming evil, which I found it impossible to quell by any effort of the reason, I perceived the huge jaws at the extremity of the proboscis suddenly expand themselves, and from them there proceeded a sound so loud and so expressive of woe, that it struck upon my nerves like a knell and as the monster disappeared at the foot of the hill, I fell at once, fainting, to the floor.

Upon recovering, my first impulse, of course, was to inform my friend of what I had seen and heard—and I can scarcely explain what feeling of repugnance it was which, in the end, operated to prevent me.

At length, one evening, some three or four days after the occurrence, we were sitting together in the room in which I had seen the apparition—I occupying the same seat at the same window, and he lounging on a sofa near at hand. The association of the place and time impelled me to give him an account of the phenomenon. He heard me to the end—at first laughed heartily—and then lapsed into an excessively grave demeanor, as if my insanity was a thing beyond suspicion. At this instant I again had a distinct view of the monster—to which, with a shout of absolute terror, I now directed his attention. He looked eagerly—but maintained that he saw nothing—although I designated minutely the course of the creature, as it made its way down the naked face of the hill.

I was now immeasurably alarmed, for I considered the vision either as an omen of my death, or, worse, as the fore-runner of an attack of mania. I threw myself passionately back in my chair, and for some moments buried my face in my hands. When I uncovered my eyes, the apparition was no longer apparent.

My host, however, had in some degree resumed the calmness of his demeanor, and questioned me very rigorously in respect to the conformation of the visionary creature. When I had fully satisfied him on this head, he sighed deeply, as if relieved of some intolerable burden, and went on to talk, with what I thought a cruel calmness, of various points of speculative philosophy, which had heretofore formed subject of discussion between us. I remember his insisting very especially (among other things) upon the idea that the principle source of error in all human investigations lay in the liability of the understanding to under-rate or to over-value the importance of an object, through mere mis-admeasurement of its propinquity. "To estimate properly, for example," he said, "the influence to be exercised on mankind at large by the thorough diffusion of Democracy, the distance of the epoch at which such diffusion may possibly be accomplished should not fail to form an item in the estimate. Yet can you tell me one writer on the subject of government who has ever thought this particular branch of the subject worthy of discussion at all?"

He here paused for a moment, stepped to a book-case, and brought forth one of the ordinary synopses of Natural History. Requesting me then to exchange seats with him, that he might the better distinguish the fine print of the volume, he took my armchair at the window, and, opening the book, resumed his discourse very much in the same tone as before.

"But for your exceeding minuteness," he said, "in describing the monster, I might never have had it in my power to demonstrate to you what it was. In the first place, let me read to you a schoolboy account of the genus Sphinx, of the family Crepuscularia of the order Lepidoptera, of the class of Insecta—or insects. The account runs thus:

"'Four membranous wings covered with little colored scales of metallic appearance; mouth forming a rolled proboscis, produced by an elongation of the jaws, upon the sides of which are found the rudiments of mandibles and downy palpi; the inferior wings retained to the superior by a stiff hair; antennae in the form of an elongated club, prismatic; abdomen pointed, The Death's-Headed Sphinx has occasioned much terror among the vulgar, at times, by the melancholy kind of cry which it utters, and the insignia of death which it wears upon its corslet.'"

He here closed the book and leaned forward in the chair, placing himself accurately in the position which I had occupied at the moment of beholding "the monster."

"Ah, here it is," he presently exclaimed—"it is reascending the face of the hill, and a very remarkable looking creature I admit it to be. Still, it is by no means so large or so distant as you imagined it,—for the fact is that, as it wriggles its way up this thread, which some spider has wrought along the window-sash, I find it to be about the sixteenth of an inch in its extreme length, and also about the sixteenth of an inch distant from the pupil of my eye."

Vocabulary

Cholera: "Cholera is a bacterial disease usually spread through contaminated water. Cholera causes severe diarrhea and dehydration. Left untreated, cholera can be fatal in a matter of hours, even in previously healthy people./ Modern sewage and water treatment have virtually eliminated cholera in industrialized countries. The last major outbreak in the United States occurred in 1911. But cholera is still present in Africa, Southeast Asia, Haiti and central Mexico." —*Mayo Clinic*

Cottage orné: "a picturesquely designed small country house of 19th century England." —*Merriam-Webster*

Ship of the line: "type of sailing warship that formed the backbone of the Western world's great navies from the mid-17th century through the mid-19th century, when it gave way to the steam-powered battleship." —*Encyclopedia Britannica*

Proboscis: "1. any long flexible snout; 2. any of various elongated or extensible tubular processes (as the sucking organ of a butterfly) of the oral region of an invertebrate." —*Merriam-Webster*

Death's Head: "a human skull or a depiction of a human skull symbolizing death." —*Merriam-Webster*

Speculative philosophy: "a philosophy professing to be founded upon intuitive or a priori insight and especially insight into the nature of the Absolute or Divine." —*Merriam-Webster*

FICTION

Comments on the Text:

Atmosphere of Horror: Gothic tales of the eighteenth century typically created a similar sense of dread by describing ghostly screams and eerie winds. In this story, Poe creates a sense of dread by describing the Cholera epidemic. Poe also creates tension in the opening paragraph by inserting the threat of death to the lives of the main characters and their friends from this disease. In some stories, there is a villain that creates dramatic tension from the get-go, but before a potential villain enters a mystery, they are frequently populated with the types of inhuman threats. The narrator's fainting later in the story is another trope or detail that frequently appears in Gothic romances.

"…an incident so entirely inexplicable…": This is a foreshadowing of an incident to be related to interest the reader in the tale that will be related later. Though in this case, the tale begins in the following paragraph. Poe calls it an "incident" and builds suspense around it instead of simply giving the account to intensify the reader's fear of what the omen might have indicated.

"some living monster of hideous conformation": Nearly all formulaic science fiction, fantasy and horror story introduce a monster early in the narrative. The monster can be a murderer, or a human that commits some other crime or evil deed. It can also be an inhuman, supernatural, or animal being. Poe begins with the vague description of this "monster" to once again attract the curiosity of the reader, before going into details in the following paragraph.

"thickly covered with metal scales": The description of the "Sphinx" is deliberately made strange as it does not match the cartoonish or mythological depictions of this creature. The *Encyclopedia Britannica* describes the original Greek and Egyptian version of the "sphinx" as having a "lion's body and a human head." It also refers to a different, earlier variety of this creature, the "winged sphinx of Boeotian Thebes." The Greek-Egyptian versions were very graceful and beautiful in contrast with the creature Poe is describing. Poe describes more of an Egyptian pyramid of a sphinx in dimensions than what a human's head on a lion's body would measure at. There are also no giant, hairy snouts on any depictions of sphinxes in classical art. Any reader that considers this description closely is likely to be struck by its absurdity, so there is some satirical criticism here of superstition and mythological perfection. The "tusks" is another odd detail that clashes with idealized sphinxes. Also, instead of a single pair of wings, this creature, has two pairs, or four of them with one above the other, connected by a strange, unnatural chain. It's no accident that planes have not been invented with two pairs of wings, with one above the other… And how can a lion's body have "metal" scales over it if this creature obeyed the rules of the myth? These abnormalities are explained in the end, when Poe confesses that he is actually describing a moth.

"synopses of Natural History": The synopsis he picked up was, *A Synopsis of Natural History: Embracing the Natural History of Animals, with Human and General Animal Physiology, Botany, Vegetable Physiology and Geology* by Céran Lemonnier (1839). This book is available for free on the Archive.org website. A search for "Sphinx" turns up some replicas of the lines the narrator's friend in the story reads. The definition can be found under "Order VII. Lepidoptera" in "Family II. Crepuscularia" which is defined as having: "Wings, during repose, horizontal or inclined; the inferior one retained to the superior by a stiff hair; antennae in the form of an elongated club, prismatic or fusiform; sometimes they are pectiniform; caterpillars always provided with sixteen feet." Then a sub-category of this family, is "Genus Sphinx," which is described as: "Antennae prismatic and terminating in airs; wings long and horizontal; abdomen pointed. The Death's-headed Sphinx has occasioned much terror in certain countries by the kind of cry which it utters, and the insignia of death upon its corselet" (138-9). Poe's wording is slightly different, as he writes: "Four membranous wings covered with little colored scales of metallic appearance; mouth forming a rolled proboscis…" The words "four," "metallic," and "scales" do not appear in the original, so this is a paraphrasing that utilizes the unique characteristics that Poe added to exaggerate the horrifying effect of the creature in his earlier description. He also added that this "Sphinx" has "occasioned much terror among the vulgar" in place of the textbook's more sensitive explanation that it frightens people who are superstitious and see an omen of death in its Death's-head "insignia." Poe is careful to name the book that he is mimicking, so that even if he is cloaking it in fiction, nobody will be able to accuse him of plagiarizing the definition. Poe and many other canonical or great writers frequently borrow ideas from newspapers and non-fiction books on the subjects they are researching. Basing fiction on real accounts makes it vivid and full of detail as no purely speculative or imaginary writing could manage to achieve. So, learn from Poe: do your research, and don't forget to cite your sources.

"the sixteenth of an inch in its extreme length, and also about the sixteenth of an inch distant from the pupil of my eye": This is a great example of a surprise ending that brings all of the details of the story together. Even the reference to the philosophy of distance and perception that the two characters discussed casually earlier on was not a random reference, but rather is the branch of philosophy that helps to explain this conclusion. Most readers, like me, probably assumed that the narrator was incorrectly describing the mythological sphinx when he offered the gigantic dimensions in his initial shocked viewing. While most of Poe's mysteries and horror stories shock with the revelation of whodunit, this shows his mastery in surprising without putting a dead body on the stage. This story is a commentary on the tricks perspective can play on the human mind, as there may be logical explanations to what might at first appear as something very odd-looking. Also, the same character or event looks very different depending on the perspective of the narrator, as every author knows. If a murder takes place in a house, the murderer, the victim, the detective and other parties will all have unique perspectives of it.

Questions for Discussion

1. Did you feel horrified or amused as you started reading "The Sphinx"? Were there clues that this was going to be a satirical story, and if so what were they?
2. Can you give an example of what happens or what is shown in a formulaic or Hollywood blockbuster film in a foreshadowing or warning regarding the likelihood of a forthcoming frightening event? How do these moments of anticipation influence your experience with the movie or book?
3. Did you assume that the narrator was seeing a mythological sphinx, an insect, or something else? Have you read about either the myth of the Sphinx or this insect family before? If Poe took this story in a different direction, and concluded that the narrator proved

to his friend the existence of Sphinxes, what would this version of this mythological creature say about Poe's aesthetics, or theory of beauty, or what is beautiful? Why did the Greeks start depicting Sphinxes as beautiful and elegant women, while some earlier versions were hairier and more like what a blend between a lion and a human would look like? If myths show ideals of beauty, why would an author like Poe choose to turn a symbol of beauty into one that's absurdly ugly? Answer any of these questions that best speak to you.

4. Find any other definition of a creature in the *Synopsis of Natural History*: https://archive.org/details/synopsisofnatura00lemo. Why do you think Poe chose the "Sphinx" in particular for this story? Would any other creature have created the same surprise ending and double meaning? You might want to try writing a paragraph of an alternative story that would have resulted if Poe chose the creature you selected.

Works Cited

Hutchisson, James M. *Poe*. Jackson: University Press of Mississippi, 2005.

Lemonnier, Céran. *A Synopsis of Natural History: Embracing the Natural History of Animals, with Human and General Animal Physiology, Botany, Vegetable Physiology and Geology*. Philadelphia: Thomas Wardle, 1839. Archive. 21 January 2017. Web.

Ostrom, John Ward, Ed. *The Letters of Edgar Allan Poe*. 2 vols. (1948). New York: Gordian, 1966.

HOP-FROG

I never knew anyone so keenly alive to a joke as the king was. He seemed to live only for joking. To tell a good story of the joke kind, and to tell it well, was the surest road to his favor. Thus it happened that his seven ministers were all noted for their accomplishments as jokers. They all took after the king, too, in being large, corpulent, oily men, as well as inimitable jokers. Whether people grow fat by joking, or whether there is something in fat itself which predisposes to a joke, I have never been quite able to determine; but certain it is that a lean joker is a *rara avis in terris*.

About the refinements, or, as he called them, the 'ghost' of wit, the king troubled himself very little. He had an especial admiration for breadth in a jest, and would often put up with length, for the sake of it. Over-niceties wearied him. He would have preferred Rabelais' *Gargantua* to the *Zadig* of Voltaire: and, upon the whole, practical jokes suited his taste far better than verbal ones.

At the date of my narrative, professing jesters had not altogether gone out of fashion at court. Several of the great continental 'powers' still retain their 'fools,' who wore motley, with caps and bells, and who were expected to be always ready with sharp witticisms, at a moment's notice, in consideration of the crumbs that fell from the royal table.

Our king, as a matter of course, retained his 'fool.' The fact is, he required something in the way of folly—if only to counterbalance the heavy wisdom of the seven wise men who were his ministers—not to mention himself.

His fool, or professional jester, was not only a fool, however. His value was trebled in the eyes of the king, by the fact of his being also a dwarf and a cripple. Dwarfs were as common at court, in those days, as fools; and many monarchs would have found it difficult to get through their days (days are rather longer at court than elsewhere) without both a jester to laugh with, and a dwarf to laugh at. But, as I have already observed, your jesters, in ninety-nine cases out of a hundred, are fat, round, and unwieldy—so that it was no small source of self-gratulation with our king that, in Hop-Frog (this was the fool's name), he possessed a triplicate treasure in one person.

I believe the name 'Hop-Frog' was not that given to the dwarf by his sponsors at baptism, but it was conferred upon him, by general consent of the several ministers, on account of his inability to walk as other men do. In fact, Hop-Frog could only get along by a sort of interjectional gait—something between a leap and a wriggle—a movement that afforded illimitable amusement, and of course consolation, to the king, for (notwithstanding the protuberance of his stomach and a constitutional swelling of the head) the king, by his whole court, was accounted a capital figure.

But although Hop-Frog, through the distortion of his legs, could move only with great pain and difficulty along a road or floor, the prodigious muscular power which nature seemed to have bestowed upon his arms, by way of compensation for deficiency in the lower limbs, enabled him to perform many feats of wonderful dexterity, where trees or ropes were in question, or any thing else to climb. At such exercises he certainly much more resembled a squirrel, or a small monkey, than a frog.

I am not able to say, with precision, from what country Hop-Frog originally came. It was from some barbarous region, however, that no person ever heard of—a vast distance from the court of our king. Hop-Frog, and a young girl, very little less dwarfish than himself (although of exquisite proportions, and a marvellous dancer), had been forcibly carried off from their respective homes in adjoining provinces, and sent as presents to the king, by one of his ever-victorious generals.

Under these circumstances, it is not to be wondered at that a close intimacy arose between the two little captives. Indeed, they soon became sworn friends. Hop-Frog, who, although he made a great deal of sport, was by no means popular, had it not in his power to render Trippetta many services; but she, on account of her grace and exquisite beauty (although a dwarf), was universally admired and petted; so she possessed much influence; and never failed to use it, whenever she could, for the benefit of Hop-Frog.

On some grand state occasion—I forgot what—the king determined to have a masquerade, and whenever a masquerade or any thing of that kind, occurred at our court, then the talents, both of Hop-Frog and Trippetta, were sure to be called into play. Hop-Frog, in especial, was so inventive in the way of getting up pageants, suggesting novel characters, and arranging costumes for masked balls, that nothing could be done, it seems, without his assistance.

The night appointed for the fete had arrived. A gorgeous hall had been fitted up, under Trippetta's eye, with every kind of device which could possibly give éclat to a masquerade. The whole court was in a fever of expectation. As for costumes and characters, it might well be supposed that everybody had come to a decision on such points. Many had made up their minds (as to what roles they should assume) a week, or even a month, in advance; and, in fact, there was not a particle of indecision anywhere—except in the case of the king and his seven minsters. Why they hesitated I never could tell, unless they did it by way of a joke. More probably, they found it difficult, on account of being so fat, to make up their minds. At all events, time flew; and, as a last resort they sent for Trippetta and Hop-Frog.

When the two little friends obeyed the summons of the king they found him sitting at his wine with the seven members of his cabinet council; but the monarch appeared to be in a very ill humor. He knew that Hop-Frog was not fond of wine, for it excited the poor cripple almost to madness; and madness is no comfortable feeling. But the king loved his practical jokes, and took pleasure in forcing Hop-Frog to drink and (as the king called it) 'to be merry.'

"Come here, Hop-Frog," said he, as the jester and his friend entered the room, "swallow this bumper to the health of your absent friends, [here Hop-Frog sighed] and then let us have the benefit of your invention. We want characters—characters, man—something novel—out of the way. We are wearied with this everlasting sameness. Come, drink! The wine will brighten your wits."

Hop-Frog endeavored, as usual, to get up a jest in reply to these advances from the king; but the effort was too much. It happened to be the poor dwarf's birthday, and the command to drink to his 'absent friends' forced the tears to his eyes. Many large, bitter drops fell into the goblet as he took it, humbly, from the hand of the tyrant.

"Ah! ha! ha!" roared the latter, as the dwarf reluctantly drained the beaker: "See what a glass of good wine can do! Why, your eyes are shining already!"

Poor fellow! His large eyes gleamed, rather than shone; for the effect of wine on his excitable brain was not more powerful than instantaneous. He placed the goblet nervously on the table, and looked round upon the company with a half-insane stare. They all seemed highly amused at the success of the king's 'joke.'

"And now to business," said the prime minister, a very fat man.

"Yes," said the King; "Come lend us your assistance. Characters, my fine fellow; we stand in need of characters—all of us—ha! ha! ha!" And as this was seriously meant for a joke, his laugh was chorused by the seven.

Hop-Frog also laughed, although feebly and somewhat vacantly.

"Come, come," said the king, impatiently, "have you nothing to suggest?"

"I am endeavoring to think of something novel," replied the dwarf, abstractedly, for he was quite bewildered by the wine.

"Endeavoring!" cried the tyrant, fiercely; "what do you mean by that? Ah, I perceive. You are sulky, and want more wine. Here, drink this!" and he poured out another goblet full and offered it to the cripple, who merely gazed at it, gasping for breath.

"Drink, I say!" shouted the monster, "or by the fiends—"

The dwarf hesitated. The king grew purple with rage. The courtiers smirked. Trippetta, pale as a corpse, advanced to the monarch's seat, and, falling on her knees before him, implored him to spare her friend.

The tyrant regarded her, for some moments, in evident wonder at her audacity. He seemed quite at a loss what to do or say—how most becomingly to express his indignation. At last, without uttering a syllable, he pushed her violently from him, and threw the contents of the brimming goblet in her face.

The poor girl got up the best she could, and, not daring even to sigh, resumed her position at the foot of the table.

There was a dead silence for about half a minute, during which the falling of a leaf, or of a feather, might have been heard. It was interrupted by a low, but harsh and protracted grating sound which seemed to come at once from every corner of the room.

"What—what—what are you making that noise for?" demanded the king, turning furiously to the dwarf.

The latter seemed to have recovered, in great measure, from his intoxication, and looking fixedly but quietly into the tyrant's face, merely ejaculated:

"I—I? How could it have been me?"

"The sound appeared to come from without," observed one of the courtiers. "I fancy it was the parrot at the window, whetting his bill upon his cage-wires."

"True," replied the monarch, as if much relieved by the

suggestion, "but, on the honor of a knight, I could have sworn that it was the gritting of this vagabond's teeth."

Hereupon the dwarf laughed (the king was too confirmed a joker to object to any one's laughing), and displayed a set of large, powerful, and very repulsive teeth. Moreover, he avowed his perfect willingness to swallow as much wine as desired. The monarch was pacified; and having drained another bumper with no very perceptible ill effect, Hop-Frog entered at once, and with spirit, into the plans for the masquerade.

"I cannot tell what was the association of idea," observed he, very tranquilly, and as if he had never tasted wine in his life, "but just after your majesty, had struck the girl and thrown the wine in her face—just after your majesty had done this, and while the parrot was making that odd noise outside the window, there came into my mind a capital diversion—one of my own country frolics, often enacted among us, at our masquerades: but here it will be new altogether. Unfortunately, however, it requires a company of eight persons and—"

"Here we are!" cried the king, laughing at his acute discovery of the coincidence. "Eight to a fraction—I and my seven ministers. Come! What is the diversion?"

"We call it," replied the cripple, "the Eight Chained Ourang-Outangs, and it really is excellent sport if well enacted."

"We will enact it," remarked the king, drawing himself up, and lowering his eyelids.

"The beauty of the game," continued Hop-Frog, "lies in the fright it occasions among the women."

"Capital!" roared in chorus the monarch and his ministry.

"I will equip you as ourang-outangs," proceeded the dwarf; "leave all that to me. The resemblance shall be so striking, that the company of masqueraders will take you for real beasts—and of course, they will be as much terrified as astonished."

"Oh, this is exquisite!" exclaimed the king. "Hop-Frog! I will make a man of you."

"The chains are for the purpose of increasing the confusion by their jangling. You are supposed to have escaped, en masse, from your keepers. Your majesty cannot conceive the effect produced, at a masquerade, by eight chained ourang-outangs, imagined to be real ones by most of the company; and rushing in with savage cries, among the crowd of delicately and gorgeously habited men and women. The contrast is inimitable!"

"It must be," said the king: and the council arose hurriedly (as it was growing late) to put in execution the scheme of Hop-Frog.

His mode of equipping the party as ourang-outangs was very simple, but effective enough for his purposes. The animals in question had, at the epoch of my story, very rarely been seen in any part of the civilized world; and as the imitations made by the dwarf were sufficiently beast-like and more than sufficiently hideous, their truthfulness to nature was thus thought to be secured.

The king and his ministers were first encased in tight-fitting stockinet shirts and drawers. They were then saturated with tar. At this stage of the process, someone of the party suggested feathers; but the suggestion was at once overruled by the dwarf, who soon convinced the eight, by ocular demonstration, that the hair of such a brute as the ourang-outang was much more efficiently represented by flu. A thick coating of the latter was accordingly plastered upon the coating of tar. A long chain was now procured. First, it was passed about the waist of the king, and tied, then about another of the party, and also tied; then about all successively, in the same manner. When this chaining arrangement was complete, and the party stood as far apart from each other as possible, they formed a circle; and to make all things appear natural, Hop-Frog passed the residue of the chain in two diameters, at right angles, across the circle, after the fashion adopted, at the present day, by those who capture Chimpanzees, or other large apes, in Borneo.

The grand saloon, in which the masquerade was to take place, was a circular room, very lofty, and receiving the light of the sun only through a single window at the top. At night (the season for which the apartment was especially designed) it was illuminated principally by a large chandelier, depending by a chain from the centre of the sky-light, and lowered, or elevated, by means of a counter-balance as usual; but (in order not to look unsightly) this latter passed outside the cupola and over the roof.

The arrangements of the room had been left to Trippetta's superintendence; but, in some particulars, it seems, she had been guided by the calmer judgment of her friend the dwarf. At his suggestion it was that, on this occasion, the chandelier was removed. Its waxen drippings (which, in weather so warm, it was quite impossible to prevent) would have been seriously detrimental to the rich dresses of the guests, who, on account of the crowded state of the saloon, could not all be expected to keep from out its centre; that is to say, from under the chandelier. Additional sconces were set in various parts of the hall, out of the way, and a flambeau, emitting sweet odor, was placed in the right hand of each of the Caryaides [Caryatides] that stood against the wall—some fifty or sixty altogether.

The eight ourang-outangs, taking Hop-Frog's advice, waited patiently until midnight (when the room was thoroughly filled with masqueraders) before making their appearance. No sooner had the clock ceased striking, however, than they rushed, or rather rolled in, all together—for the impediments of their chains caused most of the party to fall, and all to stumble as they entered.

The excitement among the masqueraders was prodigious, and filled the heart of the king with glee. As had been anticipated, there were not a few of the guests who supposed the ferocious-looking creatures to be beasts of some kind in reality, if not precisely ourang-outangs. Many of the women swooned with affright; and had not the king taken the precaution to exclude all weapons from the saloon, his party might soon have expiated their frolic in their blood. As it was, a general rush was made for the doors; but the king had ordered them to be locked immediately upon his entrance; and, at the dwarf's suggestion, the keys had been deposited with him.

While the tumult was at its height, and each masquerader attentive only to his own safety (for, in fact, there was much real danger from the pressure of the excited crowd), the chain by which the chandelier ordinarily hung, and which had been drawn up on its removal, might have been seen very gradually to descend, until its hooked extremity came within three feet of the floor.

Soon after this, the king and his seven friends having reeled about the hall in all directions, found themselves, at length, in its centre, and, of course, in immediate contact with the chain. While they were thus situated, the dwarf, who had followed noiselessly at their heels, inciting them to keep up the commotion, took hold of their own chain at the intersection of the two portions which crossed the circle diametrically and at right angles. Here, with the rapidity of thought, he inserted the hook from which the chandelier had been wont to depend; and, in an instant, by some unseen agency, the chandelier-chain was drawn so far upward as to take the hook out of reach, and, as an inevitable consequence, to drag the ourang-outangs together in close connection, and face to face.

The masqueraders, by this time, had recovered, in some measure, from their alarm; and, beginning to regard the whole matter as a well-contrived pleasantry, set up a loud shout of laughter at the predicament of the apes.

"Leave them to me!" now screamed Hop-Frog, his shrill voice making itself easily heard through all the din. "Leave them to me. I fancy I know them. If I can only get a good look at them, I can soon tell who they are."

Here, scrambling over the heads of the crowd, he managed to get to the wall; when, seizing a flambeau from one of the Caryatides, he returned, as he went, to the centre of the room—leaping, with the agility of a monkey, upon the kings head, and thence clambered a few feet up the chain; holding down the torch to examine the group of ourang-outangs, and still screaming: "I shall soon find out who they are!"

And now, while the whole assembly (the apes included) were convulsed with laughter, the jester suddenly uttered a shrill whistle; when the chain flew violently up for about thirty feet—dragging with it the dismayed and struggling ourang-outangs, and leaving them suspended in mid-air between the sky-light and the floor. Hop-Frog, clinging to the chain as it rose, still maintained his relative position in respect to the eight maskers, and still (as if nothing were the matter) continued to thrust his torch down toward them, as though endeavoring to discover who they were.

So thoroughly astonished was the whole company at this ascent, that a dead silence, of about a minute's duration, ensued. It was broken by just such a low, harsh, grating sound, as had before attracted the attention of the king and his councillors when the former threw the wine in the face of Trippetta. But, on the present occasion, there could be no question as to whence the sound issued. It came from the fang-like teeth of the dwarf, who ground them and gnashed them as he foamed at the mouth, and glared, with an expression of maniacal rage, into the upturned countenances of the king and his seven companions.

"Ah, ha!" said at length the infuriated jester. "Ah, ha! I begin to see who these people are now!" Here, pretending to scrutinize the king more closely, he held the flambeau to the flaxen coat which enveloped him, and which instantly burst into a sheet of vivid flame. In less than half a minute the whole eight ourang-outangs were blazing fiercely, amid the shrieks of the multitude who gazed at them from below, horror-stricken, and without the power to render them the slightest assistance.

At length the flames, suddenly increasing in virulence, forced the jester to climb higher up the chain, to be out of their reach; and, as he made this movement, the crowd again sank, for a brief instant, into silence. The dwarf seized his opportunity, and once more spoke:

"I now see distinctly." he said, "what manner of people these maskers are. They are a great king and his seven privy-councillors,—a king who does not scruple to strike a defenseless girl and his seven councillors who abet him in the outrage. As for myself, I am simply Hop-Frog, the jester—and this is my last jest."

Owing to the high combustibility of both the flax and the tar to which it adhered, the dwarf had scarcely made an end of his brief speech before the work of vengeance was complete. The eight corpses swung in their chains, a fetid, blackened, hideous, and indistinguishable mass. The cripple hurled his torch at them, clambered leisurely to the ceiling, and disappeared through the sky-light.

It is supposed that Trippetta, stationed on the roof of the saloon, had been the accomplice of her friend in his fiery revenge, and that, together, they effected their escape to their own country: for neither was seen again.

Vocabulary

Rara avis in terries: Latin: a rare bird in the world. This phrase appeared in Juvenal's *Satires* as a symbol for the perfect wife, which he wrote is as rare as a black swan. In this case, Poe is referring to one of the founders of the satirical genre, Juvenal, to imply that a thin joker is a rare occurrence.

Eclat: from French, meaning "dazzling effect" (*Merriam-Webster*).

Caryatides: "a draped female figure supporting an entablature," which is the "horizontal part in classical architecture that rests on the columns and consists of architrave, frieze, and cornice" (*Merriam-Webster*).

Comments on the Text:

"…his seven ministers were all noted for their accomplishments as jokers": Court jesters have appeared not only in European castles of kings but also over a millennium earlier in Egypt and in other cultures that are far removed from the West. A jester by definition is a "fool" or "a harmlessly deranged person or one lacking in common powers of understanding" (*Merriam-Webster*). By acting as somebody who is silly in his incompetence, a fool typically could deliver bad news, or insults against the monarchy or another powerful agency whereas anybody who was not a fool might have been executed for making similar treasonous remarks. In the eighteenth century, with the onset of widespread literacy and reading as the printing of cheap books became commonplace, jesters started putting their acts in writing and what resulted was the golden age of satire in Britain and in other countries. Even some of Poe's scariest short mysteries include some irony in their surprising endings and flipped plots. In this short story, Poe begins by stressing the role of the court jester and pointing out that modern jesters are too pandering to the rulers that employ them instead of taking on the task of criticizing the powerful with the tools of satire and foolery. At the same time, he writes that rulers are employing fools (meaning unintelligent people) because they are amusing in roles that are supposed to carry out very serious tasks for the good of the country. Later on, Poe stresses that the "ministers" were not fools by employment, and that this king also employs somebody specifically labeled "fool" to satirize "folly" as the function of satire is to criticize folly or evil deeds. The "ministers" would in contrast offer "heavy wisdom" or what was the right and good thing to do unlike this "fool."

"practical jokes suited his taste far better than verbal ones": In the second paragraph, Poe reviews the various elements that make for vulgar or low-brow humor. Something that is "refined" is "free from impurities" (*Merriam-Webster*). Good prose has to be proofread to delete grammatical, spelling, as well as structural problems. But, Poe's king views this type of editing as the "'ghost' of wit," a notion that contradicts eighteenth century ideas about the classical rules against "false wit" or vulgar works that were preferred by "popular taste" including "jests, riddles…, conundrums, epigrams, and cheap witticisms" (Lund 67). Poe works to cover his cynicism or critical comments with "niceties," so that he does not call the ministers "fat" directly, but rather says there is "something in fat itself which predisposes to a joke." But, the king prefers jokes that hit with an insult, rather than hiding behind the veil of propriety and gently poking fun of the victim of the joke.

Rabelais' *Gargantua* was a satire about obese giants that inspired the Brobdingnag giants in Swift's *Gulliver's Travels*; this book was judged to be obscene when it was published because of the number of direct insults and other inappropriate content. Voltaire's *Zadig* is similar to his later *Candide* novel in that it also describes the misadventures of a young traveler who discovers the varieties of cruelty and evil that exist in the world, but embraces these with a clueless heart, as if he is a jester performing for a king rather than a fully colored human being living through these torturous trials. Poe is saying that the king prefers obscene humor to more complex and delicate satire. He concludes the paragraph by saying that the king went to the extreme of preferring physical jokes without any words in them at all, this being the opposite to the finely crafted highbrow humor admired in literary circles. After explaining that the king prefers this obscene kind of humor, Poe really hits his fool subject, Hop-Frog, with insults by describing him as a "dwarf and a cripple." This story would not have been published if Poe submitted it to periodicals today because of its political incorrectness, but these insults are intentional as Poe is satirizing bad humor by performing it in the extreme. Later in the story, one of the "practical jokes" the king performs is "forcing Hop-Frog to drink" despite his distaste of it because it induces an uncomfortable "madness" on him (14). The repeating use of the adjective "fat" to refer to the ministers and the king is a rude slap-stick joke that Poe indulges in at the expense of the king, as he is describing the pleasure the king is deriving from humiliating Hop-Frog. Poe ridicules the lack of humor in the king's rhetoric as in here: "'we stand in need of characters—all of us—ha! ha! ha!' and as this was seriously meant for a joke, his laugh was chorused by the seven." The ministers laugh at anything the king says as long as they perceive that he intends them to laugh, which is apparent in this case because the king laughs at his own remarks, which have no humorous meaning behind them. (Why would needing characters for a ball be funny?)

"and of course consolation, to the king, for (notwithstanding the protuberance of his stomach and a constitutional swelling of the head) the king, by his whole court, was accounted a capital figure": This is a great example of irony, as Poe stresses in parenthesis that the king makes the opposite of a "capital figure" and yet panders to the king's vanity as if he might be executed for treason if he was more direct in his insult.

"They were then saturated with tar... someone of the party suggested feathers; but the suggestion was at once overruled by the dwarf, who soon convinced... that the hair of such a brute as the ourang-outang was much more efficiently represented by flu": The joke here is in the introduction of something the reader isn't expecting. Any American reader from Poe's period would have started thinking about "tar and feathering" as the fool proposed "tar," but Poe diverts this by instead suggesting "flu" as a material that would be more apish. Poe later calls this material "flax," which is a fibrous crop used for making different types of linen.

"low, harsh, grating sound": The earlier foreshadowing of impending maniacal, homicidal rage in Hop-Frog's heart is actualized in the later realization by the king and his ministers that the sound they hear is coming from the "fang-like teeth of the dwarf." Great story tellers frequently use a detail like this to crack a mystery by hinting that an element is mysterious in the setup for the story, and then delivering an explanation for its meaning in the resolution.

"my last jest": burning eight men to death after tarring and flaxing them is an example of a similar type of dark humor that the narrator describes the king as favoring earlier in the story. Hop-Frog adopts the tools of abuse as a form of amusement to gain revenge against the king. There has been a satirical war going on between powerful rulers and their critics since the first jesters were allowed to speak without restraint to the powerful, and the powerful have been using similar abusive criticism to cut down their detractors. Poe exaggerates this struggle and shows how criticism of a monarch can evolve into a revolutionary *coup*.

Questions for Discussion

1. In "The Sphinx," Poe began by offering some horrific tropes common to Gothic tales, including strange and frightening noises, and references to the Cholera epidemic. In contrast, "Hop-Frog" begins with a discussion on comedy and humor, with many at first light jokes about the fatness of the king and his ministers, and the like.

Why do you think Poe ends the story that begins with horror with a comedic, silly resolution, while he ends the story that starts with humor with a horrific tragic end? How did these contrasts between the expected and what is delivered impact you as their reader?
2. Summarize what Poe's theory or philosophy of satire is based on what he writes about it in "Hop-Frog"? Does Poe propagate low or highbrow satire, or works that are vulgar or those that are refined, and dark comedy or uplifting comedy? What role does the ending play in deciding the writer's intentions? Is Poe making an argument that either type of comedy can be deadly if used by an abusive hand, or is he saying that only hurtful comedy can hurt the joker by backfiring?
3. How do you interpret the tar and flaxing incident? Poe published "Hop-Frog" in 1849, three years before *Uncle Tom's Cabin* (1852). The practice of tar and feathering was applied against all sorts of radicals in until the twentieth century, when the KKK and other white power groups made it synonymous with racist violent attacks. With this in mind, why do you think Poe chose this particularly brutal method of execution? What does it say about the king and his ministers or about the jester that employed it? Does the fact that Hop-Frog was born in a different country from the king's impact your answer, and if so, how so?

Works Cited

Lund, Roger D. "The Ghosts of Epigram, False Wit, and the Augustan Mode." *Eighteenth-Century Life*, Volume 27, Number 2, Spring 2003. pp 67-95. Durham: Duke University Press. Project Muse. 23 January 2017. Web.

HOW TO WRITE A BLACKWOOD ARTICLE

"In the name of the Prophet—figs!!"
—Cry of the Turkish fig-peddler.

I PRESUME everybody has heard of me. My name is the Signora Psyche Zenobia. This I know to be a fact. Nobody but my enemies ever calls me Suky Snobbs. I have been assured that Suky is but a vulgar corruption of Psyche, which is good Greek, and means "the soul" (that's me, I'm all soul) and sometimes "a butterfly," which latter meaning undoubtedly alludes to my appearance in my new crimson satin dress, with the sky-blue Arabian mantelet, and the trimmings of green agraffas, and the seven flounces of orange-colored auriculas. As for Snobbs—any person who should look at me would be instantly aware that my name wasn't Snobbs. Miss Tabitha Turnip propagated that report through sheer envy. Tabitha Turnip indeed! Oh, the little wretch! But what can we expect from a turnip? Wonder if she remembers the old adage about "blood out of a turnip," &c.? [Mem. put her in mind of it the first opportunity.] [Mem. again—pull her nose.] Where was I? Ah! I have been assured that Snobbs is a mere corruption of Zenobia, and that Zenobia was a queen—(So am I. Dr. Moneypenny always calls me the Queen of the Hearts)—and that Zenobia, as well as Psyche, is good Greek, and that my father was "a Greek," and that consequently I have a right to our patronymic, which is Zenobia and not by any means Snobbs. Nobody but Tabitha Turnip calls me Suky Snobbs. I am the Signora Psyche Zenobia.

As I said before, everybody has heard of me. I am that very Signora Psyche Zenobia, so justly celebrated as corresponding secretary to the "Philadelphia, Regular, Exchange, Tea, Total, Young, Belles, Lettres, Universal, Experimental, Bibliographical, Association, To, Civilize, Humanity." Dr. Moneypenny made the title for us, and says he chose it because it sounded big like an empty rum-puncheon. (A vulgar man that sometimes—but he's deep.) We all sign the initials of the society after our names, in the fashion of the R. S. A., Royal Society of Arts—the S. D. U. K., Society for the Diffusion of Useful Knowledge, &c, &c. Dr. Moneypenny says that S. stands for stale, and that D. U. K. spells duck, (but it don't,) that S. D. U. K. stands for Stale Duck and not for Lord Brougham's society—but then Dr. Moneypenny is such a queer man that I am never sure when he is telling me the truth. At any rate, we always add to our names the initials P. R. E. T. T. Y. B. L. U. E. B. A. T. C. H.—that is to say, Philadelphia, Regular, Exchange, Tea, Total, Young, Belles, Lettres, Universal, Experimental, Bibliographical, Association, To, Civilize, Humanity—one letter for each word, which is a decided improvement upon Lord Brougham. Dr. Moneypenny will have it that our initials give our true character—but for my life I can't see what he means.

Notwithstanding the good offices of the Doctor, and the strenuous exertions of the association to get itself into notice, it met with no very great success until I joined it. The truth is, the members indulged in too flippant a tone of discussion. The papers read every Saturday evening were characterized less by depth than buffoonery. They were all whipped syllabub. There was no investigation of first causes, first principles. There was no investigation of anything at all. There was no attention paid to that great point, the "fitness of things." In short there was no fine writing like this. It was all low—very! No profundity, no reading, no metaphysics—nothing which the learned call spirituality, and which the unlearned choose to stigmatize as cant. [Dr. M. says I ought to spell "cant" with a capital K—but I know better.]

When I joined the society, it was my endeavor to introduce a better style of thinking and writing, and all the world knows how well I have succeeded. We get up as good papers now in the P. R. E. T. T. Y. B. L. U. E. B. A. T. C. H. as any to be found even in Blackwood. I say, Blackwood, because I have been assured that the finest writing, upon every subject, is to be discovered in the pages of that justly celebrated Magazine. We now take it for our model upon all themes, and are getting into rapid notice accordingly. And, after all, it's not so very difficult a matter to compose an article of the genuine Blackwood stamp, if one only goes properly about it. Of course I don't speak of the political articles. Everybody knows how they are managed, since Dr. Moneypenny explained it. Mr. Blackwood has a pair of tailor's-shears, and three apprentices who stand by him for orders. One hands him the *Times*, another the *Examiner* and a third a *Culley's New Compendium* of *Slang-Whang*. Mr. B. merely cuts out and intersperses. It is soon done—nothing but *Examiner, Slang-Whang,* and *Times*—then *Times, Slang-Whang,* and *Examiner*—and then *Times, Examiner,* and S*lang-Whang.*

But the chief merit of the Magazine lies in its miscellaneous articles; and the best of these come under the head of what Dr. Moneypenny calls the bizarreries (whatever that may mean) and what everybody else calls the intensities. This is a species of writing which I have long known how to appreciate, although it is only since my late visit to Mr. Blackwood (deputed by the society) that I have been made aware of the exact method of composition. This method is very simple, but not so much so as the politics. Upon my calling at Mr. B.'s, and making known to him the wishes of the society, he received me with great civility, took me into his study, and gave me a clear explanation of the whole process.

"My dear madam," said he, evidently struck with my majestic appearance, for I had on the crimson satin, with the green agraffas, and orange-colored auriclas. "My dear madam," said he, "sit down. The matter stands thus: In the first place your writer of intensities must have very black ink, and a very big pen, with a very blunt nib. And, mark me, Miss Psyche Zenobia!" he continued, after a pause, with the most expressive energy and solemnity of manner, "mark me!—that pen—must—never be mended! Herein, madam, lies the secret, the soul, of intensity. I assume upon myself to say, that no individual, of however great genius ever wrote with a good pen—understand me—a good article. You may take it for granted that when manuscript can be read, it is never worth reading. This is a leading principle in our faith, to which if you cannot readily assent, our conference is at an end."

He paused. But, of course, as I had no wish to put an end to the conference, I assented to a proposition so very obvious, and one, too, of whose truth I had all along been sufficiently aware. He seemed pleased, and went on with his instructions.

"It may appear invidious in me, Miss Psyche Zenobia, to refer you to any article, or set of articles, in the way of model or study, yet perhaps I may as well call your attention to a few cases. Let me see. There was 'The Dead Alive,' a capital thing!—the record of a gentleman's sensations when entombed before the breath was out of his body—full of tastes, terror, sentiment, metaphysics, and erudition. You would have sworn that the writer had been born and brought up in a coffin. Then we had the 'Confessions of an Opium-eater'—fine, very fine!—glorious imagination—deep philosophy, acute speculation—plenty of fire and fury, and a good spicing of the decidedly unintelligible. That was a nice bit of flummery, and went down the throats of the people delightfully. They would have it that Coleridge wrote the paper—but not so. It was composed by my pet baboon, Juniper, over a rummer of Hollands and water, 'hot, without sugar.'" [This I could scarcely have believed had it been anybody but Mr. Blackwood, who assured me of it.] "Then there was 'The Involuntary Experimentalist,' all about a gentleman who got baked in an oven, and came out alive and well, although certainly done to a turn. And then there was 'The Diary of a Late Physician,' where the merit lay in good rant, and indifferent Greek—both of them taking things with the public. And then there was 'The Man in the Bell,' a paper by-the-by, Miss Zenobia, which I cannot sufficiently recommend to your attention. It is the history of a young person who goes to sleep under the clapper of a church bell, and is awakened by its tolling for a funeral. The sound drives him mad, and, accordingly, pulling out his tablets, he gives a record of his sensations. Sensations are the great things after all. Should you ever be drowned or hung, be sure and make a note of your sensations—they will be worth to you ten guineas a sheet. If you wish to write forcibly, Miss Zenobia, pay minute attention to the sensations."

"That I certainly will, Mr. Blackwood," said I.

"Good!" he replied. "I see you are a pupil after my own heart. But I must put you au fait to the details necessary in composing what may be denominated a genuine Blackwood article of the sensation stamp—the kind which you will understand me to say I consider the best for all purposes.

"The first thing requisite is to get yourself into such a scrape as no one ever got into before. The oven, for instance,—that was a good hit. But if you have no oven or big bell, at hand, and if you cannot conveniently tumble out of a balloon, or be swallowed up in an earthquake, or get stuck fast in a chimney, you will have to be contented with simply imagining some similar misadventure. I should prefer, however, that you have the actual fact to bear you out. Nothing so well assists the fancy, as an experimental knowledge of the matter in hand. 'Truth is strange,' you know, 'stranger than fiction'—besides being more to the purpose."

Here I assured him I had an excellent pair of garters, and would go and hang myself forthwith.

"Good!" he replied: "Do so—although hanging is somewhat hackneyed. Perhaps you might do better. Take a dose of Brandreth's pills, and then give us your sensations. However, my instructions will apply equally well to any variety of misadventure, and on your way home you may easily get knocked in the head, or run over by an omnibus, or bitten by a mad dog, or drowned in a gutter. But to proceed.

"Having determined upon your subject, you must next consider the tone, or manner, of your narration. There is the tone didactic, the tone enthusiastic, the tone natural—all common-place enough. But then there is the tone laconic, or curt, which has lately come much into use. It consists in short sentences. Somehow thus: Can't be too brief. Can't be too snappish. Always a full stop. And never a paragraph.

"Then there is the tone elevated, diffusive, and interjectional. Some of our best novelists patronize this tone. The words must be all in a whirl, like a humming-top, and make a noise very similar, which answers remarkably well instead of meaning. This is the best of all possible styles where the writer is in too great a hurry to think.

"The tone metaphysical is also a good one. If you know any big words this is your chance for them. Talk of the Ionic and Eleatic schools—of Archytas, Gorgias, and Alcmaeon. Say something about objectivity and subjectivity. Be sure and abuse a man named Locke. Turn up your nose at things in general, and when you let slip anything a little too absurd, you need not be at the trouble of scratching it out, but just add a footnote and say that you are indebted for the above profound observation to the 'Kritik der reinem Vernunft,' or to the 'Metaphysithe Anfongsgrunde der Noturwissenchaft.' This would look erudite and—and—and frank.

"There are various other tones of equal celebrity, but I shall mention only two more—the tone transcendental and the tone heterogeneous. In the former the merit consists in seeing into the nature of affairs a very great deal farther than anybody else. This second sight is very efficient when properly managed. A little reading of the 'Dial' will carry you a great way. Eschew, in this case, big words; get them as small as possible, and write them upside down. Look over Channing's poems and quote what he says about a 'fat little man with a delusive show of Can.' Put in something about the Supernal Oneness. Don't say a syllable about the Infernal Twoness. Above all, study innuendo. Hint everything—assert nothing. If you feel inclined to say 'bread and butter,' do not by any means say it outright. You may say any thing and every thing approaching to 'bread and butter.' You may hint at buck-wheat cake, or you may even go so far as to insinuate oat-meal porridge, but if bread and butter be your real meaning, be cautious, my dear Miss Psyche, not on any account to say 'bread and butter!'"

I assured him that I should never say it again as long as I lived. He kissed me and continued:

"As for the tone heterogeneous, it is merely a judicious mixture, in equal proportions, of all the other tones in the world, and is consequently made up of everything deep, great, odd, piquant, pertinent, and pretty.

"Let us suppose now you have determined upon your incidents and tone. The most important portion—in fact, the soul of the whole business, is yet to be attended to—I allude to the filling up. It is not to be supposed that a lady, or gentleman either, has been leading the life of a book worm. And yet above all things it is necessary that your article have an air of erudition, or at least afford evidence of extensive general reading. Now I'll put you in the way of accomplishing this point. See here!" (Pulling down some three or four ordinary-looking volumes, and opening them at random). "By casting your eye down almost any page of any book in the world, you will be able to perceive at once a host of little scraps of either learning or bel-espritism, which are the very thing for the spicing of a Blackwood article. You might as well note down a few while I read them to you. I shall make two divisions: first, Piquant Facts for the Manufacture of Similes, and, second, Piquant Expressions to be introduced as occasion may require. Write now!"—and I wrote as he dictated.

"PIQUANT FACTS FOR SIMILES. 'There were originally but three Muses—Melete, Mneme, Aoede—meditation, memory, and singing.' You may make a good deal of that little fact if properly worked. You see it is not generally known, and looks recherché. You must be careful and give the thing with a downright improviso air.

"Again. 'The river Alpheus passed beneath the sea, and emerged without injury to the purity of its waters.' Rather stale that, to be sure, but, if properly dressed and dished up, will look quite as fresh as ever.

"Here is something better. 'The Persian Iris appears to some persons to possess a sweet and very powerful perfume, while to others it is perfectly scentless.' Fine that, and very delicate! Turn it about a little, and it will do wonders. We'll have some thing else in the botanical line.

There's nothing goes down so well, especially with the help of a little Latin. Write!

"'The Epidendrum Flos Aeris, of Java, bears a very beautiful flower, and will live when pulled up by the roots. The natives suspend it by a cord from the ceiling, and enjoy its fragrance for years.' That's capital! That will do for the similes. Now for the Piquant Expressions.

"PIQUANT EXPRESSIONS. 'The Venerable Chinese novel *Ju-Kiao-Li*.' Good! By introducing these few words with dexterity, you will evince your intimate acquaintance with the language and literature of the Chinese. With the aid of this you may either get along without either Arabic, or Sanskrit, or Chickasaw. There is no passing muster, however, without Spanish, Italian, German, Latin, and Greek. I must look you out a little specimen of each. Any scrap will answer, because you must depend upon your own ingenuity to make it fit into your article. Now write!

"'*Aussi tendre que Zaire*'—as tender as Zaire—French. Alludes to the frequent repetition of the phrase, *la tendre Zaire*, in the French tragedy of that name. Properly introduced, will show not only your knowledge of the language, but your general reading and wit. You can say, for instance, that the chicken you were eating (write an article about being choked to death by a chicken-bone) was not altogether *aussi tendre que Zaire*. Write!

> 'Van muerte tan escondida,
>   Que no te sienta venir,
> Porque el plazer del morir,
>   No mestorne a dar la vida.'¹

"That's Spanish—from Miguel de Cervantes. 'Come quickly, O death! but be sure and don't let me see you coming, lest the pleasure I shall feel at your appearance should unfortunately bring me back again to life.' This you may slip in quite a *propos* when you are struggling in the last agonies with the chicken-bone. Write!

> '*Il pover 'huomo che non sèn era accorto,*

---

1   Spanish: 'Come death so hidden,
That it does not feel you coming,
Because the pleasure of dying,
Does not give life.'

'Andava combattendo, e era morto.'[2]

"That's Italian, you perceive—from Ariosto. It means that a great hero, in the heat of combat, not perceiving that he had been fairly killed, continued to fight valiantly, dead as he was. The application of this to your own case is obvious—for I trust, Miss Psyche, that you will not neglect to kick for at least an hour and a half after you have been choked to death by that chicken-bone. Please to write!

'Und sterb'ich doch, no sterb'ich denn
Durch sie—durch sie!'[3]

"That's German—from Schiller. 'And if I die, at least I die—for thee—for thee!' Here it is clear that you are apostrophizing the cause of your disaster, the chicken. Indeed what gentleman (or lady either) of sense, wouldn't die, I should like to know, for a well fattened capon of the right Molucca breed, stuffed with capers and mushrooms, and served up in a salad-bowl, with orange-jellies *en mosaiques.* Write! (You can get them that way at Tortoni's.)—Write, if you please!

"Here is a nice little Latin phrase, and rare too, (one can't be too recherché or brief in one's Latin, it's getting so common—*ignoratio elenchi*. He has committed an *ignoratio elenchi*—that is to say, he has understood the words of your proposition, but not the idea. The man was a fool, you see. Some poor fellow whom you address while choking with that chicken-bone, and who therefore didn't precisely understand what you were talking about. Throw the *ignoratio elenchi* in his teeth, and, at once, you have him annihilated. If he dares to reply, you can tell him from Lucan (here it is) that speeches are mere *anemonae verborum*, anemone words. The anemone, with great brilliancy, has no smell. Or, if he begins to bluster, you may be down upon him with *insomnia Jovis*, reveries of Jupiter—a phrase which Silius Italicus (see here!) applies to thoughts pompous and inflated. This will be sure and cut him to the heart. He can do nothing but roll over and die. Will you be kind enough to write?

"In Greek, we must have something pretty—from Demosthenes,

---

2   Italian: 'The poor old' man who was not noticed, He went fighting, and was dead.'

3   German: "And I'll die, no I will not die Through it—through it!"

for example: *Anerh o pheugoen kai palin makesetai*. There is a tolerably good translation of it in Hudibras:

> 'For he that flies may fight again,
> Which he can never do that's slain.'

"In a Blackwood article, nothing makes so fine a show as your Greek. The very letters have an air of profundity about them. Only observe, madam, the astute look of that Epsilon! That Phi ought certainly to be a bishop! Was ever there a smarter fellow than that Omicron? Just twig that Tau! In short, there is nothing like Greek for a genuine sensation-paper. In the present case, your application is the most obvious thing in the world. Rap out the sentence, with a huge oath, and by way of ultimatum at the good-for-nothing dunder-headed villain who couldn't understand your plain English in relation to the chicken-bone. He'll take the hint and be off, you may depend upon it."

These were all the instructions Mr. B. could afford me upon the topic in question, but I felt they would be entirely sufficient. I was, at length, able to write a genuine Blackwood article, and determined to do it forthwith. In taking leave of me, Mr. B. made a proposition for the purchase of the paper when written; but as he could offer me only fifty guineas a sheet, I thought it better to let our society have it, than sacrifice it for so paltry a sum. Notwithstanding this niggardly spirit, however, the gentleman showed his consideration for me in all other respects, and indeed treated me with the greatest civility. His parting words made a deep impression upon my heart, and I hope I shall always remember them with gratitude.

"My dear Miss Zenobia," he said, while the tears stood in his eyes, "is there anything else I can do to promote the success of your laudable undertaking? Let me reflect! It is just possible that you may not be able, so soon as convenient, to—to—get yourself drowned, or—choked with a chicken-bone, or—or hung,—or—bitten by a—. But stay! Now I think me of it, there are a couple of very excellent bulldogs in the yard—fine fellows, I assure you—savage, and all that—indeed just the thing for your money—they'll have you eaten up, auricula and all, in less than five minutes (here's my watch!)—and then only think of the sensations! Here! I say—Tom!—Peter!—Dick, you villain!—Let out those"—but as I was really in a great hurry, and had not another moment to spare, I was reluctantly forced to expedite my departure,

FICTION

and accordingly took leave at once—somewhat more abruptly, I admit, than strict courtesy would have otherwise allowed.

It was my primary object upon quitting Mr. Blackwood, to get into some immediate difficulty, pursuant to his advice, and with this view I spent the greater part of the day in wandering about Edinburgh, seeking for desperate adventures—adventures adequate to the intensity of my feelings, and adapted to the vast character of the article I intended to write. In this excursion, I was attended by one negro-servant, Pompey, and my little lapdog Diana, whom I had brought with me from Philadelphia. It was not, however, until late in the afternoon that I fully succeeded in my arduous undertaking. An important event then happened of which the following Blackwood article, in the tone heterogeneous, is the substance and result.

Vocabulary

Signora Psyche Zenobia: "Signora" is Italian for "Lady." The alternative name by which only Lady Zenobia's enemies call her, "Suky," means female dog (derogatory) in Slavic languages. The presence of Zenobia's "lap-dog Diana" (30) at the end of this piece further suggests that this is the intended meaning. Poe meant to use an alternative spelling for "snob" ("Snobbs") to label her because he is doubly playing on her snobbish reference to herself as a Lady. One clue that he is deliberately using the Slavic meaning of "Suky" is that the narrator explains that it is a "vulgar corruption of Psyche," meaning that the word "psyche" sounds like Suky if somebody with poor pronunciation says it. If her enemies have assured her of these being equivalent, they might have been playing a joke on her. Psyche was the Greek goddess of the soul, but a common alternative spelling of her name is Psykhe. Poe breaks the majesty of this allusion by equating the soul with a "butterfly" and then explaining that she's like a butterfly because of the satin dress she wears. Zenobia was indeed "queen of the Roman colony of Palmyra, in present-day Syria, from 267 or 268 to 272. She conquered several of Rome's eastern provinces before she was subjugated by the emperor Aurelian" (*Encyclopedia Britannica*). A patronymic shows descent from an ancestor, but having a father who is "a" random "Greek" would certainly fail to prove an ancestral lineage to the original queen of Palmyra, so the narrator is embellishing the truth to flatter her self-image. The repetitions in this narrative are a great example of cyclical writing that keeps repeating itself; avoid making this mistake in your own research writing.

Comments on the Text

"There was no investigation of first causes, first principles… there was no fine writing like this. It was all low—very! No profundity, no reading, no metaphysics—nothing which the learned call spirituality, and which the unlearned choose to stigmatize as cant" (22): This story is deliberately confusing, nonsensical and uses unnecessary abbreviations and big words to satirize highbrow writing that has the elements described in this quote. You should think about this advice from Poe when you work on your own essays for this class. The goal of a research paper is to show evidence that supports a meaningful point, not simply to show off your rhetorical abilities by overloading the reader with "metaphysics" or "principles." Poe goes on to stress that the narrator refused to spell "cant" with a capital "K," as in Kant or Immanuel Kant, an eighteenth century philosopher whose philosophy might indeed have had some "cant" to it, as cant means: "Hypocritical and sanctimonious talk, typically of a moral, religious, or political nature" (*Oxford Living Dictionaries*).

"'You may take, it for granted, that when manuscript can be read it is never worth reading,'" Mr. Blackwood says (23): Scholarly writing frequently prides itself on being impenetrable to an average reader, and this is what's satirized here. When you write an essay, a book, or anything else for somebody else to read, be aware that clarity is the most important element of good writing; if an article cannot be read, in truth, there is no point in writing it.

"The Dead Alive": "How to Write a Blackwood Article" was published in 1838 in the *American Museum* together with a story called, "A Predicament." The title alludes to *Blackwood's Edinburgh Magazine* and its brand of sensational horror writing. In "A Predicament," Zenobia is decapitated because of her gothic curiosity, and yet her head continues to orate a speech after its separation, so the title "The Dead Alive," which he has Mr. Blackwood allude to, might be Poe referencing his own story and poking fun at himself. Poe also published a horror story, "The Premature Burial," in 1844, which plays on the same predicament of being between life and death. A few decades after Poe's early death, Wilkie Collins wrote a novella called, *The Dead Alive*; this is an interesting parallel because Poe interviewed Dickens previously, and Collins worked closely with Dickens on his periodical, so Collins is likely to have been aware of Poe's title before he adopted it. Poe's allusion to "Confessions of an Opium-eater" refers to *Confessions of an English Opium-Eater* (1821) by Thomas De Quincey, which catapulted Quincey to fame with its blatant admission of a weakness for the drug. Poe summarizes Quincey's book as "plenty of fire and fury, and a good spicing of the decidedly unintelligible" (24). The babblings of a drug addict are certainly an extreme example of unintelligible writing, and its success shows how sensibility and emotion frequently attract more readers or buyers for fiction than coherence or logic. Mr. Blackwood misattributes the "Confessions" to Samuel Taylor Coleridge, who was a poet with an opium addiction. But, Mr. Blackwood argues that the "Confessions" was actually written by his own baboon, or an African-Arabian monkey.

Mr. Blackwood also praises "The Involuntary Experimentalist," which was a short story by Samuel Ferguson that was published in *Blackwood's Edinburgh Magazine* in October of 1837, and is considered to be "the last of a number of sensational tales which were characteristic of *Blackwood's*... 'Blackwood's* fiction' became a shorthand term for a type of story which concentrated on the state of consciousness of a suffering individual in a death-bed, death-cell or similarly in extremis" (Denman 51). "The Involuntary" story is available in full in a free Google Book: *Blackwood's Edinburgh Magazine, Volume 5*. The piece indeed includes a long scene of an experimenter "burning to death for want of a ladder" (490), as he attempts to write memos to ask for deliverance, which end with: "I die, forgiving all my en..." (491). While it seems that the story ends there, he ends up being rescued after this climax, as Poe satirically points out in his brief summary of these events.

"The Diary of a Late Physician" refers to Samuel Warren's 1838 fake autobiography, but really a series of gothic tales, *Passages from the Diary of a Late Physician*, released with William Blackwood & Sons.

After giving all of these examples of exemplary sensational writing, Mr. Blackwood then tells Zenobia: "Should you ever be drowned or hung, be sure and make a note of your sensations—they will be worth to you ten guineas a sheet" (24). As a professional writer, Poe struggled with the need to write pop fiction, like these gothic works that were in demand at *Blackwood's*, but which offended his intellect because of their irrational reliance on sensationalism. If somebody is in the process of being "drowned or hung," it is hardly the time to write down the sensation one is experiencing and yet the bulk of these stories attempt this very trick. From these theoretical ideas, Poe moves into pure absurd satire, as Mr. Blackwood insists that Zenobia must put herself in a life-threatening situation to be able to write an article that *Blackwood's* might be willing to publish. Zenobia replies: "Here I assured him I had an excellent pair of garters, and would go and hang myself forthwith" (24). Writers are constantly told to write about what they know, but also that fiction has to include extreme situations that are surprising and shocking to readers, so Poe pushes these contradictory ideas by offering this female writer as a sacrifice to the Muses, "Melete, Mneme, Aoede—meditation, memory, and singing" (26). The rest of this article includes numerous other allusions, references, translations and other complex details, which I encourage you to research if you plan on writing about this story for your essay in this class.

Questions for Discussion

1. What do you think about the use of insults such as "Suky Snobbs" in the opening of this story? How is Poe's utilization of these euphemisms different from outright insults and curses that frequently appear in modern American popular films and television? Is the negative meaning strengthened when the insults are indirect or hidden; why or why not?
2. When you think about very confusing writing style, what work of fiction or non-fiction comes to mind? Do you enjoy reading clear and logical works or those that are sensational or suspenseful?
3. One of the examples from *Blackwood's* that Mr. Blackwood stresses shows some of the best writing is based on the life of an opium-user, and another is based on a man nearly burning to death. What do you think about the dark satirical humor Poe uses in these examples? Do readers frequently focus on the biographies of authors and how dramatic they were instead of on the artfulness of their compositions? Poe died an early, dramatic death that has been suspected as a homicide related to voter fraud; is it possible that in his final days Poe attempted to experience the sort of sensational near-death experience that he is joking about in this piece? Answer any

of these questions that speak to you.
4. Do a bit of research into any of the other allusions in this story, and explain what Poe meant by it in the context of "Blackwood Article." You can do a simple Google search, or search through the UTRGV Library catalog or other resources for ideas. **Allusion** is "an implied or indirect reference especially in literature" (*Merriam-Webster*).

Works Cited

Blackwood's Edinburgh Magazine, Volume 5. Edinburgh: J. Mason; New York: William Lewer, 1837. Google Books. 27 January 2017. Web.

Denman, Peter. *Samuel Ferguson: The Literary Achievement*. New York: Rowman & Littlefield, 1990.

Miguel de Cervantes

Miguel de Cervantes was born on September 29, 1547 in Alcala de Henares, in the year when the first *Index* of prohibited books was released (a step that meant a new type of censorship of the growing century-old institution of the press), and a few years before Shakespeare's birth in 1564. Miguel started writing poetry in 1567 shortly after his family moved to Madrid, and became known for it as early as in 1569 when his poetry was included in a memorial collection for Elizabeth of Valois. In 1570, he went into service under Cardinal Acquaviva in Rome amidst a war with the Turks, and was wounded by the following year. He served in different divisions after this until he was captured by Barbary pirates by the Catalonia coast in 1575, and was held captive in Algiers, where he tried to escape in 1576 and 1577. His brother, Rodrigo, was ransomed before this second unsuccessful attempt. Miguel kept trying to escape annually in 1578 and 1579, before he was finally ransomed by Trinitarian monks in 1580. Cervantes created his first play, *The Treatment of Algiers*, based on his African captivity, in 1582 in Madrid. Miguel married Catalina de Salazar in Esquivias in 1584. His first novel was a formulaic pastoral, *La Galatea* (1585). His fiction, poetry and plays were unsuccessful, so he had to make a living from public service, and a commission collecting grain for the Armada, starting in 1587, led to imprisonment for mismanagement of resources in 1592. He worked as a tax collector from 1595, and was again jailed in 1597 in Seville. The following years continued to be difficult for Cervantes as the plague broke out in 1599, then his brother, Rodrigo, died in the Battle of the Dunes in 1600, and the theaters were closed for two years because of all the warring and social turmoil. It was at the end of this set of crises, in 1602, when Cervantes wrote the first part of his best-known work, *Don Quixote*, which he only managed to publish in 1605.

DON QUIXOTE

Translated by John Ormsby

CONTENTS
Volume I.
CHAPTER I WHICH TREATS OF THE CHARACTER AND PURSUITS OF THE FAMOUS GENTLEMAN DON QUIXOTE OF LA MANCHA
CHAPTER II WHICH TREATS OF THE FIRST SALLY THE INGENIOUS DON QUIXOTE MADE FROM HOME
CHAPTER III WHEREIN IS RELATED THE DROLL WAY IN WHICH DON QUIXOTE HAD HIMSELF DUBBED A KNIGHT
CHAPTER IV OF WHAT HAPPENED TO OUR KNIGHT WHEN HE LEFT THE INN
CHAPTER V IN WHICH THE NARRATIVE OF OUR KNIGHT'S MISHAP IS CONTINUED
CHAPTER VI OF THE DIVERTING AND IMPORTANT SCRUTINY WHICH THE CURATE AND THE BARBER MADE IN THE LIBRARY OF OUR INGENIOUS GENTLEMAN
CHAPTER VII OF THE SECOND SALLY OF OUR WORTHY KNIGHT DON QUIXOTE OF LA MANCHA
CHAPTER VIII OF THE GOOD FORTUNE WHICH THE VALIANT DON QUIXOTE HAD IN THE TERRIBLE AND UNDREAMT-OF ADVENTURE OF THE WINDMILLS, WITH OTHER OCCURRENCES WORTHY TO BE FITLY RECORDED
CHAPTER IX IN WHICH IS CONCLUDED AND FINISHED THE TERRIFIC BATTLE BETWEEN THE GALLANT BISCAYAN AND THE VALIANT MANCHEGAN
CHAPTER X OF THE PLEASANT DISCOURSE THAT PASSED BETWEEN DON QUIXOTE AND HIS SQUIRE SANCHO PANZA
CHAPTER XI OF WHAT BEFELL DON QUIXOTE WITH CERTAIN GOATHERDS
CHAPTER XII OF WHAT A GOATHERD RELATED TO THOSE WITH DON QUIXOTE
CHAPTER XIII IN WHICH IS ENDED THE STORY OF THE SHEPHERDESS MARCELA, WITH OTHER INCIDENTS
CHAPTER XIV WHEREIN ARE INSERTED THE DESPAIRING VERSES OF THE DEAD SHEPHERD, TOGETHER WITH OTHER INCIDENTS NOT LOOKED FOR
CHAPTER XV IN WHICH IS RELATED THE UNFORTUNATE ADVENTURE THAT DON QUIXOTE FELL IN WITH WHEN HE FELL OUT WITH CERTAIN HEARTLESS YANGUESANS
CHAPTER XVI OF WHAT HAPPENED TO THE INGENIOUS GENTLEMAN IN THE INN WHICH HE TOOK TO BE A CASTLE
CHAPTER XVII IN WHICH ARE CONTAINED THE INNUMERABLE TROUBLES WHICH THE BRAVE DON QUIXOTE AND HIS GOOD SQUIRE SANCHO

PANZA ENDURED IN THE INN, WHICH TO HIS MISFORTUNE HE TOOK TO BE A CASTLE
CHAPTER XVIII IN WHICH IS RELATED THE DISCOURSE SANCHO PANZA HELD WITH HIS MASTER, DON QUIXOTE, AND OTHER ADVENTURES WORTH RELATING
CHAPTER XIX OF THE SHREWD DISCOURSE WHICH SANCHO HELD WITH HIS MASTER, AND OF THE ADVENTURE THAT BEFELL HIM WITH A DEAD BODY, TOGETHER WITH OTHER NOTABLE OCCURRENCES
CHAPTER XX OF THE UNEXAMPLED AND UNHEARD-OF ADVENTURE WHICH WAS ACHIEVED BY THE VALIANT DON QUIXOTE OF LA MANCHA WITH LESS PERIL THAN ANY EVER ACHIEVED BY ANY FAMOUS KNIGHT IN THE WORLD
CHAPTER XXI WHICH TREATS OF THE EXALTED ADVENTURE AND RICH PRIZE OF MAMBRINO'S HELMET, TOGETHER WITH OTHER THINGS THAT HAPPENED TO OUR INVINCIBLE KNIGHT
CHAPTER XXII OF THE FREEDOM DON QUIXOTE CONFERRED ON SEVERAL UNFORTUNATES WHO AGAINST THEIR WILL WERE BEING CARRIED WHERE THEY HAD NO WISH TO GO
CHAPTER XXIII OF WHAT BEFELL DON QUIXOTE IN THE SIERRA MORENA, WHICH WAS ONE OF THE RAREST ADVENTURES RELATED IN THIS VERACIOUS HISTORY
CHAPTER XXIV IN WHICH IS CONTINUED THE ADVENTURE OF THE SIERRA MORENA
CHAPTER XXV WHICH TREATS OF THE STRANGE THINGS THAT HAPPENED TO THE STOUT KNIGHT OF LA MANCHA IN THE SIERRA MORENA, AND OF HIS IMITATION OF THE PENANCE OF BELTENEBROS
CHAPTER XXVI IN WHICH ARE CONTINUED THE REFINEMENTS WHEREWITH DON QUIXOTE PLAYED THE PART OF A LOVER IN THE SIERRA MORENA
CHAPTER XXVII OF HOW THE CURATE AND THE BARBER PROCEEDED WITH THEIR SCHEME; TOGETHER WITH OTHER MATTERS WORTHY OF RECORD IN THIS GREAT HISTORY
CHAPTER XXVIII WHICH TREATS OF THE STRANGE AND DELIGHTFUL ADVENTURE THAT BEFELL THE CURATE AND THE BARBER IN THE SAME SIERRA
CHAPTER XXIX WHICH TREATS OF THE DROLL DEVICE AND METHOD ADOPTED TO EXTRICATE OUR LOVE-STRICKEN KNIGHT FROM THE SEVERE PENANCE HE HAD IMPOSED UPON HIMSELF
CHAPTER XXX WHICH TREATS OF ADDRESS DISPLAYED BY THE FAIR DOROTHEA, WITH OTHER MATTERS PLEASANT AND AMUSING
CHAPTER XXXI OF THE DELECTABLE DISCUSSION BETWEEN DON QUIXOTE AND SANCHO PANZA, HIS SQUIRE, TOGETHER WITH OTHER INCIDENTS
CHAPTER XXXII WHICH TREATS OF WHAT BEFELL DON QUIXOTE'S PARTY AT THE INN
CHAPTER XXXIII IN WHICH IS RELATED THE NOVEL OF "THE ILL-ADVISED CURIOSITY"
CHAPTER XXXIV IN WHICH IS CONTINUED THE NOVEL OF "THE ILL-ADVISED CURIOSITY"
CHAPTER XXXV WHICH TREATS OF THE HEROIC AND PRODIGIOUS BATTLE DON QUIXOTE HAD WITH CERTAIN SKINS OF RED WINE, AND BRINGS THE NOVEL OF "THE ILL-ADVISED CURIOSITY" TO A CLOSE
CHAPTER XXXVI WHICH TREATS OF MORE CURIOUS INCIDENTS THAT OC-

CURRED AT THE INN
CHAPTER XXXVII IN WHICH IS CONTINUED THE STORY OF THE FAMOUS PRINCESS MICOMICONA, WITH OTHER DROLL ADVENTURES
CHAPTER XXXVIII WHICH TREATS OF THE CURIOUS DISCOURSE DON QUIXOTE DELIVERED ON ARMS AND LETTERS
CHAPTER XXXIX WHEREIN THE CAPTIVE RELATES HIS LIFE AND ADVENTURES
CHAPTER XL IN WHICH THE STORY OF THE CAPTIVE IS CONTINUED.
CHAPTER XLI IN WHICH THE CAPTIVE STILL CONTINUES HIS ADVENTURES
CHAPTER XLII WHICH TREATS OF WHAT FURTHER TOOK PLACE IN THE INN, AND OF SEVERAL OTHER THINGS WORTH KNOWING
CHAPTER XLIII WHEREIN IS RELATED THE PLEASANT STORY OF THE MULETEER, TOGETHER WITH OTHER STRANGE THINGS THAT CAME TO PASS IN THE INN
CHAPTER XLIV IN WHICH ARE CONTINUED THE UNHEARD-OF ADVENTURES OF THE INN
CHAPTER XLV IN WHICH THE DOUBTFUL QUESTION OF MAMBRINO'S HELMET AND THE PACK-SADDLE IS FINALLY SETTLED, WITH OTHER ADVENTURES THAT OCCURRED IN TRUTH AND EARNEST
CHAPTER XLVI OF THE END OF THE NOTABLE ADVENTURE OF THE OFFICERS OF THE HOLY BROTHERHOOD; AND OF THE GREAT FEROCITY OF OUR WORTHY KNIGHT, DON QUIXOTE
CHAPTER XLVII OF THE STRANGE MANNER IN WHICH DON QUIXOTE OF LA MANCHA WAS CARRIED AWAY ENCHANTED, TOGETHER WITH OTHER REMARKABLE INCIDENTS
CHAPTER XLVIII IN WHICH THE CANON PURSUES THE SUBJECT OF THE BOOKS OF CHIVALRY, WITH OTHER MATTERS WORTHY OF HIS WIT
CHAPTER XLIX WHICH TREATS OF THE SHREWD CONVERSATION WHICH SANCHO PANZA HELD WITH HIS MASTER DON QUIXOTE
CHAPTER L OF THE SHREWD CONTROVERSY WHICH DON QUIXOTE AND THE CANON HELD, TOGETHER WITH OTHER INCIDENTS
CHAPTER LI WHICH DEALS WITH WHAT THE GOATHERD TOLD THOSE WHO WERE CARRYING OFF DON QUIXOTE
CHAPTER LII OF THE QUARREL THAT DON QUIXOTE HAD WITH THE GOATHERD, TOGETHER WITH THE RARE ADVENTURE OF THE PENITENTS, WHICH WITH AN EXPENDITURE OF SWEAT HE BROUGHT TO A HAPPY CONCLUSION

THE AUTHOR'S PREFACE

Idle reader: thou mayest believe me without any oath that I would this book, as it is the child of my brain, were the fairest, gayest, and cleverest that could be imagined. But I could not counteract Nature's law that everything shall beget its like; and what, then, could this sterile, ill-tilled wit of mine beget but the story of a dry, shriveled, whimsical offspring, full of thoughts of all sorts and such as never came into any other imagination—just what might be begotten in a prison, where every misery is lodged and every doleful sound makes its dwelling? Tranquillity, a cheerful retreat, pleasant fields, bright skies, murmuring brooks, peace of mind, these are the things that go far to make even the most barren muses fertile, and bring into the world births that fill it with wonder and delight. Sometimes when a father has an ugly, loutish son, the love he bears him so blindfolds his eyes that he does not see his defects, or, rather, takes them for gifts and charms of mind and body, and talks of them to his friends as wit and grace. I, however—for though I pass for the father, I am but the stepfather to "Don Quixote"—have no desire to go with the current of custom, or to implore thee, dearest reader, almost with tears in my eyes, as others do, to pardon or excuse the defects thou wilt perceive in this child of mine. Thou art neither its kinsman nor its friend, thy soul is thine own and thy will as free as any man's, whate'er he be, thou art in thine own house and master of it as much as the king of his taxes and thou knowest the common saying, "Under my cloak I kill the king;" all which exempts and frees thee from every consideration and obligation, and thou canst say what thou wilt of the story without fear of being abused for any ill or rewarded for any good thou mayest say of it.

My wish would be simply to present it to thee plain and unadorned, without any embellishment of preface or uncountable muster of customary sonnets, epigrams, and eulogies, such as are commonly put at the beginning of books. For I can tell thee, though composing it cost me some labour, I found none greater than the making of this Preface thou art now reading. Many times did I take up my pen to write it, and many did I lay it down again, not knowing what to write. One of these times, as I was pondering with the paper before me, a pen in my ear, my elbow on the desk, and my cheek in my hand, thinking of what I should say, there came in unexpectedly a certain lively, clever friend of mine, who, seeing me so deep in thought, asked the reason; to which I, making no mystery of it, answered that I was thinking of the Preface I had to make for the story of "Don Quixote," which so troubled me that I had a mind not to make any at all, nor even publish the achievements of so noble a knight.

"For, how could you expect me not to feel uneasy about what that ancient lawgiver they call the Public will say when it sees me, after slumbering so many years in the silence of oblivion, coming out now with all my years upon my back, and with a book as dry as a rush, devoid of invention, meagre in style, poor in thoughts, wholly wanting in learning and wisdom, without quotations in the margin or annotations at the end, after the fashion of other books I see, which, though all fables and profanity, are so full of maxims from Aristotle, and Plato, and the whole herd of philosophers, that they fill the readers with amazement and convince them that the authors are men of learning, erudition, and eloquence. And then, when they quote the Holy Scriptures!—anyone would say they are St. Thomases or other doctors of the Church, observing as they do a decorum so ingenious that in one sentence they describe a distracted lover and in the next deliver a devout little sermon that it is a pleasure and a treat to hear and read. Of all this there will be nothing in my book, for I have nothing to quote in the margin or to note at the end, and still less do I know what authors I follow in it, to place them at the beginning, as all do, under the letters A, B, C, beginning with Aristotle and ending with Xenophon, or Zoilus, or Zeuxis, though one was a slanderer and the other a painter. Also my book must do without sonnets at the beginning, at least sonnets whose authors are dukes, marquises, counts, bishops, ladies, or famous poets. Though if I were to ask two or three obliging friends, I know they would give me them, and such as the productions of those that have the highest reputation in our Spain could not equal.

"In short, my friend," I continued, "I am determined that Senor Don Quixote shall remain buried in the archives of his own La Mancha until Heaven provide someone to garnish him with all those things he stands in need of; because I find myself, through my shallowness and want of learning, unequal to supplying them, and because I am by nature shy and careless about hunting for authors to say what I myself can say without them. Hence the cogitation and abstraction you found me in, and reason enough, what you have heard from me."

Hearing this, my friend, giving himself a slap on the forehead and breaking into a hearty laugh, exclaimed, "Before God, Brother, now am I disabused of an error in which I have been living all this long time I have known you, all through which I have taken you to be shrewd and sensible in all you do; but now I see you are as far from that as the heaven is from the earth. It is possible that things of so little moment and so easy to set right can occupy and perplex a ripe wit like yours, fit to break through and crush far greater obstacles? By my faith, this comes, not of any want of ability, but of too much indolence and too little knowledge of life. Do you want to know if I am telling the truth?

Well, then, attend to me, and you will see how, in the opening and shutting of an eye, I sweep away all your difficulties, and supply all those deficiencies which you say check and discourage you from bringing before the world the story of your famous Don Quixote, the light and mirror of all knight-errantry."

"Say on," said I, listening to his talk; "how do you propose to make up for my diffidence, and reduce to order this chaos of perplexity I am in?"

To which he made answer, "Your first difficulty about the sonnets, epigrams, or complimentary verses which you want for the beginning, and which ought to be by persons of importance and rank, can be removed if you yourself take a little trouble to make them; you can afterwards baptise them, and put any name you like to them, fathering them on Prester John of the Indies or the Emperor of Trebizond, who, to my knowledge, were said to have been famous poets: and even if they were not, and any pedants or bachelors should attack you and question the fact, never care two maravedis for that, for even if they prove a lie against you they cannot cut off the hand you wrote it with.

"As to references in the margin to the books and authors from whom you take the aphorisms and sayings you put into your story, it is only contriving to fit in nicely any sentences or scraps of Latin you may happen to have by heart, or at any rate that will not give you much trouble to look up; so as, when you speak of freedom and captivity, to insert:

Non bene pro toto libertas venditur auro;[4]

and then refer in the margin to Horace, or whoever said it; or, if you allude to the power of death, to come in with—

Pallida mors Aequo pulsat pede pauperum tabernas, Regumque turres.[5]

"If it be friendship and the love God bids us bear to our enemy, go at once to the Holy Scriptures, which you can do with a very small amount of research, and quote no less than the words of God himself: *Ego autem dico vobis: diligite inimicos vestros.* If you speak of evil thoughts, turn to the Gospel: *De corde exeunt cogitationes malae.* If of

4   Latin: Do not sell your freedom for all the gold;
5   Latin: Pale Death is impartial: he knocks at the poor shops, and the palace-portal.

the fickleness of friends, there is Cato, who will give you his distich:

Donec eris felix multos numerabis amicos,
Tempora si fuerint nubila, solus eris.[6]

"With these and such like bits of Latin they will take you for a grammarian at all events, and that now-a-days is no small honour and profit.

"With regard to adding annotations at the end of the book, you may safely do it in this way. If you mention any giant in your book contrive that it shall be the giant Goliath, and with this alone, which will cost you almost nothing, you have a grand note, for you can put—The giant Golias or Goliath was a Philistine whom the shepherd David slew by a mighty stone-cast in the Terebinth valley, as is related in the Book of Kings—in the chapter where you find it written.

"Next, to prove yourself a man of erudition in polite literature and cosmography, manage that the river Tagus shall be named in your story, and there you are at once with another famous annotation, setting forth—'The river Tagus was so called after a King of Spain: it has its source in such and such a place and falls into the ocean, kissing the walls of the famous city of Lisbon, and it is a common belief that it has golden sands,' etc. If you should have anything to do with robbers, I will give you the story of Cacus, for I have it by heart; if with loose women, there is the Bishop of Mondoñedo, who will give you the loan of Lamia, Laida, and Flora, any reference to whom will bring you great credit; if with hard-hearted ones, Ovid will furnish you with Medea; if with witches or enchantresses, Homer has Calypso, and Virgil Circe; if with valiant captains, Julius Caesar himself will lend you himself in his own 'Commentaries,' and Plutarch will give you a thousand Alexanders. If you should deal with love, with two ounces you may know of Tuscan you can go to Leon the Hebrew, who will supply you to your heart's content; or if you should not care to go to foreign countries you have at home Fonseca's 'Of the Love of God,' in which is condensed all that you or the most imaginative mind can want on the subject. In short, all you have to do is to manage to quote these names, or refer to these stories I have mentioned, and leave it to me to insert the annotations and quotations, and I swear by all that's good to fill your margins

6 Latin: As long as you are fortunate, you will have many friends,/ When the clouds come, you will be alone.

and use up four sheets at the end of the book.

"Now let us come to those references to authors which other books have, and you want for yours. The remedy for this is very simple: You have only to look out for some book that quotes them all, from A to Z as you say yourself, and then insert the very same alphabet in your book, and though the imposition may be plain to see, because you have so little need to borrow from them, that is no matter; there will probably be some simple enough to believe that you have made use of them all in this plain, artless story of yours. At any rate, if it answers no other purpose, this long catalogue of authors will serve to give a surprising look of authority to your book. Besides, no one will trouble himself to verify whether you have followed them or whether you have not, being no way concerned in it; especially as, if I mistake not, this book of yours has no need of any one of those things you say it wants, for it is, from beginning to end, an attack upon the books of chivalry, of which Aristotle never dreamt, nor St. Basil said a word, nor Cicero had any knowledge; nor do the niceties of truth nor the observations of astrology come within the range of its fanciful vagaries; nor have geometrical measurements or refutations of the arguments used in rhetoric anything to do with it; nor does it mean to preach to anybody, mixing up things human and divine, a sort of motley in which no Christian understanding should dress itself. It has only to avail itself of truth to nature in its composition, and the more perfect the imitation the better the work will be. And as this piece of yours aims at nothing more than to destroy the authority and influence which books of chivalry have in the world and with the public, there is no need for you to go a-begging for aphorisms from philosophers, precepts from Holy Scripture, fables from poets, speeches from orators, or miracles from saints; but merely to take care that your style and diction run musically, pleasantly, and plainly, with clear, proper, and well-placed words, setting forth your purpose to the best of your power, and putting your ideas intelligibly, without confusion or obscurity. Strive, too, that in reading your story the melancholy may be moved to laughter, and the merry made merrier still; that the simple shall not be wearied, that the judicious shall admire the invention, that the grave shall not despise it, nor the wise fail to praise it. Finally, keep your aim fixed on the destruction of that ill-founded edifice of the books of chivalry, hated by some and praised by many more; for if you succeed in this you will have achieved no small success."

In profound silence I listened to what my friend said, and his observations made such an impression on me that, without attempting to question them, I admitted their soundness, and out of them I determined to make this Preface; wherein, gentle reader, thou wilt perceive my friend's good sense, my good fortune in finding such an adviser in such a time of need, and what thou hast gained in receiving, without addition or alteration, the story of the famous Don Quixote of La Mancha, who is held by all the inhabitants of the district of the Campo de Montiel to have been the chastest lover and the bravest knight that has for many years been seen in that neighbourhood. I have no desire to magnify the service I render thee in making thee acquainted with so renowned and honoured a knight, but I do desire thy thanks for the acquaintance thou wilt make with the famous Sancho Panza, his squire, in whom, to my thinking, I have given thee condensed all the squirely drolleries that are scattered through the swarm of the vain books of chivalry. And so—may God give thee health, and not forget me. Vale.

DEDICATION OF VOLUME I

TO THE DUKE OF BEJAR, MARQUIS OF GIBRALEON, COUNT OF BENALCAZAR AND BANARES, VICECOUNT OF THE PUEBLA DE ALCOCER, MASTER OF THE TOWNS OF CAPILLA, CURIEL AND BURGUILLOS

In belief of the good reception and honours that Your Excellency bestows on all sort of books, as prince so inclined to favor good arts, chiefly those who by their nobleness do not submit to the service and bribery of the vulgar, I have determined bringing to light The Ingenious Gentleman Don Quixote of la Mancha, in shelter of Your Excellency's glamorous name, to whom, with the obeisance I owe to such grandeur, I pray to receive it agreeably under his protection, so that in this shadow, though deprived of that precious ornament of elegance and erudition that clothe the works composed in the houses of those who know, it dares appear with assurance in the judgment of some who, trespassing the bounds of their own ignorance, use to condemn with more rigour and less justice the writings of others. It is my earnest

hope that Your Excellency's good counsel in regard to my honourable purpose, will not disdain the littleness of so humble a service.
—Miguel de Cervantes

VOLUME I.

CHAPTER I.

WHICH TREATS OF THE CHARACTER AND PURSUITS OF THE FAMOUS GENTLEMAN DON QUIXOTE OF LA MANCHA

In a village of La Mancha, the name of which I have no desire to call to mind, there lived not long since one of those gentlemen that keep a lance in the lance-rack, an old buckler, a lean hack, and a greyhound for coursing. An olla of rather more beef than mutton, a salad on most nights, scraps on Saturdays, lentils on Fridays, and a pigeon or so extra on Sundays, made away with three-quarters of his income. The rest of it went in a doublet of fine cloth and velvet breeches and shoes to match for holidays, while on week-days he made a brave figure in his best homespun. He had in his house a housekeeper past forty, a niece under twenty, and a lad for the field and market-place, who used to saddle the hack as well as handle the bill-hook. The age of this gentleman of ours was bordering on fifty; he was of a hardy habit, spare, gaunt-featured, a very early riser and a great sportsman. They will have it his surname was Quixada or Quesada (for here there is some difference of opinion among the authors who write on the subject), although from reasonable conjectures it seems plain that he was called Quexana. This, however, is of but little importance to our tale; it will be enough not to stray a hair's breadth from the truth in the telling of it.

You must know, then, that the above-named gentleman whenever he was at leisure (which was mostly all the year round) gave himself up to reading books of chivalry with such ardour and avidity that he almost entirely neglected the pursuit of his field-sports, and even the management of his property; and to such a pitch did his eagerness and infatuation go that he sold many an acre of tillageland to buy books of chivalry to read, and brought home as many of them as he could get. But of all there were none he liked so well as those of the famous Feliciano de Silva's composition, for their lucidity of style and complicated conceits were as pearls in his sight, particularly when in his reading he came upon courtships and cartels, where he often found passages like "the reason of the unreason with which my reason is afflicted so weakens my reason that with reason I murmur at your beauty;" or again, "the high heavens, that of your divinity divinely fortify you with the stars, render you deserving of the desert your greatness deserves." Over conceits of this sort the poor gentleman lost his wits, and used to lie awake striving to understand them and worm the meaning out of them; what Aristotle himself could not have made out or extracted had he come to life again for that special purpose. He was not at all easy about the wounds which Don Belianis gave and took, because it seemed to him that, great as were the surgeons who had cured him, he must have had his face and body covered all over with seams and scars. He commended, however, the author's way of ending his book with the promise of that interminable adventure, and many a time was he tempted to take up his pen and finish it properly as is there proposed, which no doubt he would have done, and made a successful piece of work of it too, had not greater and more absorbing thoughts prevented him.

Many an argument did he have with the curate of his village (a learned man, and a graduate of Sigüenza) as to which had been the better knight, Palmerin of England or Amadís of Gaul. Master Nicholas, the village barber, however, used to say that neither of them came up to the Knight of Phoebus, and that if there was any that could compare with him it was Don Galaor, the brother of Amadís of Gaul, because he had a spirit that was equal to every occasion, and was no finikin knight, nor lachrymose like his brother, while in the matter of valour he was not a whit behind him. In short, he became so absorbed in his books that he spent his nights from sunset to sunrise, and his days from dawn to dark, poring over them; and what with little sleep and much reading his brains got so dry that he lost his wits. His fancy grew full of what he used to read about in his books, enchantments, quarrels, battles, challenges, wounds, wooings, loves, agonies, and all sorts of impossible nonsense; and it so possessed his mind that the whole fabric of invention and fancy he read of was true, that to him no history in the world had more reality in it. He used to say the Cid Ruy Diaz was a very good knight, but that he was not to be compared with the Knight of the Burning Sword, who with one back-stroke cut in half two fierce and monstrous giants. He thought more of Bernardo del Carpio because at Roncesvalles he slew Roland in spite of enchantments, availing himself of the artifice of Hercules when he strangled Antaeus the son of Terra in his arms. He approved highly of the giant Morgante, because, although of the giant breed which is always arrogant and ill-conditioned, he alone was affable and well-bred. But above all he admired Reinaldos of Montalbán, especially when he saw him sallying forth from his castle and robbing everyone he met, and when beyond the seas he stole that image of Mahomet which, as his history says, was entirely of gold. To have a bout of kicking at that traitor of a Ganelon he would have given his housekeeper, and his niece into the bargain.

In short, his wits being quite gone, he hit upon the strangest notion that ever madman in this world hit upon, and that was that he fancied it was right and requisite, as well for the support of his own honour as for the service of his country, that he should make a knight-errant of himself, roaming the world over in full armour and on horseback in quest of adventures, and putting in practice himself all that he had read of as being the usual practices of knights-errant; righting every kind of wrong, and exposing himself to peril and danger from which, in the issue, he was to reap eternal renown and fame. Already the poor man saw himself crowned by the might of his arm Emperor of Trebizond at least; and so, led away by the intense enjoyment he found in these pleasant fancies, he set himself forthwith to put his scheme into execution.

The first thing he did was to clean up some armour that had belonged to his great-grandfather, and had been for ages lying forgotten in a corner eaten with rust and covered with mildew. He scoured and polished it as best he could, but he perceived one great defect in it, that it had no closed helmet, nothing but a simple morion. This deficiency, however, his ingenuity supplied, for he contrived a kind of half-helmet of pasteboard which, fitted on to the morion, looked like a whole one. It is true that, in order to see if it was strong and fit to stand a cut, he drew his sword and gave it a couple of slashes, the first of which undid in an instant what had taken him a week to do. The ease with which he had knocked it to pieces disconcerted him somewhat, and to guard against that danger he set to work again, fixing bars of iron on the inside until he was satisfied with its strength; and then, not caring to try any more experiments with it, he passed it and adopted it as a helmet of the most perfect construction.

He next proceeded to inspect his hack, which, with more quartos than a real and more blemishes than the steed of Gonela, that "*tantum pellis et ossa fuit*," surpassed in his eyes the Bucephalus of Alexander or the Babieca of the Cid. Four days were spent in thinking what name to give him, because (as he said to himself) it was not right that a horse belonging to a knight so famous, and one with such merits of his own, should be without some distinctive name, and he strove to adapt it so as to indicate what he had been before belonging to a knight-errant, and what he then was; for it was only reasonable that, his master taking a new character, he should take a new name, and that it should be a distinguished and full-sounding one, befitting the new order and calling he was about to follow. And so, after having composed, struck out, rejected, added to, unmade, and remade a multitude of names out of his memory and fancy, he decided upon calling him Rocinante, a name, to his thinking, lofty, sonorous, and significant of his condition as a hack before he became what he now was, the first and foremost of all the hacks in the world.

Having got a name for his horse so much to his taste, he was anxious to get one for himself, and he was eight days more pondering over this point, till at last he made up his mind to call himself "Don Quixote," whence, as has been already said, the authors of this veracious history have inferred that his name must have been beyond a doubt Quixada, and not Quesada as others would have it. Recollecting, however, that the valiant Amadís was not content to call himself curtly Amadís and nothing more, but added the name of his kingdom and country to make it famous, and called himself Amadís of Gaul, he, like a good knight, resolved to add on the name of his, and to style himself Don Quixote of La Mancha, whereby, he considered, he described accurately his origin and country, and did honour to it in taking his surname from it.

So then, his armour being furbished, his morion turned into a helmet, his hack christened, and he himself confirmed, he came to the conclusion that nothing more was needed now but to look out for a lady to be in love with; for a knight-errant without love was like a tree without leaves or fruit, or a body without a soul. As he said to himself, "If, for my sins, or by my good fortune, I come across some giant hereabouts, a common occurrence with knights-errant, and overthrow him in one onslaught, or cleave him asunder to the waist, or, in short, vanquish and subdue him, will it not be well to have someone I may send him to as a present, that he may come in and fall on his knees before my sweet lady, and in a humble, submissive voice say, 'I am the giant Caraculiambro, Lord of the island of Malindrania, vanquished in single combat by the never sufficiently extolled knight Don Quixote of La Mancha, who has commanded me to present myself before Your Grace, that Your Highness dispose of me at your pleasure'?" Oh, how our good gentleman enjoyed the delivery of this speech, especially when he had thought of someone to call his Lady! There was, so the story goes, in a village near his own a very good-looking farm-girl with whom he had been at one time in love, though, so far as is known, she never knew it nor gave a thought to the matter. Her name was Aldonza Lorenzo, and upon her he thought fit to confer the title of Lady of his Thoughts; and after some search for a name which should not be out of harmony with her own, and should suggest and indicate that of a princess and great lady, he decided upon calling her Dulcinea del Toboso—she being of El Toboso—a name, to his mind, musical, uncommon, and significant, like all those he had already bestowed upon himself and the things belonging to him.

CHAPTER II.

WHICH TREATS OF THE FIRST SALLY THE INGENIOUS DON QUIXOTE MADE FROM HOME

These preliminaries settled, he did not care to put off any longer the execution of his design, urged on to it by the thought of all the world was losing by his delay, seeing what wrongs he intended to right, grievances to redress, injustices to repair, abuses to remove, and duties to discharge. So, without giving notice of his intention to anyone, and without anybody seeing him, one morning before the dawning of the day (which was one of the hottest of the month of July) he donned his suit of armour, mounted Rocinante with his patched-up helmet on, braced his buckler, took his lance, and by the back door of the yard sallied forth upon the plain in the highest contentment and satisfaction at seeing with what ease he had made a beginning with his grand purpose. But scarcely did he find himself upon the open plain, when a terrible thought struck him, one all but enough to make him abandon the enterprise at the very outset. It occurred to him that he had not been dubbed a knight, and that according to the law of chivalry he neither could nor ought to bear arms against any knight; and that even if he had been, still he ought, as a novice knight, to wear white armour, without a device upon the shield until by his prowess he had earned one. These reflections made him waver in his purpose, but his craze being stronger than any reasoning, he made up his mind to have himself dubbed a knight by the first one he came across, following the example of others in the same case, as he had read in the books that brought him to this pass. As for white armour, he resolved, on the first opportunity, to scour his until it was whiter than an ermine; and so comforting himself he pursued his way, taking that which his horse chose, for in this he believed lay the essence of adventures.

Thus setting out, our new-fledged adventurer paced along, talking to himself and saying, "Who knows but that in time to come, when the veracious history of my famous deeds is made known, the sage who writes it, when he has to set forth my first sally in the early morning, will do it after this fashion? 'Scarce had the rubicund Apollo spread o'er the face of the broad spacious earth the golden threads of his bright hair, scarce had the little birds of painted plumage attuned their notes to hail with dulcet and mellifluous harmony the coming of the rosy Dawn, that, deserting the soft couch of her jealous spouse, was appearing to mortals at the gates and balconies of the Manchegan horizon, when the renowned knight Don Quixote of La Mancha, quitting the lazy down, mounted his celebrated steed Rocinante and began to traverse the ancient and famous Campo de Montiel,'" which in fact he was actually traversing. "Happy the age, happy the time," he continued, "in which shall be made known my deeds of fame, worthy to be moulded in brass, carved in marble, limned in pictures, for a memorial forever. And thou, O sage magician, whoever thou art, to whom it shall fall to be the chronicler of this wondrous history, forget not, I entreat thee, my good Rocinante, the constant companion of my ways and wanderings." Presently he broke out again, as if he were love-stricken in earnest, "O Princess Dulcinea, lady of this captive heart, a grievous wrong hast thou done me to drive me forth with scorn, and with inexorable obduracy banish me from the presence of thy beauty. O lady, deign to hold in remembrance this heart, thy vassal, that thus in anguish pines for love of thee."

So he went on stringing together these and other absurdities, all in the style of those his books had taught him, imitating their language as well as he could; and all the while he rode so slowly and the sun mounted so rapidly and with such fervour that it was enough to melt his brains if he had any. Nearly all day he travelled without anything remarkable happening to him, at which he was in despair, for he was anxious to encounter someone at once upon whom to try the might of his strong arm.

Writers there are who say the first adventure he met with was that of Puerto Lápice; others say it was that of the windmills; but what I have ascertained on this point, and what I have found written in the annals of La Mancha, is that he was on the road all day, and towards nightfall his hack and he found themselves dead tired and hungry, when, looking all around to see if he could discover any castle or shepherd's shanty where he might refresh himself and relieve his sore wants, he perceived not far out of his road an inn, which was as welcome as a star guiding him to the portals, if not the palaces, of his redemption; and quickening his pace he reached it just as night was setting in. At the door were standing two young women, girls of the district as they call them, on their way to Seville with some carriers who had chanced to halt that night at the inn; and as, happen what might to our adventurer, everything he saw or imaged seemed to him to be and to happen after the fashion of what he read of—the moment he saw the inn he pictured it to himself as a castle with its four turrets and pinnacles of shining silver, not forgetting the drawbridge and moat and all the belongings usually ascribed to castles of the sort. To this inn, which to him seemed a castle, he advanced, and at a short distance from it he checked Rocinante, hoping that some dwarf would show himself upon the battlements, and by sound of trumpet give notice that a knight was approaching the castle. But seeing that they were slow about it, and that Rocinante was in a hurry to reach the stable, he made for the inn door, and perceived the two gay damsels who were standing there, and who seemed to him to be two fair maidens or lovely ladies taking their ease at the castle gate.

At this moment it so happened that a swineherd who was going through the stubbles collecting a drove of pigs (for, without any apology, that is what they are called) gave a blast of his horn to bring them together, and forthwith it seemed to Don Quixote to be what he was expecting, the signal of some dwarf announcing his arrival; and so with prodigious satisfaction he rode up to the inn and to the ladies, who, seeing a man of this sort approaching in full armour and with lance and buckler, were turning in dismay into the inn, when Don Quixote, guessing their fear by their flight, raising his pasteboard visor, disclosed his dry dusty visage, and with courteous bearing and gentle voice addressed them, "Your ladyships need not fly or fear any rudeness, for that it belongs not to the order of knighthood which I profess to offer to anyone, much less to highborn maidens as your appearance proclaims you to be." The girls were looking at him and straining their eyes to make out the features which the clumsy visor obscured, but when they heard themselves called maidens, a thing so much out of their line, they could not restrain their laughter, which made Don Quixote wax indignant, and say, "Modesty becomes the fair, and moreover laughter that has little cause is great silliness; this, however, I say not to pain or anger you, for my desire is none other than to serve you."

The incomprehensible language and the unpromising looks of our cavalier only increased the ladies' laughter, and that increased his irritation, and matters might have gone farther if at that moment the landlord had not come out, who, being a very fat man, was a very peaceful one. He, seeing this grotesque figure clad in armour that did not match any more than his saddle, bridle, lance, buckler, or corselet, was not at all indisposed to join the damsels in their manifestations of amusement; but, in truth, standing in awe of such a complicated armament, he thought it best to speak him fairly, so he said, "Senor Caballero, if your worship wants lodging, bating the bed (for there is not one in the inn) there is plenty of everything else here." Don Quixote, observing the respectful bearing of the Alcaide of the fortress (for so innkeeper and inn seemed in his eyes), made answer, "Sir Castellan, for me anything will suffice, for,

'My armour is my only wear,
My only rest the fray.'"

The host fancied he called him Castellan because he took him for a "worthy of Castile," though he was in fact an Andalusian, and one from the strand of San Lúcar, as crafty a thief as Cacus and as full of tricks as a student or a page. "In that case," said he,

"'Your bed is on the flinty rock,
Your sleep to watch alway;'

and if so, you may dismount and safely reckon upon any quantity of sleeplessness under this roof for a twelvemonth, not to say for a single night." So saying, he advanced to hold the stirrup for Don Quixote, who got down with great difficulty and exertion (for he had not broken his fast all day), and then charged the host to take great care of his horse, as he was the best bit of flesh that ever ate bread in this world. The landlord eyed him over but did not find him as good as Don Quixote said, nor even half as good; and putting him up in the stable, he returned to see what might be wanted by his guest, whom the damsels, who had by this time made their peace with him, were now relieving of his armour. They had taken off his breastplate and backpiece, but they neither knew nor saw how to open his gorget or remove his make-shift helmet, for he had fastened it with green ribbons, which, as there was no untying the knots, required to be cut. This, however, he would not by any means consent to, so he remained all the evening with his helmet on, the drollest and oddest figure that can be imagined; and while they were removing his armour, taking the baggages who were about it for ladies of high degree belonging to the castle, he said to them with great sprightliness:

"Oh, never, surely, was there knight
 So served by hand of dame,
As served was he, Don Quixote hight,
 When from his town he came;
With maidens waiting on himself,
 Princesses on his hack—

or Rocinante, for that, ladies mine, is my horse's name, and Don Quixote of La Mancha is my own; for though I had no intention of declaring myself until my achievements in your service and honour had made me known, the necessity of adapting that old ballad of Lancelot to the present occasion has given you the knowledge of my name altogether prematurely. A time, however, will come for your ladyships to command and me to obey, and then the might of my arm will show my desire to serve you."

The girls, who were not used to hearing rhetoric of this sort, had nothing to say in reply; they only asked him if he wanted anything to eat. "I would gladly eat a bit of something," said Don Quixote, "for I feel it would come very seasonably." The day happened to be a Friday, and in the whole inn there was nothing but some pieces of the fish they call in Castile "abadejo," in Andalusia "bacallao," and in some places "curadillo," and in others "troutlet;" so they asked him if he thought he could eat troutlet, for there was no other fish to give him. "If there be troutlets enough," said Don Quixote, "they will be the same thing as a trout; for it is all one to me whether I am given eight reals in small change or a piece of eight; moreover, it may be that these troutlets are like veal, which is better than beef, or kid, which is better than goat. But whatever it be let it come quickly, for the burden and pressure of arms cannot be borne without support to the inside." They laid a table for him at the door of the inn for the sake of the air, and the host brought him a portion of ill-soaked and worse cooked stockfish, and a piece of bread as black and mouldy as his own armour; but a laughable sight it was to see him eating, for having his helmet on and the beaver up, he could not with his own hands put anything into his mouth unless someone else placed it there, and this service one of the ladies rendered him. But to give him anything to drink was impossible, or would have been so had not the landlord bored a reed, and putting one end in his mouth poured the wine into him through the other; all which he bore with patience rather than sever the ribbons of his helmet.

While this was going on, there came up to the inn a sowgelder, who, as he approached, sounded his reed pipe four or five times, and thereby completely convinced Don Quixote that he was in some famous castle, and that they were regaling him with music, and that the stockfish was trout, the bread the whitest, the wenches ladies, and the landlord the castellan of the castle; and consequently he held that his enterprise and sally had been to some purpose. But still it distressed him to think he had not been dubbed a knight, for it was plain to him he could not lawfully engage in any adventure without receiving the order of knighthood.

Notes on the Text
Preface-Chapter II

It was only in this late work, *Don Quixote*, that Cervantes managed to capture a readership with his anti-formulaic satire that has had its elements mimicked so many times that it is considered to be the first modern novel. It was a stark contrast to the repeating plots of the pastoral or chivalry romances that preceded it. Pastoral literature is defined as a genre that "presents the society of shepherds as free from the complexity and corruption of city life" by *Encyclopedia Britannica*, but 16th century Spain was pre-industrial so for most people living in the countryside was the norm and city life was unusual or foreign. The pastoral and agrarian themes and genres appeared in classical Greece and Rome, and popped up occasionally in various places until they were revived in the 16th century in the theater and the romance novel by authors like Torquato Tasso, who also wrote philosophical or theoretic works that complimented this genre as superior to others. Chivalry romances gained popularity in Europe starting in the 12th century France; their central heroes were knights, who gallantly fought to liberate and possess princesses against the forces of evil. Cervantes attempted a pastoral in *La Galatea* by mimicking Jorge de Montemayor's *Diana* (1559). In Cervantes' version, Elicio and Erastro, two friends who are both in love with a lady called Galatea travel across the countryside to a wedding. Duels with rivals, grief, and numerous poems carry the twisted plots. The first chapters of *Don Quixote* are a comedy that satirizes the absurdity and falsehood portrayed in formulaic chivalry tales. Later in the novel, the text becomes more complex as descriptions and philosophy behind the narrative thicken and add multiple dimensions to the central satire. I would recommend reading the rest of it for fun over a break, but it's too long even if we only read this single work in this class. The first chapters are the ones that are typically used in abridged children's and young adult versions of the novel as well as in films, so they are the best-known portion of the work. The premise is that Don Quixote has read too many chivalry tales until he started to believe that he is a Knight, and in this role he sets out on a quest with his servant, Sancho Panza, to save the world and a woman that he believes is a princess, but is really a garlic-smelling peasant girl, Dulcinea del Toboso, from evils, such as windmills.

Vocabulary

"Ego autem dico vobis: diligite inimicos vestros" (37): Latin: "But I say to you: love your enemies." This is a quote from the Bible, Matthew 5:44.

"De corde exeunt cogitationes malae" (37): Latin: "Out of the heart come evil thoughts," from Matthew 15:19. This quote continues in the Bible with the naming of the Deadly Sins.

"Donec eris felix multos numerabis amicos,/ Tempora si fuerint nubila, solus eris" (37): Cato the elder, or Marcus Porcius Cato (234 BC — 149 BC) was a Roman statesman, author and orator who made at least a couple of famous quotes about fortune.

"Golias or Goliath" (37): Golias might just be an alternative spelling of Goliath, but given how carefully Cervantes is choosing his words in this "Preface," it seems more likely that it might be a reference to a 12th century Latin and French poem, *Apocalypse of Golias the Bishop*, which satirized the clergy. Goliath refers to the Biblical Philistinian giant warrior who was defeated by the relatively small Israelites' future king David with his sling shot.

Cacus: "The Roman poet Virgil (*Aeneid*, Book VIII) described Cacus as the son of the flame god Vulcan and as a monstrous fire-breathing brigand who terrorized the countryside. He stole some of the giant Geryon's cattle from the hero Hercules and hid them in his lair on the Aventine Hill; but a lowing cow betrayed Cacus, and Hercules, bursting in, killed him" (*Encyclopedia Britannica*).

"tantum pellis et ossa fuit" (44): Latin for: it was only skin and bones. This is how the narrator is describing Quixote's horse or "hack," Rocinante, which is a frequent source of slap-stick humor for the rest of the novel.

Comments on the Text

"Under my cloak I kill the king" (34): *Selected Proverbs of All Nations* (1824) by Thomas Fielding cites this quote in the future tense with "I'll…" instead of the present tense used in this translation of "I kill…" Fielding explains that it is a Spanish proverb that means that "as a man's thoughts cannot be controlled, he may kill the king in imagination" (47). It is amazing that this sharply radical statement in the "Preface" passed by the censors that could prevent any anti-establishment book from being printed. Open threats of rebellion or against the life of the king were frequently met with imprisonments on sedition and treason charges, even when they were satirical or subversively cloaked as belonging to somebody else, as in this case, a proverb that belongs to the Spanish folkloric tradition. Many critics have discussed this proverb, typically concluding that Cervantes was commenting on the wrongful publication of chivalry tales with the approval of the king despite them not being grounded in fact. The Inquisition was putting writers to death for writing fantasies, science, or other matter that contradicted the Church's version of the truth, so it seemed hypocritical for radical writers such as Cervantes that the fanciful and fantastic chivalry tales passed the censors. Later on, the narrator's friend explains that *Quixote* is an "attack" on books of chivalry, and their tendency for "mixing up things human and divine" (38). In the first chapter, Cervantes re-states the problem of falsehood in chivalry tales: "His fancy grew full of what he used to read about in his books, enchantments, quarrels, battles, challenges, wounds, wooings, loves, agonies, and all sorts of impossible nonsense; and it so possessed his mind that the whole fabric of invention and fancy he read of was true, that to him no history in the world had more reality in it." (42). If chivalry authors could lie in print, then certainly it was acceptable to depict the murder of a king in fiction or to describe the damage some of the approved chivalry tales could have had on a weak mind, such as that of the main character, Don Quixote. Later, in the "Preface", the narrator describes his hesitation regarding even offering this book up for publication, perhaps because of the fear he had of being censored or charged for its contents.

"any sentences or scraps of Latin you may happen to have by heart, or at any rate that will not give you much trouble to look up" (36): Many popular fiction and scholarly books include quotations from the classics, and in Cervantes' time many of these were in Latin. Cervantes included a great deal of poetry and other types of the front matter, annotations, quotations and the like he speaks about here in his first formulaic chivalry novel, but it failed despite his obedience to these stylistic rules. Cervantes did include some honorary poems to Quixote at the end of the novel, but he decided against them at the start, opting for a plain version that was more likely to appeal to the average reader, who might not have been educated in Latin and highbrow conventions. One of the short stories we read from Poe, "How to Write a Blackwood Article," also poked fun at such deep quotes from foreign languages.

"Strive, too, that in reading your story the melancholy may be moved to laughter, and the merry made merrier still; that the simple shall not be wearied, that the judicious shall admire the invention, that the grave shall not despise it, nor the wise fail to praise it" (39): This is great advice for any writer, including some guidance for you as you start writing your first essay for this class. This is also a great summary as to why *Don Quixote* has remained relevant and read for so many centuries.

Questions for Discussion

1. The description of how Don Quixote fixed his great-grandfather's broken morion into a helmet shows the type of realistic details that this novel popularized and that is a characteristic common to many non-formulaic, classical novels. What do you think this helmet-making craft-project signifies in terms of Quixote's character or the larger story? Why does Cervantes stop the narrative to zoom into this detail? Why do most modern popular formulaic novels or films speed up and avoid such narrations?
2. How does Quixote explain to himself the necessity of having a Lady love interest before he sets out on his knightly quest? Why do you think Cervantes did not allow Quixote to pick an actual Lady as his obsessive love interest? A "Lady," according to *Merriam-Webster* was defined at the time as: "any of various titled women in Great Britain [or Spain for Cervantes]—used as the customary title of (1) a marchioness, countess, viscountess, or baroness or (2) the wife of a knight, baronet, member of the peerage, or one having the

courtesy title of lord and used as a courtesy title for the daughter of a duke, marquess, or earl." Is there comedy in failed or reversed expectations?

3. What other deceptions does Quixote suffer from in Chapter II? How does he interpret the inn and the "girls of the district" (48)? Quixote's mind interprets everyday details as signs of something more significant. Do modern films, video games and the like have a similar impact on today's youths?

4. Don Quixote is aching after a full day on horseback. He also discovers that all the inn has to feed him is "troutlet," but he insists that to him it is as good as "trout" (50). Why is Cervantes constantly showing Don Quixote's ceaseless optimism, which only finally wavers at the tragic end of the novel? Would Quixote continue this journey if he saw it in a darker light? Is his optimism and "patience" related to his delusion that makes him see castles instead of inns? If Quixote did not maintain this "knightly" patience as wine is being poured into his mouth through a reed and the like, much of the comedy in this satire would have been lost. What other reasons might there be for this element in the novel?

5. At the same time, Quixote's occasional worries regarding things like not yet being named a knight create motives for him to continue on the adventure. Is this Quixote's only worry up to page 51? Does this thread of concern make you anxious to find out how Quixote might be knighted in the coming chapters? Does it help to create suspense?

6. How do you think Cervantes' life experiences impact the elements, such as the storyline, characters, and meaning of *Don Quixote*? What misadventures might Cervantes be reliving through Quixote's quest? Do you think Cervantes felt as if he had himself been fooled into a life of illusion by chivalry tales?

7. Briefly describe how pastoral and chivalry themes, plots, characters or the like are satirized in the first two chapters of this novel. How do you interpret Cervantes' introductory proverb, "Under my cloak I kill the king" (34)? Do you think Cervantes is making a subversive threat against the king's life? If not, what was he trying to say here?

Works Cited

Fielding, Thomas. *Selected Proverbs of All Nations: Illustrated with Notes and Comments to which is Added a Summary of Ancient Pastimes Holidays and Customs with an Analysis of the Wisdom of the Ancients and of the Fathers of the Church.* London: Longman Thirst Rels Orme, 1824. Google Books. 3 February 2017. Web.

CHAPTER III.

WHEREIN IS RELATED THE DROLL WAY IN WHICH DON QUIXOTE HAD HIMSELF DUBBED A KNIGHT

Harassed by this reflection, he made haste with his scanty pothouse supper, and having finished it called the landlord, and shutting himself into the stable with him, fell on his knees before him, saying, "From this spot I rise not, valiant knight, until your courtesy grants me the boon I seek, one that will redound to your praise and the benefit of the human race." The landlord, seeing his guest at his feet and hearing a speech of this kind, stood staring at him in bewilderment, not knowing what to do or say, and entreating him to rise, but all to no purpose until he had agreed to grant the boon demanded of him. "I looked for no less, my lord, from your High Magnificence," replied Don Quixote, "and I have to tell you that the boon I have asked and your liberality has granted is that you shall dub me knight to-morrow morning, and that to-night I shall watch my arms in the chapel of this your castle; thus tomorrow, as I have said, will be accomplished what I so much desire, enabling me lawfully to roam through all the four quarters of the world seeking adventures on behalf of those in distress, as is the duty of chivalry and of knights-errant like myself, whose ambition is directed to such deeds."

The landlord, who, as has been mentioned, was something of a wag, and had already some suspicion of his guest's want of wits, was quite convinced of it on hearing talk of this kind from him, and to make sport for the night he determined to fall in with his humour. So he told him he was quite right in pursuing the object he had in view, and that such a motive was natural and becoming in cavaliers as distinguished as he seemed and his gallant bearing showed him to be; and that he himself in his younger days had followed the same honourable calling, roaming in quest of adventures in various parts of the world, among others the Curing-grounds of Malaga, the Isles of Riaran, the Precinct of Seville, the Little Market of Segovia, the Olivera of Valencia, the Rondilla of Granada, the Strand of San Lucar, the Colt of Cordova, the Taverns of Toledo, and divers other quarters, where he had proved the nimbleness of his feet and the lightness of his fingers, doing many wrongs, cheating many widows, ruining maids and swindling minors, and, in short, bringing himself under the notice of almost every tribunal and court of justice in Spain; until at last he had retired to this castle of his, where he was living upon his property and upon that of others; and where he received all knights-errant of whatever rank or condition they might be, all for the great love he bore them and that they might share their substance with him in return for his benevolence. He told him, moreover, that in this castle of his there was no chapel in which he could watch his armour, as it had been pulled down in order to be rebuilt, but that in a case of necessity it might, he knew, be watched anywhere, and he might watch it that night in a courtyard of the castle, and in the morning, God willing, the requisite ceremonies might be performed so as to have him dubbed a knight, and so thoroughly dubbed that nobody could be more so. He asked if he had any money with him, to which Don Quixote replied that he had not a farthing, as in the histories of knights-errant he had never read of any of them carrying any. On this point the landlord told him he was mistaken; for, though not recorded in the histories, because in the author's opinion there was no need to mention anything so obvious and necessary as money and clean shirts, it was not to be supposed therefore that they did not carry them, and he might regard it as certain and established that all knights-errant (about whom there were so many full and unimpeachable books) carried well-furnished purses in case of emergency, and likewise carried shirts and a little box of ointment to cure the wounds they received. For in those plains and deserts where they engaged in combat and came out wounded, it was not always that there was someone to cure them, unless indeed they had for a friend some sage magician to succour them at once by fetching through the air upon a cloud some damsel or dwarf with a vial of water of such virtue that by tasting one drop of it they were cured of their hurts and wounds in an instant and left as sound as if they had not received any damage whatever. But in case this should not occur, the knights of old took care to see that their squires were provided with money and other requisites, such as lint and ointments for healing purposes; and when it happened that knights had no squires (which was rarely and seldom the case) they themselves carried everything in cunning saddle-bags that were hardly seen on the horse's croup, as if it were something else of more importance, because, unless for some such reason, carrying saddle-bags was not very favourably regarded among knights-errant. He therefore advised him (and, as his godson so soon to be, he might even command him) never from that time forth to travel without money and the usual requirements, and he would find the advantage of them when he least expected it.

Don Quixote promised to follow his advice scrupulously, and it was arranged forthwith that he should watch his armour in a large yard at one side of the inn; so, collecting it all together, Don Quixote placed it on a trough that stood by the side of a well, and bracing his buckler on his arm he grasped his lance and began with a stately air to march up and down in front of the trough, and as he began his march night began to fall.

The landlord told all the people who were in the inn about the craze of his guest, the watching of the armour, and the dubbing ceremony he contemplated. Full of wonder at so strange a form of madness, they flocked to see it from a distance, and observed with what composure he sometimes paced up and down, or sometimes, leaning on his lance, gazed on his armour without taking his eyes off it for ever so long; and as the night closed in with a light from the moon so brilliant that it might vie with his that lent it, everything the novice knight did was plainly seen by all.

Meanwhile one of the carriers who were in the inn thought fit to water his team, and it was necessary to remove Don Quixote's armour as it lay on the trough; but he seeing the other approach hailed him in a loud voice, "O thou, whoever thou art, rash knight that comest to lay hands on the armour of the most valorous errant that ever girt on sword, have a care what thou dost; touch it not unless thou wouldst lay down thy life as the penalty of thy rashness." The carrier gave no heed to these words (and he would have done better to heed them if he had been heedful of his health), but seizing it by the straps flung the armour some distance from him. Seeing this, Don Quixote raised his eyes to heaven, and fixing his thoughts, apparently, upon his lady Dulcinea, exclaimed, "Aid me, lady mine, in this the first encounter that presents itself to this breast which thou holdest in subjection; let not thy favour and protection fail me in this first jeopardy;" and, with these words and others to the same purpose, dropping his buckler he lifted his lance with both hands and with it smote such a blow on the carrier's head that he stretched him on the ground, so stunned that had he followed it up with a second there would have been no need of a surgeon to cure him. This done, he picked up his armour and returned to his beat with the same serenity as before.

Shortly after this, another, not knowing what had happened (for the carrier still lay senseless), came with the same object of giving water to his mules, and was proceeding to remove the armour in order to clear the trough, when Don Quixote, without uttering a word or imploring aid from anyone, once more dropped his buckler and once more lifted his lance, and without actually breaking the second carrier's head into pieces, made more than three of it, for he laid it open in four. At the noise all the people of the inn ran to the spot, and among them the landlord. Seeing this, Don Quixote braced his buckler on his arm, and with his hand on his sword exclaimed, "O Lady of Beauty, strength and support of my faint heart, it is time for thee to turn the eyes of thy greatness on this thy captive knight on the brink of so mighty an adventure." By this he felt himself so inspired that he would not have flinched if all the carriers in the world had assailed him. The comrades of the wounded perceiving the plight they were in began from a distance to shower stones on Don Quixote, who screened himself as best he could with his buckler, not daring to quit the trough and leave his armour unprotected. The landlord shouted to them to leave him alone, for he had already told them that he was mad, and as a madman he would not be accountable even if he killed them all. Still louder shouted Don Quixote, calling them knaves and traitors, and the lord of the castle, who allowed knights-errant to be treated in this fashion, a villain and a low-born knight whom, had he received the order of knighthood, he would call to account for his treachery. "But of you," he cried, "base and vile rabble, I make no account; fling, strike, come on, do all ye can against me, ye shall see what the reward of your folly and insolence will be." This he uttered with so much spirit and boldness that he filled his assailants with a terrible fear, and as much for this reason as at the persuasion of the landlord they left off stoning him, and he allowed them to carry off the wounded, and with the same calmness and composure as before resumed the watch over his armour.

But these freaks of his guest were not much to the liking of the landlord, so he determined to cut matters short and confer upon him at once the unlucky order of knighthood before any further misadventure could occur; so, going up to him, he apologised for the rudeness which, without his knowledge, had been offered to him by these low people, who, however, had been well punished for their audacity. As he had already told him, he said, there was no chapel in the castle, nor was it needed for what remained to be done, for, as he understood the ceremonial of the order, the whole point of being dubbed a knight lay in the accolade and in the slap on the shoulder, and that could be administered in the middle of a field; and that he had now done all that was needful as to watching the armour, for all requirements were satisfied by a watch of two hours only, while he had been more than four about it. Don Quixote believed it all, and told him he stood there ready to obey him, and to make an end of it with as much despatch as possible; for, if he were again attacked, and felt himself to be dubbed knight, he would not, he thought, leave a soul alive in the castle, except such as out of respect he might spare at his bidding.

Thus warned and menaced, the castellan forthwith brought out a book in which he used to enter the straw and barley he served out to the carriers, and, with a lad carrying a candle-end, and the two damsels already mentioned, he returned to where Don Quixote stood, and bade him kneel down. Then, reading from his account-book as if he were repeating some devout prayer, in the middle of his delivery he raised his hand and gave him a sturdy blow on the neck, and then, with his own sword, a smart slap on the shoulder, all the while muttering between his teeth as if he was saying his prayers. Having done this, he directed one of the ladies to gird on his sword, which she did with great self-possession and gravity, and not a little was required to prevent a burst of laughter at each stage of the ceremony; but what they had already seen of the novice knight's prowess kept their laughter within bounds. On girding him with the sword the worthy lady said to him, "May God make your worship a very fortunate knight, and grant you success in battle." Don Quixote asked her name in order that he might from that time forward know to whom he was beholden for the favour he had received, as he meant to confer upon her some portion of the honour he acquired by the might of his arm. She answered with great humility that she was called La Tolosa, and that she was the daughter of a cobbler of Toledo who lived in the stalls of Sanchobienaya, and that wherever she might be she would serve and esteem him as her lord. Don Quixote said in reply that she would do him a favour if thenceforward she assumed the "Don" and called herself Dona Tolosa. She promised she would, and then the other buckled on his spur, and with her followed almost the same conversation as with the lady of the sword. He asked her name, and she said it was La Molinera, and that she was the daughter of a respectable miller of Antequera; and of her likewise Don Quixote requested that she would adopt the "Don" and call herself Dona Molinera, making offers to her further services and favours.

Having thus, with hot haste and speed, brought to a conclusion these never-till-now-seen ceremonies, Don Quixote was on thorns until he saw himself on horseback sallying forth in quest of adventures; and saddling Rocinante at once he mounted, and embracing his host, as he returned thanks for his kindness in knighting him, he addressed him in language so extraordinary that it is impossible to convey an idea of it or report it. The landlord, to get him out of the inn, replied with no less rhetoric though with shorter words, and without calling upon him to pay the reckoning, let him go with a "Godspeed."

CHAPTER IV.

OF WHAT HAPPENED TO OUR KNIGHT WHEN HE LEFT THE INN

Day was dawning when Don Quixote quitted the inn, so happy, so gay, so exhilarated at finding himself now dubbed a knight, that his joy was like to burst his horse-girths. However, recalling the advice of his host as to the requisites he ought to carry with him, especially that referring to money and shirts, he determined to go home and provide himself with all, and also with a squire, for he reckoned upon securing a farm-labourer, a neighbour of his, a poor man with a family, but very well qualified for the office of squire to a knight. With this object he turned his horse's head towards his village, and Rocinante, thus reminded of his old quarters, stepped out so briskly that he hardly seemed to tread the earth.

He had not gone far, when out of a thicket on his right there seemed to come feeble cries as of someone in distress, and the instant he heard them he exclaimed, "Thanks be to heaven for the favour it accords me, that it so soon offers me an opportunity of fulfilling the obligation I have undertaken, and gathering the fruit of my ambition. These cries, no doubt, come from some man or woman in want of help, and needing my aid and protection," and wheeling, he turned Rocinante in the direction whence the cries seemed to proceed. He had gone but a few paces into the wood, when he saw a mare tied to an oak, and tied to another, and stripped from the waist upwards, a youth of about fifteen years of age, from whom the cries came. Nor were they without cause, for a lusty farmer was flogging him with a belt and following up every blow with scoldings and commands, repeating, "Your mouth shut and your eyes open!" while the youth made answer, "I won't do it again, master mine; by God's passion I won't do it again, and I'll take more care of the flock another time."

Seeing what was going on, Don Quixote said in an angry voice, "Discourteous knight, it ill becomes you to assail one who cannot defend himself; mount your steed and take your lance" (for there was a lance leaning against the oak to which the mare was tied), "and I will make you know that you are behaving as a coward." The farmer, seeing before him this figure in full armour brandishing a lance over his head, gave himself up for dead, and made answer meekly, "Sir Knight, this youth that I am chastising is my servant, employed by me to watch a flock of sheep that I have hard by, and he is so careless that I lose one every day, and when I punish him for his carelessness and knavery he says I do it out of niggardliness, to escape paying him the wages I owe him, and before God, and on my soul, he lies."

"Lies before me, base clown!" said Don Quixote. "By the sun that shines on us I have a mind to run you through with this lance. Pay him at once without another word; if not, by the God that rules us I will make an end of you, and annihilate you on the spot; release him instantly."

The farmer hung his head, and without a word untied his servant, of whom Don Quixote asked how much his master owed him.

He replied, nine months at seven reals a month. Don Quixote added it up, found that it came to sixty-three reals, and told the farmer to pay it down immediately, if he did not want to die for it.

The trembling clown replied that as he lived and by the oath he had sworn (though he had not sworn any) it was not so much; for there were to be taken into account and deducted three pairs of shoes he had given him, and a real for two blood-lettings when he was sick.

"All that is very well," said Don Quixote; "but let the shoes and the blood-lettings stand as a setoff against the blows you have given him without any cause; for if he spoiled the leather of the shoes you paid for, you have damaged that of his body, and if the barber took blood from him when he was sick, you have drawn it when he was sound; so on that score he owes you nothing."

"The difficulty is, Sir Knight, that I have no money here; let Andres come home with me, and I will pay him all, real by real."

"I go with him!" said the youth. "Nay, God forbid! No, senor, not for the world; for once alone with me, he would ray me like a Saint Bartholomew."

"He will do nothing of the kind," said Don Quixote; "I have only to command, and he will obey me; and as he has sworn to me by the order of knighthood which he has received, I leave him free, and I guarantee the payment."

"Consider what you are saying, señor," said the youth; "this master of mine is not a knight, nor has he received any order of knighthood; for he is Juan Haldudo the Rich, of Quintanar."

"That matters little," replied Don Quixote; "there may be Haldudos knights; moreover, everyone is the son of his works."

"That is true," said Andres; "but this master of mine—of what works is he the son, when he refuses me the wages of my sweat and labour?"

"I do not refuse, brother Andres," said the farmer, "be good enough to come along with me, and I swear by all the orders of knighthood there are in the world to pay you as I have agreed, real by real, and perfumed."

"For the perfumery I excuse you," said Don Quixote; "give it to him in reals, and I shall be satisfied; and see that you do as you have sworn; if not, by the same oath I swear to come back and hunt you out and punish you; and I shall find you though you should lie closer than a lizard. And if you desire to know who it is lays this command upon you, that you be more firmly bound to obey it, know that I am the valorous Don Quixote of La Mancha, the undoer of wrongs and injustices; and so, God be with you, and keep in mind what you have promised and sworn under those penalties that have been already declared to you."

So saying, he gave Rocinante the spur and was soon out of reach. The farmer followed him with his eyes, and when he saw that he had cleared the wood and was no longer in sight, he turned to his boy Andres, and said, "Come here, my son, I want to pay you what I owe you, as that undoer of wrongs has commanded me."

"My oath on it," said Andres, "your worship will be well advised to obey the command of that good knight—may he live a thousand years—for, as he is a valiant and just judge, by Roque, if you do not pay me, he will come back and do as he said."

"My oath on it, too," said the farmer; "but as I have a strong affection for you, I want to add to the debt in order to add to the payment;" and seizing him by the arm, he tied him up again, and gave him such a flogging that he left him for dead.

"Now, Master Andres," said the farmer, "call on the undoer of wrongs; you will find he won't undo that, though I am not sure that I have quite done with you, for I have a good mind to flay you alive." But at last he untied him, and gave him leave to go look for his judge in order to put the sentence pronounced into execution.

Andres went off rather down in the mouth, swearing he would go to look for the valiant Don Quixote of La Mancha and tell him exactly what had happened, and that all would have to be repaid him sevenfold; but for all that, he went off weeping, while his master stood laughing.

Thus did the valiant Don Quixote right that wrong, and, thoroughly satisfied with what had taken place, as he considered he had made a very happy and noble beginning with his knighthood, he took the road towards his village in perfect self-content, saying in a low voice, "Well mayest thou this day call thyself fortunate above all on earth, O Dulcinea del Toboso, fairest of the fair! since it has fallen to thy lot to hold subject and submissive to thy full will and pleasure a knight so renowned as is and will be Don Quixote of La Mancha, who, as all the world knows, yesterday received the order of knighthood, and hath to-day righted the greatest wrong and grievance that ever injustice conceived and cruelty perpetrated: who hath to-day plucked the rod from the hand of yonder ruthless oppressor so wantonly lashing that tender child."

He now came to a road branching in four directions, and immediately he was reminded of those cross-roads where knights-errant used to stop to consider which road they should take. In imitation of them he halted for a while, and after having deeply considered it, he gave Rocinante his head, submitting his own will to that of his hack, who followed out his first intention, which was to make straight for his own stable. After he had gone about two miles Don Quixote perceived a large party of people, who, as afterwards appeared, were some Toledo traders, on their way to buy silk at Murcia. There were six of them coming along under their sunshades, with four servants mounted, and three muleteers on foot. Scarcely had Don Quixote descried them when the fancy possessed him that this must be some new adventure; and to help him to imitate as far as he could those passages he had read of in his books, here seemed to come one made on purpose, which he resolved to attempt. So with a lofty bearing and determination he fixed himself firmly in his stirrups, got his lance ready, brought his buckler before his breast, and planting himself in the middle of the road, stood waiting the approach of these knights-errant, for such he now considered and held them to be; and when they had come near enough to see and hear, he exclaimed with a haughty gesture, "All the world stand, unless all the world confess that in all the world there is no maiden fairer than the Empress of La Mancha, the peerless Dulcinea del Toboso."

The traders halted at the sound of this language and the sight of the strange figure that uttered it, and from both figure and language at once guessed the craze of their owner; they wished, however, to learn quietly what was the object of this confession that was demanded of them, and one of them, who was rather fond of a joke and was very sharp-witted, said to him, "Sir Knight, we do not know who this good lady is that you speak of; show her to us, for, if she be of such beauty as you suggest, with all our hearts and without any pressure we will confess the truth that is on your part required of us."

"If I were to show her to you," replied Don Quixote, "what merit would you have in confessing a truth so manifest? The essential point is that without seeing her you must believe, confess, affirm, swear, and defend it; else ye have to do with me in battle, ill-conditioned, arrogant rabble that ye are; and come ye on, one by one as the order of knighthood requires, or all together as is the custom and vile usage of your breed, here do I bide and await you relying on the justice of the cause I maintain."

"Sir Knight," replied the trader, "I entreat your worship in the name of this present company of princes, that, to save us from charging our consciences with the confession of a thing we have never seen or heard of, and one moreover so much to the prejudice of the Empresses and Queens of the Alcarria and Estremadura, your worship will be pleased to show us some portrait of this lady, though it be no bigger than a grain of wheat; for by the thread one gets at the ball, and in this way we shall be satisfied and easy, and you will be content and pleased;

nay, I believe we are already so far agreed with you that even though her portrait should show her blind of one eye, and distilling vermilion and sulphur from the other, we would nevertheless, to gratify your worship, say all in her favour that you desire."

"She distils nothing of the kind, vile rabble," said Don Quixote, burning with rage, "nothing of the kind, I say, only ambergris and civet in cotton; nor is she one-eyed or humpbacked, but straighter than a Guadarrama spindle: but ye must pay for the blasphemy ye have uttered against beauty like that of my lady."

And so saying, he charged with levelled lance against the one who had spoken, with such fury and fierceness that, if luck had not contrived that Rocinante should stumble midway and come down, it would have gone hard with the rash trader. Down went Rocinante, and over went his master, rolling along the ground for some distance; and when he tried to rise he was unable, so encumbered was he with lance, buckler, spurs, helmet, and the weight of his old armour; and all the while he was struggling to get up he kept saying, "Fly not, cowards and caitiffs! Stay, for not by my fault, but my horse's, am I stretched here."

One of the muleteers in attendance, who could not have had much good nature in him, hearing the poor prostrate man blustering in this style, was unable to refrain from giving him an answer on his ribs; and coming up to him he seized his lance, and having broken it in pieces, with one of them he began so to belabour our Don Quixote that, notwithstanding and in spite of his armour, he milled him like a measure of wheat. His masters called out not to lay on so hard and to leave him alone, but the muleteers blood was up, and he did not care to drop the game until he had vented the rest of his wrath, and gathering up the remaining fragments of the lance he finished with a discharge upon the unhappy victim, who all through the storm of sticks that rained on him never ceased threatening heaven, and earth, and the brigands, for such they seemed to him. At last the muleteer was tired, and the traders continued their journey, taking with them matter for talk about the poor fellow who had been cudgelled. He when he found himself alone made another effort to rise; but if he was unable when whole and sound, how was he to rise after having been thrashed and well-nigh knocked to pieces? And yet he esteemed himself fortunate, as it seemed to him that this was a regular knight-errant's mishap, and entirely, he considered, the fault of his horse. However, battered in body as he was, to rise was beyond his power.

CHAPTER V.

IN WHICH THE NARRATIVE OF OUR KNIGHT'S MISHAP IS CONTINUED

Finding then that, in fact, he could not move, he thought himself of having recourse to his usual remedy, which was to think of some passage in his books, and his craze brought to his mind that about Baldwin and the Marquis of Mantua, when Carloto left him wounded on the mountain side, a story known by heart by the children, not forgotten by the young men, and lauded and even believed by the old folk; and for all that not a whit truer than the miracles of Mahomet. This seemed to him to fit exactly the case in which he found himself, so, making a show of severe suffering, he began to roll on the ground and with feeble breath repeat the very words which the wounded knight of the wood is said to have uttered:

> Where art thou, lady mine, that thou
>   My sorrow dost not rue?
> Thou canst not know it, lady mine,
>   Or else thou art untrue.

And so he went on with the ballad as far as the lines:

> O noble Marquis of Mantua,
> My Uncle and liege lord!

As chance would have it, when he had got to this line there happened to come by a peasant from his own village, a neighbour of his, who had been with a load of wheat to the mill, and he, seeing the man stretched there, came up to him and asked him who he was and what was the matter with him that he complained so dolefully.

Don Quixote was firmly persuaded that this was the Marquis of Mantua, his uncle, so the only answer he made was to go on with his ballad, in which he told the tale of his misfortune, and of the loves of the Emperor's son and his wife all exactly as the ballad sings it.

The peasant stood amazed at hearing such nonsense, and relieving him of the visor, already battered to pieces by blows, he wiped his face, which was covered with dust, and as soon as he had done so he recognised him and said, "Senor Quixada" (for so he appears to have been called when he was in his senses and had not yet changed from a quiet country gentleman into a knight-errant), "who has brought your worship to this pass?" But to all questions the other only went on with his ballad.

Seeing this, the good man removed as well as he could his breastplate and backpiece to see if he had any wound, but he could perceive no blood nor any mark whatever. He then contrived to raise him from the ground, and with no little difficulty hoisted him upon his ass, which seemed to him to be the easiest mount for him; and collecting the arms, even to the splinters of the lance, he tied them on Rocinante, and leading him by the bridle and the ass by the halter he took the road for the village, very sad to hear what absurd stuff Don Quixote was talking.

Nor was Don Quixote less so, for what with blows and bruises he could not sit upright on the ass, and from time to time he sent up sighs to heaven, so that once more he drove the peasant to ask what ailed him. And it could have been only the devil himself that put into his head tales to match his own adventures, for now, forgetting Baldwin, he bethought himself of the Moor Abindarraez, when the Alcaide of Antequera, Rodrigo de Narvaez, took him prisoner and carried him away to his castle; so that when the peasant again asked him how he was and what ailed him, he gave him for reply the same words and phrases that the captive Abindarraez gave to Rodrigo de Narvaez, just as he had read the story in the "Diana" of Jorge de Montemayor where it is written, applying it to his own case so aptly that the peasant went along cursing his fate that he had to listen to such a lot of nonsense; from which, however, he came to the conclusion that his neighbour was mad, and so made all haste to reach the village to escape the wearisomeness of this harangue of Don Quixote's; who, at the end of it, said, "Senor Don Rodrigo de Narvaez, your worship must know that this fair Xarifa I have mentioned is now the lovely Dulcinea del Toboso, for whom I have done, am doing, and will do the most famous deeds of chivalry that in this world have been seen, are to be seen, or ever shall be seen."

To this the peasant answered, "Senor—sinner that I am!—cannot your worship see that I am not Don Rodrigo de Narvaez nor the Marquis of Mantua, but Pedro Alonso, your neighbour, and that your worship is neither Baldwin nor Abindarraez, but the worthy gentleman Senor Quixada?"

"I know who I am," replied Don Quixote, "and I know that I may be not only those I have named, but all the Twelve Peers of France and even all the Nine Worthies, since my achievements surpass all that they have done all together and each of them on his own account."

With this talk and more of the same kind they reached the village just as night was beginning to fall, but the peasant waited until it was a little later that the belaboured gentleman might not be seen riding in such a miserable trim. When it was what seemed to him the proper time he entered the village and went to Don Quixote's house, which he found all in confusion, and there were the curate and the village barber, who were great friends of Don Quixote, and his housekeeper was saying to them in a loud voice, "What does your worship think can have befallen my master, Senor Licentiate Pero Perez?" for so the curate was called; "it is three days now since anything has been seen of him, or the hack, or the buckler, lance, or armour. Miserable me! I am certain of it, and it is as true as that I was born to die, that these accursed books of chivalry he has, and has got into the way of reading so constantly, have upset his reason; for now I remember having often heard him saying to himself that he would turn knight-errant and go all over the world in quest of adventures. To the devil and Barabbas with such books, that have brought to ruin in this way the finest understanding there was in all La Mancha!"

The niece said the same, and, more: "You must know, Master Nicholas"—for that was the name of the barber—"it was often my uncle's way to stay two days and nights together poring over these unholy books of misventures, after which he would fling the book away and snatch up his sword and fall to slashing the walls; and when he was tired out he would say he had killed four giants like four towers; and the sweat that flowed from him when he was weary he said was the blood of the wounds he had received in battle; and then he would drink a great jug of cold water and become calm and quiet, saying that this water was a most precious potion which the sage Esquife, a great magician and friend of his, had brought him. But I take all the blame upon myself for never having told your worships of my uncle's vagaries, that you might put a stop to them before things had come to this pass, and burn all these accursed books—for he has a great number—that richly deserve to be burned like heretics."

"So say I too," said the curate, "and by my faith to-morrow shall not pass without public judgment upon them, and may they be condemned to the flames lest they lead those that read to behave as my good friend seems to have behaved."

All this the peasant heard, and from it he understood at last what was the matter with his neighbour, so he began calling aloud, "Open, your worships, to Senor Baldwin and to Senor the Marquis of Mantua, who comes badly wounded, and to Senor Abindarraez, the Moor, whom the valiant Rodrigo de Narvaez, the Alcaide of Antequera, brings captive."

At these words they all hurried out, and when they recognised their friend, master, and uncle, who had not yet dismounted from the ass because he could not, they ran to embrace him.

"Hold!" said he, "for I am badly wounded through my horse's fault; carry me to bed, and if possible send for the wise Urganda to cure and see to my wounds."

"See there! Plague on it!" cried the housekeeper at this. "Did not my heart tell the truth as to which foot my master went lame of? To bed with your worship at once, and we will contrive to cure you here without fetching that Hurgada. A curse I say once more, and a hundred times more, on those books of chivalry that have brought your worship to such a pass."

They carried him to bed at once, and after searching for his wounds could find none, but he said they were all bruises from having had a severe fall with his horse Rocinante when in combat with ten giants, the biggest and the boldest to be found on earth.

"So, so!" said the curate. "Are there giants in the dance? By the sign of the Cross I will burn them to-morrow before the day over."

They put a host of questions to Don Quixote, but his only answer to all was—give him something to eat, and leave him to sleep, for that was what he needed most. They did so, and the curate questioned the peasant at great length as to how he had found Don Quixote. He told him, and the nonsense he had talked when found and on the way home, all which made the licentiate the more eager to do what he did the next day, which was to summon his friend the barber, Master Nicholas, and go with him to Don Quixote's house.

Notes on the Text
Chapter III-V

Vocabulary

carrier: letter, parcel and the like carrier or deliverer.

Dona: "a Spanish woman of rank—used as a title prefixed to the Christian name. Origin: Spanish, from Latin *domina*. First Known Use: 1606" (*Merriam-Webster*).

blood-lettings: The removal of blood with leeches or by piercing the skin was used for many centuries. The use of leeches for bleedings reached a peak of popularity in the nineteenth century around the world, and blood-lettings are still occasionally used in medicine today. The idea was that when somebody is ill, their blood is poisoned, and if the old blood is let out the new blood the body will create will be healthier and the person would return to good health. In reality, patients frequently died of too many or too copious of blood-lettings. So, this is not so much a joke about the farmer asking the youth, Andres, to pay him for making him bleed, as an actual medical expense that he wants to be subsidized for.

"distilling vermilion and sulphur" (62): This seems to be a reference to vermilion red or mercury sulphide (HgS), a popular red color in painting. The saying is a bit confusing because sulphur was one of the ingredients that made-up vermilion, so he would have been distilling or extracting sulphur back out of vermilion. Either way, the trader is saying that red paint is leaking out of this supposed painted lady's good eye.

"ambergris and civet in cotton" (62): Civet is a catlike mammal that lives in Africa and Asia that secretes a musky fluid out of which perfumes are made. Ambergris is an amber produced by sperm whales, which sweetens as it ages and is used to make perfumes last longer. Don Quixote is saying that his lady produces ingredients of perfume rather than something vile.

Forces of Muhammed IX, Sultan of Granada, at the Battle of Higueruela 1431, as depicted in fresco paintings by Fabrizio Castello. 1582.

Comments on the Text

The description of how Don Quixote is dubbed as a knight by the innkeeper is probably a tough one for modern readers to understand because we live in a far-removed time and place. Cervantes is satirizing the knightly traditions by exaggerating them. A knight would have to do vigil in a Church before being dubbed. An innkeeper was not likely to have been qualified to dub Quixote because he would have had to be related to the king, nobility or to a knight. Some exceptions were made to this rule, so that occasionally even a corrupt innkeeper might have been allowed to perform this essentially religious ceremony. This liberal dubbing of people who might not have been worthy of the title of "knight" is what Cervantes is satirizing. Here is a quote from Grace E. Coolidge's *The Formation of the Child in Early Modern Spain* that should help to explain Cervantes' perspective:

> Service in the king's armies had at its origins the conscripted roles of soldiers and military leaders carried out by both the lower classes and the nobility in the late fifteenth and early sixteenth centuries. Continued recruitment through commissions, contracts, or compulsion, whether due to the enticement of the New World or to dispatches to European battlefields, resulted in the constant drain of manpower during the sixteenth century… by 1630, Spain relied on over 150,000 soldiers, not counting its naval fleet… As a soldier who enlisted in his early twenties, Cervantes was well aware that military service offered poor youths a mean of employment, no matter how miserly… (73).

Portrait of Francisco de los Cobos y Molina. 1532.

There was a difference between serving in the army as a lower-class employee and volunteering to serve the king as a noble knight. The latter received honors, while the first group performed most of the fighting. The tools of the knight that Quixote mimics were starting to be outdated by the time Cervantes wrote this novel, as the lance was giving way to more practical weapons. The innkeeper supports Quixote's delusions by falsely confirming that he was indeed a knight that had many successful adventures. The innkeeper also says the vigil is actually just a matter of watching one's arms and that it can be performed in the courtyard, rather than in an actual church. The satire is in the contradiction between the structured courtly ritual of dubbing and this very casual and absurd dubbing that involves made-up changes to the approved rituals.

"Then, reading from his account-book as if he were repeating some devout prayer, in the middle of his delivery he raised his hand and gave him a sturdy blow on the neck, and then, with his own sword, a smart slap on the shoulder, all the while muttering between his teeth as if he was saying his prayers" (56): This is a great example of the type of humor consistently used in *Don Quixote*. Some writers were persecuted for blasphemy for joking about religious subjects, so Cervantes is making a controversial statement for his time by saying that the innkeeper read from his account-book as if it was a prayer-book. In this period, few people were literate, so most probably muttered things between their teeth when they were asked to read from a prayer book, thus this was a humorous problem that was recognizable to less educated readers. The outrageous nature of the statement is what makes it absurd and unexpected, thus creating a humorous contradiction. The violence in this novel is such that it is harsher than it would normally be in some instances, and lighter or more like clownish stumbling in fights where Quixote attempts to play the knight. He only succeeds if his victims are caught off guard, and more frequently fails and is severely beat up when he encounters armed or powerful opponents. In this case, knighting did not include any blows with the hand, and the sword is supposed to lightly touch the shoulder rather than "slap" it (with potential for doing harm to the future knight).

"battered in body as he was, to rise was beyond his power" (63):

This is an example of a cliffhanger. A **cliffhanger** is when the reader is left in suspense for fear that the main character will die or his suffering might increase in the last lines of a scene, a chapter or an episode. The intention is to keep the reader reading onto the next chapter. This trick became more important in the nineteenth century as periodicals printed novels on a weekly basis and the ends (before the week's reading concluded) had to encourage readers to purchase the next installment. The same trick is important today in TV series that profit if viewers stay with the show through commercial breaks and into the following episodes.

"by my faith to-morrow shall not pass without public judgment upon them, and may they be condemned to the flames lest they lead those that read to behave as my good friend seems to have behaved" (67): Book burnings were (and in places remain) common religious or political punishments against transgressing, blasphemous or otherwise supposedly in-need-of-censorship books. Anticipating that his own book might fall to this fate, Cervantes inserts these calls to burn all books of chivalry for their use of magicians and other blasphemous, untrue matter that drives people mad (as exemplified by Don Quixote's case). This way, any objectors have to first defend books of chivalry (an unlikely scenario), before they could attempt to criticize the radical anti-chivalry stance Cervantes is taking.

Questions for Discussion

1. Why does Don Quixote react to an intrusion upon his armor by striking a couple of carriers unconscious? Is violence one of the driving forces of suspense in this novel? Would the story lack momentum if the threat of death to Quixote and those he attacks was absent? There is around one violent or otherwise life-threatening clash in most of the following chapters of this novel.
2. Find a sentence in this section of the reading that you thought was funny (not something that I discussed in my comments), and explain what kind of humor is used and why the sentence made you laugh, giggle, or think that it is amusing.
3. Sancho Panza is mentioned in the preface, as the "famous… squire" of Don Quixote. And Quixote states that he plans on taking on a servant to assist in his adventures on the innkeeper's advice. Mean-

while, Don Quixote takes up paragraphs in the first chapters on monologues wherein he glorifies his Dulcinea del Toboso, as he does on page 61: "it has fallen to thy lot to hold subject and submissive to thy full will and pleasure a knight so renowned as is and will be Don Quixote of La Mancha." Do you think Cervantes might have decided he needed a sidekick to make light of these prolonged speeches for the novel to be more humorous and satirical? Is dialogue (rather than monologue) necessary for the character's ideas to be dynamic and engaging? Give an example of another monologue or dialogue that illustrates this from the assigned *Don Quixote* chapters. A **monologue** is when a single character talks to himself or the audience. A **dialogue** is when two or more characters talk with each other.

4. Discuss a cliffhanger that you thought was particularly suspenseful from this section of the reading. Was the main character's or somebody else's life in danger? Do you think a cliffhanger can be based on the anticipation of potential love or feelings other than fear? Why or why not?

5. What do you think about the curate's plan to burn books of chivalry because they are blasphemous, or in violation of the Christian doctrine? Do you think it is immoral to fool some people into insanity with fantasy, science fiction or other speculative books? These books are very popular today, as are institutionalization and drugs for various delusions and other mental illnesses? Would the world be a saner place if all fantastic books that related untrue things were banned? Why or why not?

Works Cited

Coolidge, Grace E. *The Formation of the Child in Early Modern Spain*. New York: Ashgate Publishing, 2014. *Google Books*. 6 February 2017. Web.

Portrait of Prince Elector Moritz of Saxony. 1578.

Jonathan Swift

Jonathan Swift lived between 1667 and 1745 predominantly in Dublin, Ireland. The last year of his MA studies at Trinity College, Dublin, was disturbed by the Glorious Revolution, which saw the overthrow of the rightful heir to the throne, James II of England by an invading Dutch usurper, William III. The conflict was in part over James' policies of religious tolerance due to his own Catholicism, in contrast with the strong Protestant tradition that ruled over the United Kingdom (a weak union at this time between Scotland, Ireland, Wales and England, which was only solidified with the Acts of Union in 1707) in prior decades. After James was deposed, he continued fighting on the Irish and later Scottish fronts, trying to garner support, and these attempts incited a strong negative backlash against all Protestants, as Catholics were a majority in Ireland. Since Swift was a Protestant, he left Ireland and continued his MA studies at the University of Oxford. As a student, and before he was ordained as a pastor, in 1695, Swift wrote some poetry, a form that was highly respected at this time for the skill necessary to execute its precise structure and artistic elements. Swift then turned to satire in short stories self-published in anonymous pamphlets, such as *A Tale of a Tub* (1704). This genre was thought of as the craft of the scholarly critic, as its task was to ridicule with harsh parody another writer's or politician's work to stress its flaws. Swift disguised his identity because while satire was practiced by both radicals and conservative supporters of Church and State, those who opposed the established doctrine were occasionally prosecuted for blasphemy or treason and could be put to death if their authorship was discovered. In 1699, Swift worked as the secretary and chaplain of the Earl of Berkeley. When the Tories briefly rose to power in 1710, Swift became their chief propagandist, writing many of the pamphlets that worked to convince the people of the Tories' cause in his position as the editor of the *Examiner* and in pamphlets such as *The Conduct of the Allies* (1711). This public service resulted in Swift's appointment to the post of Dean of St. Patrick's Cathedral in Dublin, a title he held long after this brief political stint ended. The rapid decline of the Tories and the dashing of Swift's further political or clergy ambitions left him bitter, so that his later satirical works include the much darker *A Modest Proposal* (about the wealthy contemplating eating poor Irish children) and *Gulliver's Travels*. The Whigs put many of the Tories that criticized them when they were in power on trial for sedition (or for assisting in Jacobite schemes) and related crimes. There was a series of Jacobite uprisings in the decades after the Revolution and the 1689-92 Irish rising; the later risings took place in 1708, 1715, 1719, 1744, 1745, and 1759. All of these risings failed, but they did set the stage for the Scottish and Irish independence movements. The risings touched on nationalist issues as well as religious, party and other concerns. They were extremely divisive and strongly influenced Swift as he was writing this novel in their midst. Most of Sir Walter Scott's historical *Waverley* novels are about these Jacobite risings. He started writing them in 1714, over sixty years after the risings ended. This topic was too contentious to mention it in 1726 when Swift composed his story, so he deliberately made the characters fantastic to avoid directly criticizing the winning party in this ongoing dispute. Regardless of this, if Swift remained in political favor, he might not have had time to write these late masterpieces, and the bitterness Swift felt made for very dramatic writing.

GULLIVER'S TRAVELS

INTO SEVERAL REMOTE NATIONS OF THE WORLD

By Jonathan Swift, D. D.,

DEAN OF ST. PATRICK'S, DUBLIN.

1726-7

THE PUBLISHER TO THE READER

The author of these Travels, Mr. Lemuel Gulliver, is my ancient and intimate friend; there is likewise some relation between us on the mother's side. About three years ago, Mr. Gulliver, growing weary of the concourse of curious people coming to him at his house in Redriff, made a small purchase of land, with a convenient house, near Newark, in Nottinghamshire, his native country; where he now lives retired, yet in good esteem among his neighbours.

Although Mr. Gulliver was born in Nottinghamshire, where his father dwelt, yet I have heard him say his family came from Oxfordshire; to confirm which, I have observed in the churchyard at Banbury in that county, several tombs and monuments of the Gullivers.

Before he quitted Redriff, he left the custody of the following papers in my hands, with the liberty to dispose of them as I should think fit. I have carefully perused them three times. The style is very plain and simple; and the only fault I find is, that the author, after the manner of travellers, is a little too circumstantial. There is an air of truth apparent through the whole; and indeed, the author was so distinguished for his veracity, that it became a sort of proverb among his neighbours at Redriff, when any one affirmed a thing, to say, it was as true as if Mr. Gulliver had spoken it.

By the advice of several worthy persons, to whom, with the author's permission, I communicated these papers, I now venture to send them into the world, hoping they may be, at least for some time, a better entertainment to our young noblemen, than the common scribbles of politics and party.

This volume would have been at least twice as large, if I had not made bold to strike out innumerable passages relating to the winds and tides, as well as to the variations and bearings in the several voyages, together with the minute descriptions of the management of the ship in storms, in the style of sailors; likewise, the account of longitudes and latitudes; wherein I have reason to apprehend, that Mr. Gulliver may be a little dissatisfied. But I was resolved to fit the work as much as possible to the general capacity of readers. However, if my own ignorance in sea affairs shall have led me to commit some mistakes, I alone am answerable for them. And if any traveller hath a curiosity to see the whole work at large, as it came from the hands of the author, I will be ready to gratify him.

As for any further particulars relating to the author, the reader will receive satisfaction from the first pages of the book.

RICHARD SYMPSON.

A LETTER FROM CAPTAIN GULLIVER TO HIS COUSIN SYMPSON

Written in the Year 1727.

I hope you will be ready to own publicly, whenever you shall be called to it, that by your great and frequent urgency you prevailed on me to publish a very loose and uncorrect account of my travels, with directions to hire some young gentleman of either university to put them in order, and correct the style, as my cousin Dampier did, by my advice, in his book called *A Voyage Round the World*. But I do not remember I gave you power to consent that any thing should be omitted, and much less that any thing should be inserted; therefore, as to the latter, I do here renounce everything of that kind; particularly a paragraph about her majesty Queen Anne, of most pious and glorious memory; although I did reverence and esteem her more than any of human species. But you, or your interpolator, ought to have considered, that it was not my inclination, so was it not decent to praise any animal of our composition before my master *Houyhnhnm*: And besides, the fact was altogether false; for to my knowledge, being in England during some part of her majesty's reign, she did govern by a chief minister; nay even by two successively, the first whereof was the lord of Godolphin, and the second the lord of Oxford; so that you have made me say the thing that was not. Likewise, in the account of the academy of projectors, and several passages of my discourse to my master *Houyhnhnm*, you have either omitted some material circumstances, or minced or changed them in such a manner, that I do hardly know my own work. When I formerly hinted to you something of this in a letter, you were pleased to answer that you were afraid of giving offence; that people in power were very watchful over the press, and apt not only to interpret, but to punish everything which looked like an *innuendo* (as I think you call it). But, pray how could that which I spoke so many years ago, and at about five thousand leagues distance, in another reign, be applied to any of the *Yahoos*, who now are said to govern the herd; especially at a time when I little thought, or feared, the unhappiness of living under them? Have not I the most reason to complain, when I see these very *Yahoos* carried by *Houyhnhnms* in a vehicle, as if they were brutes, and those the rational creatures? And indeed, to avoid so monstrous and detestable a sight was one principal motive of my retirement hither.

Thus much I thought proper to tell you in relation to yourself, and to the trust I reposed in you.

I do, in the next place, complain of my own great want of judgment, in being prevailed upon by the entreaties and false reasoning of you and some others, very much against my own opinion, to suffer my travels to be published. Pray bring to your mind how often I desired you to consider, when you insisted on the motive of public good, that the *Yahoos* were a species of animals utterly incapable of amendment by precept or example: and so it has proved; for, instead of seeing a full stop put to all abuses and corruptions, at least in this little island, as I had reason to expect; behold, after above six months warning, I cannot learn that my book has produced one single effect according to my intentions. I desired you would let me know, by a letter, when party and faction were extinguished; judges learned and upright; pleaders honest and modest, with some tincture of common sense, and Smithfield blazing with pyramids of law books; the young nobility's education entirely changed; the physicians banished; the female *Yahoos* abounding in virtue, honour, truth, and good sense; courts and levees of great ministers thoroughly weeded and swept; wit, merit, and learning rewarded; all disgracers of the press in prose and verse condemned to eat nothing but their own cotton, and quench their thirst with their own ink. These, and a thousand other reformations, I firmly counted upon by your encouragement; as indeed they were plainly deducible from the precepts delivered in my book. And it must be owned, that seven months were a sufficient time to correct every vice and folly to which *Yahoos* are subject, if their natures had been capable of the least disposition to virtue or wisdom. Yet, so far have you been from answering my expectation in any of your letters; that on the contrary you are loading our carrier every week with libels, and keys, and reflections, and memoirs, and second parts; wherein I see myself accused of reflecting upon great state folk; of degrading human nature (for so they have still the confidence to style it), and of abusing the female sex. I find likewise that the writers of those bundles are not agreed among themselves; for some of them will not allow me to be the author of my own travels; and others make me author of books to which I am wholly a stranger.

I find likewise that your printer has been so careless as to confound the times, and mistake the dates, of my several voyages and returns; neither assigning the true year, nor the true month, nor day of the month: and I hear the original manuscript is all destroyed since the publication of my book; neither have I any copy left: however, I have sent you some corrections, which you may insert, if ever there should be a second edition: and yet I cannot stand to them; but shall leave that matter to my judicious and candid readers to adjust it as they please.

I hear some of our sea *Yahoos* find fault with my sea-language, as not proper in many parts, nor now in use. I cannot help it. In my first voyages, while I was young, I was instructed by the oldest mariners, and learned to speak as they did. But I have since found that the sea *Yahoos* are apt, like the land ones, to become new-fangled in their words, which the latter change every year; insomuch, as I remember upon each return to my own country their old dialect was so altered, that I could hardly understand the new. And I observe, when any *Yahoo* comes from London out of curiosity to visit me at my house, we neither of us are able to deliver our conceptions in a manner intelligible to the other.

If the censure of the *Yahoos* could any way affect me, I should have great reason to complain, that some of them are so bold as to think my book of travels a mere fiction out of mine own brain, and have gone so far as to drop hints, that the *Houyhnhnms* and *Yahoos* have no more existence than the inhabitants of Utopia.

Indeed I must confess, that as to the people of *Lilliput, Brobdingrag* (for so the word should have been spelt, and not erroneously *Brobdingnag*), and *Laputa*, I have never yet heard of any *Yahoo* so presumptuous as to dispute their being, or the facts I have related concerning them; because the truth immediately strikes every reader with conviction. And is there less probability in my account of the *Houyhnhnms* or *Yahoos*, when it is manifest as to the latter, there are so many thousands even in this country, who only differ from their brother brutes in *Houyhnhnmland*, because they use a sort of jabber, and do not go naked? I wrote for their amendment, and not their approbation. The united praise of the whole race would be of less consequence to me, than the neighing of those two degenerate *Houyhnhnms* I keep in my stable; because from these, degenerate as they are, I still improve in some virtues without any mixture of vice.

Do these miserable animals presume to think, that I am so degenerated as to defend my veracity? *Yahoo* as I am, it is well known through all *Houyhnhnmland*, that, by the instructions and example of my illustrious master, I was able in the compass of two years (although I confess with the utmost difficulty) to remove that infernal habit of lying, shuffling, deceiving, and equivocating, so deeply rooted in the very souls of all my species; especially the Europeans.

I have other complaints to make upon this vexatious occasion; but I forbear troubling myself or you any further. I must freely confess, that since my last return, some corruptions of my *Yahoo* nature have revived in me by conversing with a few of your species, and particularly those of my own family, by an unavoidable necessity; else I should never have attempted so absurd a project as that of reforming the *Yahoo* race in this kingdom. But I have now done with all such visionary schemes for ever.

April 2, 1727

PART I. A VOYAGE TO LILLIPUT

CHAPTER I

The author gives some account of himself and family. His first inducements to travel. He is shipwrecked, and swims for his life. Gets safe on shore in the country of Lilliput; is made a prisoner, and carried up the country.

My father had a small estate in Nottinghamshire: I was the third of five sons. He sent me to Emanuel College in Cambridge at fourteen years old, where I resided three years, and applied myself close to my studies; but the charge of maintaining me, although I had a very scanty allowance, being too great for a narrow fortune, I was bound apprentice to Mr. James Bates, an eminent surgeon in London, with whom I continued four years. My father now and then sending me small sums of money, I laid them out in learning navigation, and other parts of the mathematics, useful to those who intend to travel, as I always believed it would be, some time or other, my fortune to do. When I left Mr. Bates, I went down to my father: where, by the assistance of him and my uncle John, and some other relations, I got forty pounds, and a promise of thirty pounds a year to maintain me at Leyden: there I studied physic two years and seven months, knowing it would be useful in long voyages.

Soon after my return from Leyden, I was recommended by my good master, Mr. Bates, to be surgeon to the Swallow, Captain Abraham Pannel, commander; with whom I continued three years and a half, making a voyage or two into the Levant, and some other parts. When I came back I resolved to settle in London; to which Mr. Bates, my master, encouraged me, and by him I was recommended to several patients. I took part of a small house in the Old Jewry; and being advised to alter my condition, I married Mrs. Mary Burton, second daughter to Mr. Edmund Burton, hosier, in Newgate Street, with whom I received four hundred pounds for a portion.

But my good master Bates dying in two years after, and I having few friends, my business began to fail; for my conscience would not suffer me to imitate the bad practice of too many among my brethren. Having therefore consulted with my wife, and some of my acquaintance, I determined to go again to sea. I was surgeon successively in two ships, and made several voyages, for six years, to the East and West Indies, by which I got some addition to my fortune. My hours of leisure I spent in reading the best authors, ancient and modern, being always provided with a good number of books; and when I was ashore, in observing the manners and dispositions of the people, as well as learning their language; wherein I had a great facility, by the strength of my memory.

The last of these voyages not proving very fortunate, I grew weary of the sea, and intended to stay at home with my wife and family. I removed from the Old Jewry to Fetter Lane, and from thence to Wapping, hoping to get business among the sailors; but it would not turn to account. After three years' expectation that things would mend, I accepted an advantageous offer from Captain William Prichard, master of the Antelope, who was making a voyage to the South Sea. We set sail from Bristol, May 4, 1699, and our voyage was at first very prosperous.

It would not be proper, for some reasons, to trouble the reader with the particulars of our adventures in those seas; let it suffice to inform him, that in our passage from thence to the East Indies, we were driven by a violent storm to the north-west of Van Diemen's Land. By an observation, we found ourselves in the latitude of 30 degrees 2 minutes south. Twelve of our crew were dead by immoderate labour and ill food; the rest were in a very weak condition. On the 5th of November, which was the beginning of summer in those parts, the weather being very hazy, the seamen spied a rock within half a cable's length of the ship; but the wind was so strong, that we were driven directly upon it, and immediately split. Six of the crew, of whom I was one, having let down the boat into the sea, made a shift to get clear of the ship and the rock. We rowed, by my computation, about three leagues, till we were able to work no longer, being already spent with labour while we were in the ship. We therefore trusted ourselves to the mercy of the waves, and in about half an hour the boat was overset by a sudden flurry from the north. What became of my companions in the boat, as well as of those who escaped on the rock, or were left in the vessel, I cannot tell; but conclude they were all lost. For my own part, I swam as fortune directed me, and was pushed forward by wind and tide. I often let my legs drop, and could feel no bottom; but when I was almost gone, and able to struggle no longer, I found myself within my depth; and by this time the storm was much abated. The declivity was so small, that I walked near a mile before I got to the shore, which I conjectured was about eight o'clock in the evening. I then advanced forward near half a mile, but could not discover any sign of houses or inhabitants; at least I was in so weak a condition, that I did not observe them. I was extremely tired, and with that, and the heat of the weather, and about half a pint of brandy that I drank as I left the ship, I found myself much inclined to sleep. I lay down on the grass, which was very short and soft, where I slept sounder than ever I remembered to have done in my life, and, as I reckoned, about nine hours; for when I awaked, it was just day-light. I attempted to rise, but was not able to stir: for, as I happened to lie on my back, I found my arms and legs were strongly fastened on each side to the ground; and my hair, which was long and thick, tied down in the same manner. I likewise felt several slender ligatures across my body, from my arm-pits to my thighs. I could only look upwards; the sun began to grow hot, and the light offended my eyes. I heard a confused noise about me; but in the posture I lay, could see nothing except the sky. In a little time, I felt something alive moving on my left leg, which, advancing gently forward over my breast, came almost up to my chin; when, bending my eyes downwards as much as I could, I perceived it to be a human creature not six inches high, with a bow and arrow in his hands, and a quiver at his back. In the meantime, I felt at least forty more of the same kind (as I conjectured) following the first. I was in the utmost astonishment, and roared so loud, that they all ran back in a fright; and some of them, as I was afterwards told, were hurt with the falls they got by leaping from my sides upon the ground. However, they soon returned, and one of them, who ventured so far as to get a full sight of my face, lifting up his hands and eyes by way of admiration, cried out in a shrill but distinct voice, *Hekinah degul!* The others repeated the same words several times, but then I knew not what they meant. I lay all this while, as the reader may believe, in great uneasiness. At length, struggling to get loose, I had the fortune to break the strings, and wrench out the pegs that fastened my left arm to the ground; for, by lifting it up to my face, I discovered the methods they had taken to bind me, and at the same time with a violent pull, which gave me excessive pain, I a little loosened the strings that tied down my hair on the left side, so that I was just able to turn my head about two inches. But the creatures ran off a second time, before I could seize them; whereupon there was a great shout in a very shrill accent, and after it ceased I heard one of them cry aloud, *Tolgo phonac*, when in an instant, I felt above a hundred arrows discharged on my left hand, which pricked me like so many needles; and besides, they shot another flight into the air, as we do bombs in Europe, whereof many, I suppose, fell on my body, (though I felt them not), and some on my face, which I immediately covered with my left hand. When this shower of arrows was over, I fell a groaning with grief and pain; and then striving again to get loose, they discharged another volley larger than the first, and some of them attempted with spears to stick me in the sides; but by good luck I had on a buff jerkin, which they could not pierce. I thought it the most prudent method to lie still, and my design was to continue so till night, when, my left hand being already loose, I could easily free myself: and as for the inhabitants, I had reason to believe I might be a match for the greatest army they could bring against me, if they were all of the same size with him that I saw. But fortune disposed otherwise of me. When the people observed I was quiet, they discharged no more arrows; but, by the noise I heard, I knew their numbers increased; and about four yards from me, over against my right ear, I heard a knocking for above an hour, like that of people at work; when turning my head that way, as well as the pegs and strings would permit me, I saw a stage erected about a foot and a half from the ground, capable of holding four of the inhabitants, with two or three ladders to mount it: from whence one of them, who seemed to be a person of quality, made me a long speech, whereof I understood not one syllable. But I should have mentioned, that before the principal person began his oration, he cried out three times, *Langro dehul san* (these words and the former were afterwards repeated and explained to me); whereupon, immediately, about fifty of the inhabitants came and cut the strings that fastened the left side of my head, which gave me the liberty of turning it to the right, and of observing the person and gesture of him that was to speak. He appeared to be of a middle age, and taller than any of the other three who attended him, whereof one was a page that held up his train, and seemed to be somewhat longer than my middle finger; the other two stood one on each side to support him. He acted every part of an orator, and I could observe many periods of threatenings, and others of promises, pity, and kindness. I answered in a few words, but in the most submissive manner, lifting up my left hand, and both my eyes to the sun, as calling him for a witness; and being almost famished with hunger, having not eaten a morsel for some hours before I left the ship, I found the demands of nature so strong upon me, that I could not forbear showing my impatience (perhaps against the strict rules of decency) by putting my finger frequently to my mouth, to signify that I wanted food. The *hurgo* (for so they call a great lord, as I afterwards learnt) understood me very well. He descended from the stage, and commanded that several ladders should be applied to my sides, on which above a hundred of the inhabitants mounted and walked towards my mouth, laden with baskets full of meat, which had been provided and sent thither by the king's orders, upon the first intelligence he received of me. I observed there was the flesh of several animals, but could not distinguish them by the taste. There were shoulders, legs, and loins, shaped like those of mutton, and very well dressed, but smaller than the wings of a lark. I ate them by two or three at a mouthful, and took three loaves at a time, about the bigness of musket bullets. They supplied me as fast as they could, showing a thousand marks of wonder and astonishment at my bulk and appetite. I then made another sign, that I wanted drink. They found by my eating that a small quantity would not suffice me; and being a most ingenious people, they slung up, with great dexterity, one of their largest hogsheads, then rolled it towards my hand, and beat out the top; I drank it off at a draught, which I might well do, for it did not hold half a pint, and tasted like a small wine of Burgundy, but much more delicious. They brought me a second hogshead, which I drank in the same manner, and made signs for more; but they had none to give me. When I had performed these wonders, they shouted for joy, and danced upon my breast, repeating several times as they did at first, *Hekinah degul!* They made me a sign that I should throw down the two hogsheads, but first warning the people below to stand out of the way, crying aloud, *Borach mevolah*; and when they saw the vessels in the air, there was a universal shout of *Hekinah degul!* I confess I was often tempted, while they were passing backwards and forwards on my body, to seize forty or fifty of the first that came in my reach, and dash them against the ground. But the remembrance of what I had felt, which probably might not be the worst they could do, and the promise of honour I made them—for so I interpreted my submissive behaviour—soon drove out these imaginations. Besides, I now considered myself as bound by the laws of hospitality, to a people who had treated me with so much expense and magnificence. However, in my thoughts I could not sufficiently wonder at the intrepidity of these diminutive mortals, who durst venture to mount and walk upon my body, while one of my hands was at liberty, without trembling at the very sight of so prodigious a creature as I must appear to them. After some time, when they observed that I made no more demands for meat, there appeared before me a person of high rank from his imperial majesty. His excellency, having mounted on the small of my right leg, advanced forwards up to my face, with about a dozen of his retinue; and producing his credentials under the signet royal, which he applied close to my eyes, spoke about ten minutes without any signs of anger, but with a kind of determinate resolution, often pointing forwards, which, as I afterwards found, was towards the capital city, about half a mile distant; whither it was agreed by his majesty in council that I must be conveyed. I answered in few words, but to no purpose, and made a sign with my hand that was loose, putting it to the other (but over his excellency's head for fear of hurting him or his train) and then to my own head and body, to signify that I desired my liberty. It appeared that he understood me well enough, for he shook his head by way of disapprobation, and held his hand in a posture to show that I must be carried as a prisoner. However, he made other signs to let me understand that I should have meat and drink enough, and very good treatment. Whereupon I once more thought of attempting to break my bonds; but again, when I felt the smart of their arrows upon my face and hands, which were all in blisters, and many of the darts still sticking in them, and observing likewise that the number of my enemies increased, I gave tokens to let them know that they might do with me what they pleased. Upon this, the *hurgo* and his train withdrew, with much civility and cheerful countenances. Soon after I heard a general shout, with frequent repetitions of the words *Peplom selan*; and I felt great numbers of people on my left side relaxing the cords to such a degree, that I was able to turn upon my right, and to ease myself with making water; which I very plentifully did, to the great astonishment of the people; who, conjecturing by my motion what I was going to do, immediately opened to the right and left on that side, to avoid the torrent, which fell with such noise and violence from me. But before this, they had daubed my face and both my hands with a sort of ointment, very pleasant to the smell, which, in a few minutes, removed all the smart of their arrows. These circumstances, added to the refreshment I had received by their victuals and drink, which were very nourishing, disposed me to sleep. I slept about eight hours, as I was afterwards assured; and it was no wonder, for the physicians, by the emperor's order, had mingled a sleepy potion in the hogsheads of wine.

It seems, that upon the first moment I was discovered sleeping on the ground, after my landing, the emperor had early notice of it by an express; and determined in council, that I should be tied in the manner I have related, (which was done in the night while I slept;) that plenty of meat and drink should be sent to me, and a machine prepared to carry me to the capital city.

This resolution perhaps may appear very bold and dangerous, and I am confident would not be imitated by any prince in Europe on the like occasion. However, in my opinion, it was extremely prudent, as well as generous: for, supposing these people had endeavoured to kill me with their spears and arrows, while I was asleep, I should certainly have awaked with the first sense of smart, which might so far have roused my rage and strength, as to have enabled me to break the strings wherewith I was tied; after which, as they were not able to make resistance, so they could expect no mercy.

These people are most excellent mathematicians, and arrived to a great perfection in mechanics, by the countenance and encouragement of the emperor, who is a renowned patron of learning. This prince has several machines fixed on wheels, for the carriage of trees and other great weights. He often builds his largest men of war, whereof some are nine feet long, in the woods where the timber grows, and has them carried on these engines three or four hundred yards to the sea. Five hundred carpenters and engineers were immediately set at work to prepare the greatest engine they had. It was a frame of wood raised three inches from the ground, about seven feet long, and four wide, moving upon twenty-two wheels. The shout I heard was upon the arrival of this engine, which, it seems, set out in four hours after my landing. It was brought parallel to me, as I lay. But the principal difficulty was to raise and place me in this vehicle. Eighty poles, each of one foot high, were erected for this purpose, and very strong cords, of the bigness of packthread, were fastened by hooks to many bandages, which the workmen had girt round my neck, my hands, my body, and my legs.

Nine hundred of the strongest men were employed to draw up these cords, by many pulleys fastened on the poles; and thus, in less than three hours, I was raised and slung into the engine, and there tied fast. All this I was told; for, while the operation was performing, I lay in a profound sleep, by the force of that soporiferous medicine infused into my liquor. Fifteen hundred of the emperor's largest horses, each about four inches and a half high, were employed to draw me towards the metropolis, which, as I said, was half a mile distant.

About four hours after we began our journey, I awaked by a very ridiculous accident; for the carriage being stopped a while, to adjust something that was out of order, two or three of the young natives had the curiosity to see how I looked when I was asleep; they climbed up into the engine, and advancing very softly to my face, one of them, an officer in the guards, put the sharp end of his half-pike a good way up into my left nostril, which tickled my nose like a straw, and made me sneeze violently; whereupon they stole off unperceived, and it was three weeks before I knew the cause of my waking so suddenly. We made a long march the remaining part of the day, and, rested at night with five hundred guards on each side of me, half with torches, and half with bows and arrows, ready to shoot me if I should offer to stir. The next morning at sun-rise we continued our march, and arrived within two hundred yards of the city gates about noon. The emperor, and all his court, came out to meet us; but his great officers would by no means suffer his majesty to endanger his person by mounting on my body.

At the place where the carriage stopped there stood an ancient temple, esteemed to be the largest in the whole kingdom; which, having been polluted some years before by an unnatural murder, was, according to the zeal of those people, looked upon as profane, and therefore had been applied to common use, and all the ornaments and furniture carried away. In this edifice it was determined I should lodge. The great gate fronting to the north was about four feet high, and almost two feet wide, through which I could easily creep. On each side of the gate was a small window, not above six inches from the ground: into that on the left side, the king's smith conveyed fourscore and eleven chains, like those that hang to a lady's watch in Europe, and almost as large, which were locked to my left leg with six-and-thirty padlocks. Over against this temple, on the other side of the great highway, at twenty feet distance, there was a turret at least five feet high. Here the emperor ascended, with many principal lords of his court, to have an opportunity of viewing me, as I was told, for I could not see them. It was reckoned that above a hundred thousand inhabitants came out of the town upon the same errand; and, in spite of my guards, I believe there could not be fewer than ten thousand at several times, who mounted my body by the help of ladders. But a proclamation was soon issued, to forbid it upon pain of death. When the workmen found it was impossible for me to break loose, they cut all the strings that bound me; whereupon I rose up, with as melancholy a disposition as ever I had in my life. But the noise and astonishment of the people, at seeing me rise and walk, are not to be expressed. The chains that held my left leg were about two yards long, and gave me not only the liberty of walking backwards and forwards in a semicircle, but, being fixed within four inches of the gate, allowed me to creep in, and lie at my full length in the temple.

CHAPTER II

The emperor of Lilliput, attended by several of the nobility, comes to see the author in his confinement. The emperor's person and habit described. Learned men appointed to teach the author their language. He gains favour by his mild disposition. His pockets are searched, and his sword and pistols taken from him.

When I found myself on my feet, I looked about me, and must confess I never beheld a more entertaining prospect. The country around appeared like a continued garden, and the enclosed fields, which were generally forty feet square, resembled so many beds of flowers. These fields were intermingled with woods of half a stang, and the tallest trees, as I could judge, appeared to be seven feet high. I viewed the town on my left hand, which looked like the painted scene of a city in a theatre.

I had been for some hours extremely pressed by the necessities of nature; which was no wonder, it being almost two days since I had last disburdened myself. I was under great difficulties between urgency and shame. The best expedient I could think of, was to creep into my house, which I accordingly did; and shutting the gate after me, I went as far as the length of my chain would suffer, and discharged my body of that uneasy load. But this was the only time I was ever guilty of so uncleanly an action; for which I cannot but hope the candid reader will give some allowance, after he has maturely and impartially considered my case, and the distress I was in. From this time my constant practice was, as soon as I rose, to perform that business in open air, at the full extent of my chain; and due care was taken every morning before company came, that the offensive matter should be carried off in wheel-barrows, by two servants appointed for that purpose. I would not have dwelt so long upon a circumstance that, perhaps, at first sight, may appear not very momentous, if I had not thought it necessary to justify my character, in point of cleanliness, to the world; which, I am told, some of my maligners have been pleased, upon this and other occasions, to call in question.

When this adventure was at an end, I came back out of my house, having occasion for fresh air. The emperor was already descended from the tower, and advancing on horseback towards me, which had like to have cost him dear; for the beast, though very well trained, yet wholly unused to such a sight, which appeared as if a mountain moved before him, reared up on its hinder feet: but that prince, who is an excellent horseman, kept his seat, till his attendants ran in, and held the bridle, while his majesty had time to dismount. When he alighted, he surveyed me round with great admiration; but kept beyond the length of my chain. He ordered his cooks and butlers, who were already prepared, to give me victuals and drink, which they pushed forward in a sort of vehicles upon wheels, till I could reach them. I took these vehicles and soon emptied them all; twenty of them were filled with meat, and ten with liquor; each of the former afforded me two or three good mouthfuls; and I emptied the liquor of ten vessels, which was contained in earthen vials, into one vehicle, drinking it off at a draught; and so I did with the rest. The empress, and young princes of the blood of both sexes, attended by many ladies, sat at some distance in their chairs; but upon the accident that happened to the emperor's horse, they alighted, and came near his person, which I am now going to describe. He is taller by almost the breadth of my nail, than any of his court; which alone is enough to strike an awe into the beholders. His features are strong and masculine, with an Austrian lip and arched nose, his complexion olive, his countenance erect, his body and limbs well proportioned, all his motions graceful, and his deportment majestic. He was then past his prime, being twenty-eight years and three quarters old, of which he had reigned about seven in great felicity, and generally victorious. For the better convenience of beholding him, I lay on my side, so that my face was parallel to his, and he stood but three yards off: however, I have had him since many times in my hand, and therefore cannot be deceived in the description. His dress was very plain and simple, and the fashion of it between the Asiatic and the European; but he had on his head a light helmet of gold, adorned with jewels, and a plume on the crest. He held his sword drawn in his hand to defend himself, if I should happen to break loose; it was almost three inches long; the hilt and scabbard were gold enriched with diamonds. His voice was shrill, but very clear and articulate; and I could distinctly hear it when I stood up. The ladies and courtiers were all most magnificently clad; so that the spot they stood upon seemed to resemble a petticoat spread upon the ground, embroidered with figures of gold and silver. His imperial majesty spoke often to me, and I returned answers: but neither of us could understand a syllable. There were several of his priests and lawyers present (as I conjectured by their habits), who were commanded to address themselves to me; and I spoke to them in as many languages as I had the least smattering of, which were High and Low Dutch, Latin, French, Spanish, Italian, and Lingua Franca, but all to no purpose. After about two hours the court retired, and I was left with a strong guard, to prevent the impertinence, and probably the malice of the rabble, who were very impatient to crowd about me as near as they durst; and some of them had the impudence to shoot their arrows at me, as I sat on the ground by the door of my house, whereof one very narrowly missed my left eye. But the colonel ordered six of the ringleaders to be seized, and thought no punishment so proper as to deliver them bound into my hands; which some of his soldiers accordingly did, pushing them forward with the butt-ends of their pikes into my reach. I took them all in my right hand, put five of them into my coat-pocket; and as to the sixth, I made a countenance as if I would eat him alive. The poor man squalled terribly, and the colonel and his officers were in much pain, especially when they saw me take out my penknife: but I soon put them out of fear; for, looking mildly, and immediately cutting the strings he was bound with, I set him gently on the ground, and away he ran. I treated the rest in the same manner, taking them one by one out of my pocket; and I observed both the soldiers and people were highly delighted at this mark of my clemency, which was represented very much to my advantage at court.

Towards night I got with some difficulty into my house, where I lay on the ground, and continued to do so about a fortnight; during which time, the emperor gave orders to have a bed prepared for me. Six hundred beds of the common measure were brought in carriages, and worked up in my house; a hundred and fifty of their beds, sewn together, made up the breadth and length; and these were four double: which, however, kept me but very indifferently from the hardness of the floor, that was of smooth stone. By the same computation, they provided me with sheets, blankets, and coverlets, tolerable enough for one who had been so long inured to hardships.

As the news of my arrival spread through the kingdom, it brought prodigious numbers of rich, idle, and curious people to see me; so that the villages were almost emptied; and great neglect of tillage and household affairs must have ensued, if his imperial majesty had not provided, by several proclamations and orders of state, against this inconveniency. He directed that those who had already beheld me should return home, and not presume to come within fifty yards of my house, without license from the court; whereby the secretaries of state got considerable fees.

In the meantime the emperor held frequent councils, to debate what course should be taken with me; and I was afterwards assured by a particular friend, a person of great quality, who was as much in the secret as any, that the court was under many difficulties concerning me. They apprehended my breaking loose; that my diet would be very expensive, and might cause a famine. Sometimes they determined to starve me; or at least to shoot me in the face and hands with poisoned arrows, which would soon despatch me; but again, they considered that the stench of so large a carcass might produce a plague in the metropolis, and probably spread through the whole kingdom. In the midst of these consultations, several officers of the army went to the door of the great council-chamber, and two of them being admitted, gave an account of my behaviour to the six criminals above-mentioned; which made so favourable an impression in the breast of his majesty and the whole board, in my behalf, that an imperial commission was issued out, obliging all the villages, nine hundred yards round the city, to deliver in every morning six beeves, forty sheep, and other victuals for my sustenance; together with a proportionable quantity of bread, and wine, and other liquors; for the due payment of which, his majesty gave assignments upon his treasury—for this prince lives chiefly upon his own demesnes; seldom, except upon great occasions, raising any subsidies upon his subjects, who are bound to attend him in his wars at their own expense. An establishment was also made of six hundred persons to be my domestics, who had board-wages allowed for their maintenance, and tents built for them very conveniently on each side of my door. It was likewise ordered, that three hundred tailors should make me a suit of clothes, after the fashion of the country; that six of his majesty's greatest scholars should be employed to instruct me in their language; and lastly, that the emperor's horses, and those of the nobility and troops of guards, should be frequently exercised in my sight, to accustom themselves to me. All these orders were duly put in execution; and in about three weeks I made a great progress in learning their language; during which time the emperor frequently honoured me with his visits, and was pleased to assist my masters in teaching me. We began already to converse together in some sort; and the first words I learnt, were to express my desire "that he would please give me my liberty," which I every day repeated on my knees. His answer, as I could comprehend it, was, "that this must be a work of time, not to be thought on without the advice of his council, and that first I must *lumos kelmin pesso desmar lon emposo*;" that is, swear a peace with him and his kingdom. However, that I should be used with all kindness. And he advised me to "acquire, by my patience and discreet behaviour, the good opinion of himself and his subjects." He desired "I would not take it ill, if he gave orders to certain proper officers to search me; for probably I might carry about me several weapons, which must needs be dangerous things, if they answered the bulk of so prodigious a person." I said, "His majesty should be satisfied; for I was ready to strip myself, and turn up my pockets before him." This I delivered part in words, and part in signs. He replied, "that, by the laws of the kingdom, I must be searched by two of his officers; that he knew this could not be done without my consent and assistance; and he had so good an opinion of my generosity and justice, as to trust their persons in my hands; that whatever they took from me, should be returned when I left the country, or paid for at the rate which I would set upon them." I took up the two officers in my hands, put them first into my coat-pockets, and then into every other pocket about me, except my two fobs, and another secret pocket, which I had no mind should be searched, wherein I had some little necessaries that were of no consequence to any but myself.

In one of my fobs there was a silver watch, and in the other a small quantity of gold in a purse. These gentlemen, having pen, ink, and paper, about them, made an exact inventory of every thing they saw; and when they had done, desired I would set them down, that they might deliver it to the emperor. This inventory I afterwards translated into English, and is, word for word, as follows:

"*Imprimis*: In the right coat-pocket of the great man-mountain" (for so I interpret the words *quinbus flestrin*,) "after the strictest search, we found only one great piece of coarse-cloth, large enough to be a foot-cloth for your majesty's chief room of state. In the left pocket we saw a huge silver chest, with a cover of the same metal, which we, the searchers, were not able to lift. We desired it should be opened, and one of us stepping into it, found himself up to the mid leg in a sort of dust, some part whereof flying up to our faces set us both a sneezing for several times together. In his right waistcoat-pocket we found a prodigious bundle of white thin substances, folded one over another, about the bigness of three men, tied with a strong cable, and marked with black figures; which we humbly conceive to be writings, every letter almost half as large as the palm of our hands. In the left there was a sort of engine, from the back of which were extended twenty long poles, resembling the pallisados before your majesty's court: wherewith we conjecture the man-mountain combs his head; for we did not always trouble him with questions, because we found it a great difficulty to make him understand us. In the large pocket, on the right side of his middle cover" (so I translate the word *ranfulo*, by which they meant my breeches,) "we saw a hollow pillar of iron, about the length of a man, fastened to a strong piece of timber larger than the pillar; and upon one side of the pillar, were huge pieces of iron sticking out, cut into strange figures, which we know not what to make of. In the left pocket, another engine of the same kind. In the smaller pocket on the right side, were several round flat pieces of white and red metal, of different bulk; some of the white, which seemed to be silver, were so large and heavy, that my comrade and I could hardly lift them. In the left pocket were two black pillars irregularly shaped: we could not, without difficulty, reach the top of them, as we stood at the bottom of his pocket. One of them was covered, and seemed all of a piece: but at the upper end of the other there appeared a white round substance, about twice the bigness of our heads. Within each of these was enclosed a prodigious plate of steel; which, by our orders, we obliged him to show us, because we apprehended they might be dangerous engines. He took them out of their cases, and told us, that in his own country his practice was to shave his beard with one of these, and cut his meat with the other. There were two pockets which we could not enter: these he called his fobs; they were two large slits cut into the top of his middle cover, but squeezed close by the pressure of his belly. Out of the right fob hung a great silver chain, with a wonderful kind of engine at the bottom. We directed him to draw out whatever was at the end of that chain; which appeared to be a globe, half silver, and half of some transparent metal; for, on the transparent side, we saw certain strange figures circularly drawn, and thought we could touch them, till we found our fingers stopped by the lucid substance. He put this engine into our ears, which made an incessant noise, like that of a water-mill: and we conjecture it is either some unknown animal, or the god that he worships; but we are more inclined to the latter opinion, because he assured us, (if we understood him right, for he expressed himself very imperfectly) that he seldom did anything without consulting it. He called it his oracle, and said, it pointed out the time for every action of his life. From the left fob he took out a net almost large enough for a fisherman, but contrived to open and shut like a purse, and served him for the same use: we found therein several massy pieces of yellow metal, which, if they be real gold, must be of immense value.

"Having thus, in obedience to your majesty's commands, diligently searched all his pockets, we observed a girdle about his waist made of the hide of some prodigious animal, from which, on the left side, hung a sword of the length of five men; and on the right, a bag or pouch divided into two cells, each cell capable of holding three of your majesty's subjects. In one of these cells were several globes, or balls, of a most ponderous metal, about the bigness of our heads, and requiring a strong hand to lift them: the other cell contained a heap of certain black grains, but of no great bulk or weight, for we could hold above fifty of them in the palms of our hands.

"This is an exact inventory of what we found about the body of the man-mountain, who used us with great civility, and due respect to your majesty's commission. Signed and sealed on the fourth day of the eighty-ninth moon of your majesty's auspicious reign.

CLEFRIN FRELOCK, MARSI FRELOCK."

When this inventory was read over to the emperor, he directed me, although in very gentle terms, to deliver up the several particulars. He first called for my scimitar, which I took out, scabbard and all. In the meantime he ordered three thousand of his choicest troops (who then attended him) to surround me at a distance, with their bows and arrows just ready to discharge; but I did not observe it, for mine eyes were wholly fixed upon his majesty. He then desired me to draw my scimitar, which, although it had got some rust by the sea water, was, in most parts, exceeding bright. I did so, and immediately all the troops gave a shout between terror and surprise; for the sun shone clear, and the reflection dazzled their eyes, as I waved the scimitar to and fro in my hand. His majesty, who is a most magnanimous prince, was less daunted than I could expect: he ordered me to return it into the scabbard, and cast it on the ground as gently as I could, about six feet from the end of my chain. The next thing he demanded was one of the hollow iron pillars; by which he meant my pocket pistols. I drew it out, and at his desire, as well as I could, expressed to him the use of it; and charging it only with powder, which, by the closeness of my pouch, happened to escape wetting in the sea (an inconvenience against which all prudent mariners take special care to provide,) I first cautioned the emperor not to be afraid, and then I let it off in the air. The astonishment here was much greater than at the sight of my scimitar. Hundreds fell down as if they had been struck dead; and even the emperor, although he stood his ground, could not recover himself for some time. I delivered up both my pistols in the same manner as I had done my scimitar, and then my pouch of powder and bullets; begging him that the former might be kept from fire, for it would kindle with the smallest spark, and blow up his imperial palace into the air. I likewise delivered up my watch, which the emperor was very curious to see, and commanded two of his tallest yeomen of the guards to bear it on a pole upon their shoulders, as draymen in England do a barrel of ale. He was amazed at the continual noise it made, and the motion of the minute-hand, which he could easily discern; for their sight is much more acute than ours: he asked the opinions of his learned men about it, which were various and remote, as the reader may well imagine without my repeating; although indeed I could not very perfectly understand them. I then gave up my silver and copper money, my purse, with nine large pieces of gold, and some smaller ones; my knife and razor, my comb and silver snuff-box, my handkerchief and journal-book. My scimitar, pistols, and pouch, were conveyed in carriages to his majesty's stores; but the rest of my goods were returned me.

    I had as I before observed, one private pocket, which escaped their search, wherein there was a pair of spectacles (which I sometimes use for the weakness of mine eyes,) a pocket perspective, and some other little conveniences; which, being of no consequence to the emperor, I did not think myself bound in honour to discover, and I apprehended they might be lost or spoiled if I ventured them out of my possession.

Notes on Text
To the Reader-Chapter II

Traveler's tales were very popular in 1726, when Swift published *Gulliver's Travels*. Some readers were fooled by these and other fantastic accounts, and trusted writers that worlds existed overseas that were full of giants, and other fantastical creatures. It was easy to fool the public because so few had the basic education necessary to tell truth from fiction, and because so little was known about the New World that had not been fully charted yet, and about the various other cultures that only a few Europeans had visited at this point. In part, Swift is satirizing the gullibility of uneducated readers who trusted tales that pretend to be true narratives.

    Gulliver's Travels is a great novel for students of literature because it is dense with allusions, symbolism and other forms of figurative language. Because the novel was a new invention at this time, few readers could comprehend the symbolic satirical elements of this novel. This is connected to their inability to separate true travel accounts from fantasies or invented travelogues. Swift studied these complex literary techniques in the best schools of England, and he mastered them better than has any modern writer. Books were censored in this period for politically or religiously sensitive materials and were denied the right to publication if they were problematic. The censors typically were overwhelmed with their workload of manuscripts to review and were frequently barely literate, so they were likely to miss the figurative language in which Swift hid his radical messages. Once the novel was published, it was an immediate success. The figurative suggestions were explained in the main periodicals in the United Kingdom, so by that point, it was too late for censors to retract their approval.

The "Introduction" to Paul Turner's 1998 edition of *Gulliver's Travels* explains that Swift disguised his identity when he offered the book to Benjamin Motte, printer and bookseller (the person who printed and sold books) to protect himself against potential censorship the book might face for its strong anti-Whig criticisms. Motte made some edits to Swift's version of the text that deleted some of the more controversial portions to avoid being prosecuted or censored post-publication; Swift objected and released an edition without Motte's omissions and substitutions a decade later (xiii). Turner also claims that the first in the travelers' tale genre was Lucian's *True History*, from the 2nd century AD. Turner also shows parallels with Sir Thomas More's *Utopia* (1516), which was satirized and was the inspiration for Gulliver's journey. Swift's novel was unique because it combined utopian elements with elements from realistic travel accounts such as *Robinson Crusoe* (xvii). Turner explains that the tale of Lilliput parallels the Jacobite or Whig versus Tory struggles that plagued Swift's times. Turner explains that the Whig King George is represented in the tyranny of the King of Laputa, while the Tory Queen Anne can be seen in the Lilliputian Empress. Jacobite rebellions and particularly the trial of one of the rebels, Bishop Atterbury, who led yet another attempt to restore James to his throne, is portrayed in Chapter 6 of Part III (which we won't be reading) (xviii).

Illustration by Louis Rhead in Gulliver's Travels (*Harper Brothers* 1913)

As with *Don Quixote*, the first voyage to Lilliput, or the first part of the novel is best-known and most often used in abridged versions

Van Diemen's Land (Tasmania, 1644) by Melchisedech Thevenot, Paris

intended for younger readers. Thus, it is appropriate to read this part in our class study, as it is more recognizable if you were to discuss this book with anybody who might not have studied it in a specialized class.

In a letter on the purpose of this novel, composed on September 29, 1725, Swift wrote to his friend and fellow radical, Alexander Pope: "I have ever hated all Nations, professions and Communities and all my love is towards individuals; for instance, I hate the tribe of Lawyers, but I love Councilor such a one, Judge… Soldiers, English, Scotch, French and the rest but principally I hate and detest that animal called man, although I heartily love John, Peter, Thomas and so forth…" (Bloom 25). Swift shows his pessimism about humanity, and a similar detestation for all forms of human evil is depicted in his dark satire.

Vocabulary

Van Diemen's Land (75): Gulliver claims that the first island of Lilliput that he is stranded on is 30 degrees, or 2,071 miles south of the then newly discovered island of Tasmania (now a state in the Commonwealth of Australia, and known as Van Diemen's Land back in Swift's time), lying below the Australian mainland. I looked up the 72 South, 147 East degrees' directions that the author offers, and ended up far inland on the Antarctica continent. Swift might have projected that there were islands there because some explorers started finding islands in the region prior to the authorship of the novel. The landmass of the continent of Antarctica was first spotted in 1820. Thus, Swift assumed that there were islands rather than a giant landmass in the spot he named, and he probably did not anticipate that it would be an ice-covered land rather than a place fit for the tiny Lilliputians. Gulliver's later travels take him as far as Japan, so Swift is basically naming areas of the world map that had newly discovered islands on them and where back in that century there might have still been some islands that could have been uncovered by curious travelers. Gulliver warns readers of his lack of nautical knowledge at the start of the book, so these locations might have been deliberately absurd to avoid actual countries being blamed for the sins of the fantastical characters Swift invented.

Borach mevolah (78): When I read this exclamation, it immediately sounded familiar. I entered it into a Google Translate search and it came up as Polish; this was clearly incorrect as I know it does not sound Slavic, but this made me realize that *Borach* or rather *Boruch* is a word frequently used in Hebrew prayers, which means *blessed*. It is a bit foreign when spelled out in English letters rather than in Hebrew; the words are also mutated, so that they are unrecognizable without searching for similar Hebrew words. I ran a search for the term, and found an article on ProQuest that credited the discovery that the Lilliputians' and Brobdingnags' languages are based on Hebrew to professor Irving Rothman at the University of Houston only in the 2015 issue of *Swift Studies*, rather than in the centuries that this novel must have been read by thousands of Hebrew speakers. This goes to show that new discoveries are possible even when studying books that have had thousands of scholarly studies done on them. Swift studied Hebrew at Trinity College, where it was a common course for an Anglican minister. Many of the Hebrew terms Swift uses are related to God, worship and rightful actions, and indicate that Swift was ridiculing people for their ungodly behavior without directly preaching to them. Take a look at the article cited below from the *US Fed News Service* for a detailed explanation. However, it would be too simplistic to say that all of the supposedly invented words in this novel are of Hebrew origins. A better explanation is to say that they are a lingua franca mixture of the languages to which Swift was exposed. For example, "*lumos kelmin pesso desmar lon emposo*" (87) according to Google Translate includes the words "person fainting" (*pessoa desmaiar*) in Portuguese and a word similar to "husband" (*esposo*) in Spanish. Gulliver translates this phrase as: "swear a peace with him and his kingdom." This might be a joke about the emperor proclaiming his love for Gulliver, if my translation is correct. Later in the text, Gulliver is called, "quinbus flestrin" (87), which Google Translate interprets in Hebrew to mean, "Occupation of Palestine." Although, it might also include the words "these schemes" if it is in Icelandic. The Icelandic translation is nonsensical, but the Hebrew translation fits with the term "man-mountain" that Gulliver translates it to mean, as it seems to be an allusion to Moses going to the mountain to obtain the word of God, or an allusion to the occupation of the Holy Land by the Turks in Swift's period or Gulliver's similar occupation of the Lilliputians' primary church. The Ottoman Empire had control over what is now known as Palestine, but at that time also included Jerusalem; most Europeans could not easily travel into this region.

Lingua Franca (85): The dominant language in a given region. In this case, Swift is referring to English because French and the other popular languages in Europe in this period are mentioned separately. Lingua Franca can be a single commonly used language, or it can be a mixture of popular languages (i.e. Spanglish) that are combined so that merchants could understand each other, without fully learning all of the languages of the countries they visited.

two fobs (87): A chain with an attached item such as a decoration or a pocket watch than was hung from a pocket in the waistcoat. When they are first mentioned, Gulliver writes that he did not show the inspectors these fobs as well as another secret pocket, but at the end of the chapter he describes in detail how the inspectors did inspect the fobs and how the emperor took some of his possessions from them. This contradiction might have a figurative meaning, or it might simply be a typo on Swift's part.

Comments on the Text

Richard Sympson: The preface is attributed to Richard Sympson, who claims to be Mr. Lemuel Gulliver's "relation" on the "mother's side." Harvey Irlen explained that Sympson only appears twice in the novel, at the start to argue that Gulliver's tale is truthful and in a letter at the end that only appeared in the second 1735 edition of the novel to state that Gulliver is also too prideful (and perhaps a bit mad) and therefore a flawed narrator. It has never been fully proven if Sympson was Swift or if one of his friends wrote these parts as he or she was helping Swift sell the work despite Swift's hesitations. In his letter of response to Sympson, Gulliver objects that Sympson should not have edited his book as much as he did, particularly objecting to the insertion of praise for Queen Anne. These objections make it sound as if Sympson was actually Motte, Swift's publisher, who made heavy edits to the book before releasing it to the public. But Swift, Motte, and others involved in the publication succeeded in keeping their anonymity. Motte was publicly acknowledged as the printer and bookseller, but never claimed that Sympson was his pseudonym. Whoever Sympson was, the name might have been an allusion to Richard Sympson (1553-88), an English priest who was executed for his radical Catholic beliefs, before being declared a martyr for his sacrifice.

"without license from the court; whereby the secretaries of state got considerable fees" (86): This might be a reference to the practice of the Church collecting fees from visitors to Churches where holy relics were on display. Swift is equating Gulliver's appearance to a holy coming as the Lilliputians are calling him "blessed" and are paying homage to him; but at the same time, they are constantly shooting or otherwise hurting him, so there is room for other interpretations, such as that the emperor is treating him as a circus act and profiting from visitors' fees.

Questions for Discussion

1. If the Lilliput city is half a mile away from Gulliver's original resting place, why do you think Swift decide to have the Lilliputians construct an engine to carry him there instead of simply asking him to walk there himself? Were you able to suspend your disbelief as the story of how quickly (4 hours) the Lilliputians managed to construct this enormous (for them) engine and organize hundreds of workers and horses for the task? Did you doubt the narrator's truthfulness (aside for it being a fantasy), and if so are the details intentionally unbelievable to force the reader to see them as absurd, humorous and symbols rather than a real traveler's account? **Suspension of disbelief** is the state of believing in fictitious or fantastical events as you are reading a narrative for the sake of fully immersing yourself in a fictional world.
2. Gulliver is shot with arrows and restrained in extremely uncom-

fortable circumstances by the Lilliputians without any other cause than his relatively large size. Plenty of very brilliant, radical people were similarly imprisoned in Ireland and England of Swift's day. Describe a modern imprisonment or prosecution against somebody that was bigger in mind or heart than those restraining his or her freedom? Explain the parallel with Gulliver's experience.

3. Chapter II begins with the usual summary of the chapter's contents: "The emperor of Lilliput, attended by several of the nobility, comes to see the author in his confinement." Inserting these brief descriptions was common in the 17th through 19th centuries (*Don Quixote* also included these), but is very rare today. What are the benefits or negatives for readers of having these summaries? *Cliff Notes*, *Wikipedia* and other sources that summarize books are in contrast very popular today, so why have authors stopped adding these types of helpful components for comprehension themselves?

4. Gulliver describes discharging his "body of that uneasy load" inside of his church-house, and then in the open air in public, writing that the latter was less shameful, and asking for "allowance" from the reader for engaging in this topic. Venturing into discussions of bodily functions was common in these early days of publishing in satires. Later in *Don Quixote*, there are also a few instances of awkward bodily function-related jokes. Do you think this act inside of a church has a symbolic or blasphemous significance? Is the humor enhanced or dampened by such crude digressions?

5. After threatening to eat one of the Lilliputians that hit him with an arrow, he shows mercy and lets him run away (85). Does this incident really show "clemency" or a positive character? Is Gulliver a hero or an anti-hero? In other words, does he show positive characteristics or are there major flaws in his character? He might not be aware of having problems, but does Swift intend for the reader to dislike him or to see his faults as well as to sympathize with him as the outsider or "fish-out-of-water"? Can you describe an incident that you think best summarizes his character?

6. What do you think about the Lilliputian language Swift is using? Can you spot any words in Spanish or another language that sound familiar? Do you think he's using a *lingua franca* combination that merchants that possessed many languages might have understood (or that Swift hoped would understand) so that he could convey subversive hidden messages for an intellectual audience while cen-

sors might not have understood the apparently nonsensical language?
7. Read the "Idea Invention" pages. Think of 2-3 ideas that you might want to write about for Essay 1. Describe these ideas briefly here.

Works Cited

Luebering, J. E. *The 100 Most Influential Writers of All Time*. New York, NY: Britannica Educational Publishing, 2010. *eBook Collection (EBSCOhost)*. Web. 13 Feb. 2017.

Turner, Paul and Jonathan Swift. *Gulliver's Travels*. Oxford: Oxford University Press, 1998. *eBook Collection (EBSCOhost)*. Web. 15 Feb. 2017.

Bloom, Harold. *Jonathan Swift's Gulliver's Travels*. New York: Facts on File, Inc, 1996. *eBook Collection (EBSCOhost)*. Web. 15 Feb. 2017.

Irlen, Harvey Stuart. "Gulliver's Cousin Sympson." *South Atlantic Bulletin*, vol. 36, no. 2, 1971, pp. 21—23. *JStor*. Web. 16 Feb. 2017.

"University of Houston Linguist Explains Secret Language of Gulliver's Travels." 12 Aug. 2015. *US Fed News Service, Including US State News. ProQuest*. Web. 16 Feb. 2017.

CHAPTER III

The author diverts the emperor, and his nobility of both sexes, in a very uncommon manner. The diversions of the court of Lilliput described. The author has his liberty granted him upon certain conditions.

My gentleness and good behaviour had gained so far on the emperor and his court, and indeed upon the army and people in general, that I began to conceive hopes of getting my liberty in a short time. I took all possible methods to cultivate this favourable disposition. The natives came, by degrees, to be less apprehensive of any danger from me. I would sometimes lie down, and let five or six of them dance on my hand; and at last the boys and girls would venture to come and play at hide-and-seek in my hair. I had now made a good progress in understanding and speaking the language. The emperor had a mind one day to entertain me with several of the country shows, wherein they exceed all nations I have known, both for dexterity and magnificence. I was diverted with none so much as that of the rope-dancers, performed upon a slender white thread, extended about two feet, and twelve inches from the ground. Upon which I shall desire liberty, with the reader's patience, to enlarge a little.

This diversion is only practised by those persons who are candidates for great employments, and high favour at court. They are trained in this art from their youth, and are not always of noble birth, or liberal education. When a great office is vacant, either by death or disgrace (which often happens,) five or six of those candidates petition the emperor to entertain his majesty and the court with a dance on the rope; and whoever jumps the highest, without falling, succeeds in the office. Very often the chief ministers themselves are commanded to show their skill, and to convince the emperor that they have not lost their faculty. Flimnap, the treasurer, is allowed to cut a caper on the straight rope, at least an inch higher than any other lord in the whole empire. I have seen him do the summerset several times together, upon a trencher fixed on a rope which is no thicker than a common packthread in England. My friend Reldresal, principal secretary for private affairs, is, in my opinion, if I am not partial, the second after the treasurer; the rest of the great officers are much upon a par.

These diversions are often attended with fatal accidents, whereof great numbers are on record. I myself have seen two or three candidates break a limb. But the danger is much greater, when the ministers themselves are commanded to show their dexterity; for, by contending to excel themselves and their fellows, they strain so far that there is hardly one of them who has not received a fall, and some of them two or three. I was assured that, a year or two before my arrival, Flimnap would infallibly have broken his neck, if one of the king's cushions, that accidentally lay on the ground, had not weakened the force of his fall.

There is likewise another diversion, which is only shown before the emperor and empress, and first minister, upon particular occasions. The emperor lays on the table three fine silken threads of six inches long; one is blue, the other red, and the third green. These threads are proposed as prizes for those persons whom the emperor has a mind to distinguish by a peculiar mark of his favour. The ceremony is performed in his majesty's great chamber of state, where the candidates are to undergo a trial of dexterity very different from the former, and such as I have not observed the least resemblance of in any other country of the new or old world. The emperor holds a stick in his hands, both ends parallel to the horizon, while the candidates advancing, one by one, sometimes leap over the stick, sometimes creep under it, backward and forward, several times, according as the stick is advanced or depressed. Sometimes the emperor holds one end of the stick, and his first minister the other; sometimes the minister has it entirely to himself. Whoever performs his part with most agility, and holds out the longest in leaping and creeping, is rewarded with the blue-coloured silk; the red is given to the next, and the green to the third, which they all wear girt twice round about the middle; and you see few great persons about this court who are not adorned with one of these girdles.

The horses of the army, and those of the royal stables, having been daily led before me, were no longer shy, but would come up to my very feet without starting. The riders would leap them over my hand, as I held it on the ground; and one of the emperor's huntsmen, upon a large courser, took my foot, shoe and all; which was indeed a prodigious leap. I had the good fortune to divert the emperor one day after a very extraordinary manner. I desired he would order several sticks of two feet high, and the thickness of an ordinary cane, to be brought to me; whereupon his majesty commanded the master of his woods to give directions accordingly; and the next morning six woodmen arrived with as many carriages, drawn by eight horses to each. I took nine of these sticks, and fixing them firmly in the ground in a quadrangular figure, two feet and a half square, I took four other sticks, and tied them parallel at each corner, about two feet from the ground; then I fastened my handkerchief to the nine sticks that stood erect; and extended it on all sides, till it was tight as the top of a drum; and the four parallel sticks, rising about five inches higher than the handkerchief, served as ledges on each side. When I had finished my work, I desired the emperor to let a troop of his best horses twenty-four in number, come and exercise upon this plain. His majesty approved of the proposal, and I took them up, one by one, in my hands, ready mounted and armed, with the proper officers to exercise them. As soon as they got into order they divided into two parties, performed mock skirmishes, discharged blunt arrows, drew their swords, fled and pursued, attacked and retired, and in short discovered the best military discipline I ever beheld. The parallel sticks secured them and their horses from falling over the stage; and the emperor was so much delighted, that he ordered this entertainment to be repeated several days, and once was pleased to be lifted up and give the word of command; and with great difficulty persuaded even the empress herself to let me hold her in her close chair within two yards of the stage, when she was able to take a full view of the whole performance. It was my good fortune, that no ill accident happened in these entertainments; only once a fiery horse, that belonged to one of the captains, pawing with his hoof, struck a hole in my handkerchief, and his foot slipping, he overthrew his rider and himself; but I immediately relieved them both, and covering the hole with one hand, I set down the troop with the other, in the same manner as I took them up. The horse that fell was strained in the left shoulder, but the rider got no hurt; and I repaired my handkerchief as well as I could: however, I would not trust to the strength of it any more, in such dangerous enterprises.

About two or three days before I was set at liberty, as I was entertaining the court with this kind of feat, there arrived an express to inform his majesty that some of his subjects, riding near the place where I was first taken up, had seen a great black substance lying on the around, very oddly shaped, extending its edges round, as wide as his majesty's bedchamber, and rising up in the middle as high as a man; that it was no living creature, as they at first apprehended, for it lay on the grass without motion; and some of them had walked round it several times; that, by mounting upon each other's shoulders, they had got to the top, which was flat and even, and, stamping upon it, they found that it was hollow within; that they humbly conceived it might be something belonging to the man-mountain; and if his majesty pleased, they would undertake to bring it with only five horses. I presently knew what they meant, and was glad at heart to receive this intelligence. It seems, upon my first reaching the shore after our shipwreck, I was in such confusion, that before I came to the place where I went to sleep, my hat, which I had fastened with a string to my head while I was rowing, and had stuck on all the time I was swimming, fell off after I came to land; the string, as I conjecture, breaking by some accident, which I never observed, but thought my hat had been lost at sea. I entreated his imperial majesty to give orders it might be brought to me as soon as possible, describing to him the use and the nature of it: and the next day the waggoners arrived with it, but not in a very good condition; they had bored two holes in the brim, within an inch and half of the edge, and fastened two hooks in the holes; these hooks were tied by a long cord to the harness, and thus my hat was dragged along for above half an English mile; but, the ground in that country being extremely smooth and level, it received less damage than I expected.

Two days after this adventure, the emperor, having ordered that part of his army which quarters in and about his metropolis, to be in readiness, took a fancy of diverting himself in a very singular manner. He desired I would stand like a Colossus, with my legs as far asunder as I conveniently could. He then commanded his general (who was an old experienced leader, and a great patron of mine) to draw up the troops in close order, and march them under me; the foot by twenty-four abreast, and the horse by sixteen, with drums beating, colours flying, and pikes advanced. This body consisted of three thousand foot, and a thousand horse. His majesty gave orders, upon pain of death, that every soldier in his march should observe the strictest decency with regard to my person; which however could not prevent some of the younger officers from turning up their eyes as they passed under me: and, to confess the truth, my breeches were at that time in so ill a condition, that they afforded some opportunities for laughter and admiration.

I had sent so many memorials and petitions for my liberty, that his majesty at length mentioned the matter, first in the cabinet, and then in a full council; where it was opposed by none, except Skyresh Bolgolam, who was pleased, without any provocation, to be my mortal enemy. But it was carried against him by the whole board, and confirmed by the emperor. That minister was *galbet*, or admiral of the realm, very much in his master's confidence, and a person well versed in affairs, but of a morose and sour complexion. However, he was at length persuaded to comply; but prevailed that the articles and conditions upon which I should be set free, and to which I must swear, should be drawn up by himself. These articles were brought to me by Skyresh Bolgolam in person attended by two under-secretaries, and several persons of distinction. After they were read, I was demanded to swear to the performance of them; first in the manner of my own country, and afterwards in the method prescribed by their laws; which was, to hold my right foot in my left hand, and to place the middle finger of my right hand on the crown of my head, and my thumb on the tip of my right ear. But because the reader may be curious to have some idea of the style and manner of expression peculiar to that people, as well as to know the article upon which I recovered my liberty, I have made a translation of the whole instrument, word for word, as near as I was able, which I here offer to the public.

"Golbasto Momarem Evlame Gurdilo Shefin Mully Ully Gue, most mighty Emperor of Lilliput, delight and terror of the universe, whose dominions extend five thousand *blustrugs* (about twelve miles in circumference) to the extremities of the globe; monarch of all monarchs, taller than the sons of men; whose feet press down to the centre, and whose head strikes against the sun; at whose nod the princes of the earth shake their knees; pleasant as the spring, comfortable as the summer, fruitful as autumn, dreadful as winter: his most sublime majesty proposes to the man-mountain, lately arrived at our celestial dominions, the following articles, which, by a solemn oath, he shall be obliged to perform:

"1st, The man-mountain shall not depart from our dominions, without our license under our great seal.

"2nd, He shall not presume to come into our metropolis, without our express order; at which time, the inhabitants shall have two hours warning to keep within doors.

"3rd, The said man-mountain shall confine his walks to our principal high roads, and not offer to walk, or lie down, in a meadow or field of corn.

"4th, As he walks the said roads, he shall take the utmost care not to trample upon the bodies of any of our loving subjects, their horses, or carriages, nor take any of our subjects into his hands without their own consent.

"5th, If an express requires extraordinary despatch, the man-mountain shall be obliged to carry, in his pocket, the messenger and horse a six days' journey, once in every moon, and return the said messenger back (if so required) safe to our imperial presence.

"6th, He shall be our ally against our enemies in the island of Blefuscu, and do his utmost to destroy their fleet, which is now preparing to invade us.

"7th, That the said man-mountain shall, at his times of leisure, be aiding and assisting to our workmen, in helping to raise certain great stones, towards covering the wall of the principal park, and other our royal buildings.

"8th, That the said man-mountain shall, in two moons' time, deliver in an exact survey of the circumference of our dominions, by a computation of his own paces round the coast.

"Lastly, That, upon his solemn oath to observe all the above articles, the said man-mountain shall have a daily allowance of meat and drink sufficient for the support of 1724 of our subjects, with free access to our royal person, and other marks of our favour. Given at our palace at Belfaborac, the twelfth day of the ninety-first moon of our reign."

I swore and subscribed to these articles with great cheerfulness and content, although some of them were not so honourable as I could have wished; which proceeded wholly from the malice of Skyresh Bolgolam, the high-admiral: whereupon my chains were immediately unlocked, and I was at full liberty. The emperor himself, in person, did me the honour to be by at the whole ceremony. I made my acknowledgements by prostrating myself at his majesty's feet: but he commanded me to rise; and after many gracious expressions, which, to avoid the censure of vanity, I shall not repeat, he added that he, "hoped I should prove a useful servant, and well deserve all the favours he had already conferred upon me, or might do for the future."

The reader may please to observe, that, in the last article of the recovery of my liberty, the emperor stipulates to allow me a quantity of meat and drink sufficient for the support of 1724 Lilliputians. Some time after, asking a friend at court how they came to fix on that determinate number, he told me that his majesty's mathematicians, having taken the height of my body by the help of a quadrant, and finding it to exceed theirs in the proportion of twelve to one, they concluded from the similarity of their bodies, that mine must contain at least 1724 of theirs, and consequently would require as much food as was necessary to support that number of Lilliputians. By which the reader may conceive an idea of the ingenuity of that people, as well as the prudent and exact economy of so great a prince.

CHAPTER IV

Mildendo, the metropolis of Lilliput, described, together with the emperor's palace. A conversation between the author and a principal secretary, concerning the affairs of that empire. The author's offers to serve the emperor in his wars.

The first request I made, after I had obtained my liberty, was, that I might have license to see Mildendo, the metropolis; which the emperor easily granted me, but with a special charge to do no hurt either to the inhabitants or their houses. The people had notice, by proclamation, of my design to visit the town. The wall which encompassed it is two feet and a half high, and at least eleven inches broad, so that a coach and horses may be driven very safely round it; and it is flanked with strong towers at ten feet distance. I stepped over the great western gate, and passed very gently, and sidling, through the two principal streets, only in my short waistcoat, for fear of damaging the roofs and eaves of the houses with the skirts of my coat. I walked with the utmost circumspection, to avoid treading on any stragglers who might remain in the streets, although the orders were very strict, that all people should keep in their houses, at their own peril. The garret windows and tops of houses were so crowded with spectators, that I thought in all my travels I had not seen a more populous place. The city is an exact square, each side of the wall being five hundred feet long. The two great streets, which run across and divide it into four quarters, are five feet wide. The lanes and alleys, which I could not enter, but only view them as I passed, are from twelve to eighteen inches. The town is capable of holding five hundred thousand souls: the houses are from three to five stories: the shops and markets well provided.

The emperor's palace is in the centre of the city where the two great streets meet. It is enclosed by a wall of two feet high, and twenty feet distance from the buildings. I had his majesty's permission to step over this wall; and, the space being so wide between that and the palace, I could easily view it on every side. The outward court is a square of forty feet, and includes two other courts: in the inmost are the royal apartments, which I was very desirous to see, but found it extremely difficult; for the great gates, from one square into another, were but eighteen inches high, and seven inches wide. Now the buildings of the outer court were at least five feet high, and it was impossible for me to stride over them without infinite damage to the pile, though the walls were strongly built of hewn stone, and four inches thick. At the same time the emperor had a great desire that I should see the magnificence of his palace; but this I was not able to do till three days after, which I spent in cutting down with my knife some of the largest trees in the royal park, about a hundred yards distant from the city. Of these trees I made two stools, each about three feet high, and strong enough to bear my weight. The people having received notice a second time, I went again through the city to the palace with my two stools in my hands. When I came to the side of the outer court, I stood upon one stool, and took the other in my hand; this I lifted over the roof, and gently set it down on the space between the first and second court, which was eight feet wide. I then stepped over the building very conveniently from one stool to the other, and drew up the first after me with a hooked stick. By this contrivance, I got into the inmost court; and, lying down upon my side, I applied my face to the windows of the middle stories, which were left open on purpose, and discovered the most splendid apartments that can be imagined. There I saw the empress and the young princes, in their several lodgings, with their chief attendants about them. Her imperial majesty was pleased to smile very graciously upon me, and gave me out of the window her hand to kiss.

But I shall not anticipate the reader with further descriptions of this kind, because I reserve them for a greater work, which is now almost ready for the press; containing a general description of this empire, from its first erection, through a long series of princes; with a particular account of their wars and politics, laws, learning, and religion; their plants and animals; their peculiar manners and customs, with other matters very curious and useful; my chief design at present being only to relate such events and transactions as happened to the public or to myself during a residence of about nine months in that empire.

One morning, about a fortnight after I had obtained my liberty, Reldresal, principal secretary (as they style him) for private affairs, came to my house attended only by one servant. He ordered his coach to wait at a distance, and desired I would give him an hour's audience, which I readily consented to, on account of his quality and personal merits, as well as of the many good offices he had done me during my solicitations at court. I offered to lie down that he might the more conveniently reach my ear, but he chose rather to let me hold him in my hand during our conversation. He began with compliments on my liberty; said he "might pretend to some merit in it;" but, however, added, "that if it had not been for the present situation of things at court, perhaps" I "might not have obtained it so soon. For," said he, "as flourishing a condition as we may appear to be in to foreigners, we labour under two mighty evils: a violent faction at home, and the danger of an invasion, by a most potent enemy, from abroad. As to the first, you are to understand, that for about seventy moons past there have been two struggling parties in this empire, under the names of *Tramecksan* and *Slamecksan*, from the high and low heels of their shoes, by which they distinguish themselves. It is alleged, indeed, that the high heels are most agreeable to our ancient constitution; but, however this be, his majesty has determined to make use only of low heels in the administration of the government, and all offices in the gift of the crown, as you cannot but observe; and particularly that his majesty's imperial heels are lower at least by a *drurr* than any of his court (*drurr* is a measure about the fourteenth part of an inch). The animosities between these two parties run so high, that they will neither eat, nor drink, nor talk with each other. We compute the *Tramecksan*, or high heels, to exceed us in number; but the power is wholly on our side. We apprehend his imperial highness, the heir to the crown, to have some tendency towards the high heels; at least we can plainly discover that one of his heels is higher than the other, which gives him a hobble in his gait. Now, in the midst of these intestine disquiets, we are threatened with an invasion from the island of Blefuscu, which is the other great empire of the universe, almost as large and powerful as this of his majesty. For as to what we have heard you affirm, that there are other kingdoms and states in the world inhabited by human creatures as large as yourself, our philosophers are in much doubt, and would rather conjecture that you dropped from the moon, or one of the stars; because it is certain, that a hundred mortals of your bulk would in a short time destroy all the fruits and cattle of his majesty's dominions; besides, our histories of six thousand moons make no mention of any other regions than the two great empires of Lilliput and Blefuscu. Which two mighty powers have, as I was going to tell you, been engaged in a most obstinate war for six-and-thirty moons past. It began upon the following occasion. It is allowed on all hands, that the primitive way of breaking eggs, before we eat them, was upon the larger end; but his present majesty's grandfather, while he was a boy, going to eat an egg, and breaking it according to the ancient practice, happened to cut one of his fingers. Whereupon the emperor, his father, published an edict, commanding all his subjects, upon great penalties, to break the smaller end of their eggs. The people so highly resented this law, that our histories tell us, there have been six rebellions raised on that account; wherein one emperor lost his life, and another his crown. These civil commotions were constantly fomented by the monarchs of Blefuscu; and when they were quelled, the exiles always fled for refuge to that empire. It is computed that eleven thousand persons have at several times suffered death, rather than submit to break their eggs at the smaller end. Many hundred large volumes have been published upon this controversy: but the books of the Big-endians have been long forbidden, and the whole party rendered incapable by law of holding employments. During the course of these troubles, the emperors of Blefuscu did frequently expostulate by their ambassadors, accusing us of making a schism in religion, by offending against a fundamental doctrine of our great prophet Lustrog, in the fifty-fourth chapter of the Blundecral (which is their Alcoran). This, however, is thought to be a mere strain upon the text; for the words are these: 'that all true believers break their eggs at the convenient end.' And which is the convenient end, seems, in my humble opinion to be left to every man's conscience, or at least in the power of the chief magistrate to determine. Now, the Big-endian exiles have found so much credit in the emperor of Blefuscu's court, and so much private assistance and encouragement from their party here at home, that a bloody war has been carried on between the two empires for six-and-thirty moons, with various success; during which time we have lost forty capital ships, and a much a greater number of smaller vessels, together with thirty thousand of our best seamen and soldiers; and the damage received by the enemy is reckoned to be somewhat greater than ours. However, they have now equipped a numerous fleet, and are just preparing to make a descent upon us; and his imperial majesty, placing great confidence in your valour and strength, has commanded me to lay this account of his affairs before you."

I desired the secretary to present my humble duty to the emperor; and to let him know, "that I thought it would not become me, who was a foreigner, to interfere with parties; but I was ready, with the hazard of my life, to defend his person and state against all invaders."

CHAPTER V

The author, by an extraordinary stratagem, prevents an invasion. A high title of honour is conferred upon him. Ambassadors arrive from the emperor of Blefuscu, and sue for peace. The empress's apartment on fire by an accident; the author instrumental in saving the rest of the palace.

The empire of Blefuscu is an island situated to the north-east of Lilliput, from which it is parted only by a channel of eight hundred yards wide. I had not yet seen it, and upon this notice of an intended invasion, I avoided appearing on that side of the coast, for fear of being discovered, by some of the enemy's ships, who had received no intelligence of me; all intercourse between the two empires having been strictly forbidden during the war, upon pain of death, and an embargo laid by our emperor upon all vessels whatsoever. I communicated to his majesty a project I had formed of seizing the enemy's whole fleet; which, as our scouts assured us, lay at anchor in the harbour, ready to sail with the first fair wind. I consulted the most experienced seamen upon the depth of the channel, which they had often plumbed; who told me, that in the middle, at high-water, it was seventy *glumgluffs* deep, which is about six feet of European measure; and the rest of it fifty *glumgluffs* at most. I walked towards the north-east coast, over against Blefuscu, where, lying down behind a hillock, I took out my small perspective glass, and viewed the enemy's fleet at anchor, consisting of about fifty men of war, and a great number of transports: I then came back to my house, and gave orders (for which I had a warrant) for a great quantity of the strongest cable and bars of iron. The cable was about as thick as packthread and the bars of the length and size of a knitting-needle. I trebled the cable to make it stronger, and for the same reason I twisted three of the iron bars together, bending the extremities into a hook. Having thus fixed fifty hooks to as many cables, I went back to the north-east coast, and putting off my coat, shoes, and stockings, walked into the sea, in my leathern jerkin, about half an hour before high water. I waded with what haste I could, and swam in the middle about thirty yards, till I felt ground. I arrived at the fleet in less than half an hour. The enemy was so frightened when they saw me, that they leaped out of their ships, and swam to shore, where there could not be fewer than thirty thousand souls. I then took my tackling, and, fastening a hook to the hole at the prow of each, I tied all the cords together at the end. While I was thus employed, the enemy discharged several thousand arrows, many of which stuck in my hands and face, and, beside the excessive smart, gave me much disturbance in my work. My greatest apprehension was for mine eyes, which I should have infallibly lost, if I had not suddenly thought of an expedient. I kept, among other little necessaries, a pair of spectacles in a private pocket, which, as I observed before, had escaped the emperor's searchers. These I took out and fastened as strongly as I could upon my nose, and thus armed, went on boldly with my work, in spite of the enemy's arrows, many of which struck against the glasses of my spectacles, but without any other effect, further than a little to discompose them. I had now fastened all the hooks, and, taking the knot in my hand, began to pull; but not a ship would stir, for they were all too fast held by their anchors, so that the boldest part of my enterprise remained. I therefore let go the cord, and leaving the hooks fixed to the ships, I resolutely cut with my knife the cables that fastened the anchors, receiving about two hundred shots in my face and hands; then I took up the knotted end of the cables, to which my hooks were tied, and with great ease drew fifty of the enemy's largest men of war after me.

The Blefuscudians, who had not the least imagination of what I intended, were at first confounded with astonishment. They had seen me cut the cables, and thought my design was only to let the ships run adrift or fall foul on each other: but when they perceived the whole fleet moving in order, and saw me pulling at the end, they set up such a scream of grief and despair as it is almost impossible to describe or conceive. When I had got out of danger, I stopped awhile to pick out the arrows that stuck in my hands and face; and rubbed on some of the same ointment that was given me at my first arrival, as I have formerly mentioned. I then took off my spectacles, and waiting about an hour, till the tide was a little fallen, I waded through the middle with my cargo, and arrived safe at the royal port of Lilliput.

The emperor and his whole court stood on the shore, expecting the issue of this great adventure. They saw the ships move forward in a large half-moon, but could not discern me, who was up to my breast in water. When I advanced to the middle of the channel, they were yet more in pain, because I was under water to my neck. The emperor concluded me to be drowned, and that the enemy's fleet was approaching in a hostile manner: but he was soon eased of his fears; for the channel growing shallower every step I made, I came in a short time within hearing, and holding up the end of the cable, by which the fleet was fastened, I cried in a loud voice, "Long live the most puissant king of Lilliput!" This great prince received me at my landing with all possible encomiums, and created me a *nardac* upon the spot, which is the highest title of honour among them.

His majesty desired I would take some other opportunity of bringing all the rest of his enemy's ships into his ports. And so unmeasureable is the ambition of princes, that he seemed to think of nothing less than reducing the whole empire of Blefuscu into a province, and governing it, by a viceroy; of destroying the Big-endian exiles, and compelling that people to break the smaller end of their eggs, by which he would remain the sole monarch of the whole world. But I endeavoured to divert him from this design, by many arguments drawn from the topics of policy as well as justice; and I plainly protested that "I would never be an instrument of bringing a free and brave people into slavery." And, when the matter was debated in council, the wisest part of the ministry were of my opinion.

This open bold declaration of mine was so opposite to the schemes and politics of his imperial majesty, that he could never forgive me. He mentioned it in a very artful manner at council, where I was told that some of the wisest appeared, at least by their silence, to be of my opinion; but others, who were my secret enemies, could not forbear some expressions which, by a side-wind, reflected on me. And from this time began an intrigue between his majesty and a junto of ministers, maliciously bent against me, which broke out in less than two months, and had like to have ended in my utter destruction. Of so little weight are the greatest services to princes, when put into the balance with a refusal to gratify their passions.

About three weeks after this exploit, there arrived a solemn embassy from Blefuscu, with humble offers of a peace, which was soon concluded, upon conditions very advantageous to our emperor, wherewith I shall not trouble the reader. There were six ambassadors, with a train of about five hundred persons, and their entry was very magnificent, suitable to the grandeur of their master, and the importance of their business. When their treaty was finished, wherein I did them several good offices by the credit I now had, or at least appeared to have, at court, their excellencies, who were privately told how much I had been their friend, made me a visit in form. They began with many compliments upon my valour and generosity, invited me to that kingdom in the emperor their master's name, and desired me to show them some proofs of my prodigious strength, of which they had heard so many wonders; wherein I readily obliged them, but shall not trouble the reader with the particulars.

When I had for some time entertained their excellencies, to their infinite satisfaction and surprise, I desired they would do me the honour to present my most humble respects to the emperor their master, the renown of whose virtues had so justly filled the whole world with admiration, and whose royal person I resolved to attend, before I returned to my own country. Accordingly, the next time I had the honour to see our emperor, I desired his general license to wait on the Blefuscudian monarch, which he was pleased to grant me, as I could perceive, in a very cold manner; but could not guess the reason, till I had a whisper from a certain person, "that Flimnap and Bolgolam had represented my intercourse with those ambassadors as a mark of disaffection;" from which I am sure my heart was wholly free. And this was the first time I began to conceive some imperfect idea of courts and ministers.

It is to be observed, that these ambassadors spoke to me, by an interpreter, the languages of both empires differing as much from each other as any two in Europe, and each nation priding itself upon the antiquity, beauty, and energy of their own tongue, with an avowed contempt for that of their neighbour; yet our emperor, standing upon the advantage he had got by the seizure of their fleet, obliged them to deliver their credentials, and make their speech, in the Lilliputian tongue. And it must be confessed, that from the great intercourse of trade and commerce between both realms, from the continual reception of exiles which is mutual among them, and from the custom, in each empire, to send their young nobility and richer gentry to the other, in order to polish themselves by seeing the world, and understanding men and manners; there are few persons of distinction, or merchants, or seamen, who dwell in the maritime parts, but what can hold conversation in both tongues; as I found some weeks after, when I went to pay my respects to the emperor of Blefuscu, which, in the midst of great misfortunes, through the malice of my enemies, proved a very happy adventure to me, as I shall relate in its proper place.

The reader may remember, that when I signed those articles upon which I recovered my liberty, there were some which I disliked, upon account of their being too servile; neither could anything but an extreme necessity have forced me to submit. But being now a *nardac* of the highest rank in that empire, such offices were looked upon as below my dignity, and the emperor (to do him justice), never once mentioned them to me. However, it was not long before I had an opportunity of doing his majesty, at least as I then thought, a most signal service. I was alarmed at midnight with the cries of many hundred people at my door; by which, being suddenly awaked, I was in some kind of terror. I heard the word *Burglum* repeated incessantly: several of the emperor's court, making their way through the crowd, entreated me to come immediately to the palace, where her imperial majesty's apartment was on fire, by the carelessness of a maid of honour, who fell asleep while she was reading a romance. I got up in an instant; and orders being given to clear the way before me, and it being likewise a moonshine night, I made a shift to get to the palace without trampling on any of the people. I found they had already applied ladders to the walls of the apartment, and were well provided with buckets, but the water was at some distance. These buckets were about the size of large thimbles, and the poor people supplied me with them as fast as they could: but the flame was so violent that they did little good. I might easily have stifled it with my coat, which I unfortunately left behind me for haste, and came away only in my leathern jerkin. The case seemed wholly desperate and deplorable; and this magnificent palace would have infallibly been burnt down to the ground, if, by a presence of mind unusual to me, I had not suddenly thought of an expedient. I had, the evening before, drunk plentifully of a most delicious wine called *glimigrim*, (the Blefuscudians call it *flunec*, but ours is esteemed the better sort,) which is very diuretic. By the luckiest chance in the world, I had not discharged myself of any part of it. The heat I had contracted by coming very near the flames, and by labouring to quench them, made the wine begin to operate by urine; which I voided in such a quantity, and applied so well to the proper places, that in three minutes the fire was wholly extinguished, and the rest of that noble pile, which had cost so many ages in erecting, preserved from destruction.

It was now day-light, and I returned to my house without waiting to congratulate with the emperor: because, although I had done a very eminent piece of service, yet I could not tell how his majesty might resent the manner by which I had performed it: for, by the fundamental laws of the realm, it is capital in any person, of what quality soever, to make water within the precincts of the palace. But I was a little comforted by a message from his majesty, "that he would give orders to the grand justiciary for passing my pardon in form:" which, however, I could not obtain; and I was privately assured, "that the empress, conceiving the greatest abhorrence of what I had done, removed to the most distant side of the court, firmly resolved that those buildings should never be repaired for her use: and, in the presence of her chief confidents could not forbear vowing revenge."

Notes on the Text
Chapter III-V

high heels (100): A large portion of this reading is a discussion of the manners, customs, language and dress of the Lilliputians. These matters very hotly debated and inflated in the period when Swift wrote this book. What attendants wore to court would frequently shape their political positions more so than what they said or did. Swift shows his frustration with this system by ridiculing the heel size division. He might also be alluding to the "Whig" party. The first main Whig politician was also the first Prime Minister of Britain, Robert Walpole. The Whigs were proponents of a constitutional rather than an absolute monarchy. Since Swift was a Tory, the losing party by this point, he might be poking fun at the Whigs name, as something trivial that should not be a defining symbol of a serious political party.

"…upon great penalties, to break the smaller end of their eggs. The people so highly resented this law, that our histories tell us, there have been six rebellions raised on that account…" (101): This is a satire on the Jacobite rebellions that were protests that had some similarly absurd inspirations, in addition to very serious political divisions.

George I [with a blue ribbon] by Georg Wilhelm Lafontaine, Royal Collection Object

Swift was one of the "exiles" that was forced to flee for "refuge" from this type of turmoil. The divisions included small differences in religious rituals between the Catholic and Protestant faiths. The reference to the banning of books by the losing party was also something that touched Swift as he lost his editorial position. And he may be talking about his own failure to advance in the new administration when he writes about the "party rendered incapable by law of holding employments" (101).

King George I by Godfrey Kneller, National Portrait Gallery, Wikipedia

PLAY

A play is presented in full to show the detail of its dramatic plotline. Aristophanes' Lysistrata is one of the only surviving examples of Old Comedy from Greece. It was written when basic comedic and tragic story structures were first being formed. These early ideas spread across the world and influence various types of fiction being reproduced today. This play is about women withholding sex from men in order to stop a war. It brings up many questions about gender roles and the meaning of warfare. Some of the ideas Aristophanes expresses are still being debated to this day, and some of his notions are more radical and taboo today than they were in 300-500 BC, when he wrote them. Thus, this story is very contemporary and a fun read.

The same type of analysis is offered for Aristophanes' play as for the fiction section. After reading this play, students should proceed to the "Close Reading of Lysistrata: Essay 2: Assignment." As the title suggests, this essay asks for a close examination of the content of this play. Instructions are offered on how this can best be achieved.

Drama Terms

Any essay that closely examines a play has to be informed with dramatic terms and concepts. For example, the symbols and allegory in *Lysistrata* enlarge this work into a globally relevant feminist tract out of simply a story about a group of men and women. It is impossible to compose any literary criticism without knowing the definitions of some of the other terms like "theme" and "form." Additionally, Greek mythology is an important contextual element of the play, so this had to be explained. Finally, a Greek play was a very different type of performance from modern theater, so information is provided on how it was staged, and on how staging can be discussed in a literary criticism essay. As in other sections, "Questions for Discussion" offer fruit for further thought or topics for the students' essays.

Symbolism: According to the *Oxford Dictionary*, a symbol is: "A thing that represents or stands for something else, especially a material object representing something abstract." There are numerous symbols in this play, and many probably escape modern readers because symbolic meanings fade as the myths they represent fade into pre-history. One example of a symbolic meaning in *Lysistrata* is: "A sword with myrtle-branches wreathed forever in my hand" (145). It might seem strange that the Old Men are stating that they will be walking around with myrtle-branch wreathed swords, unless the reader understands that wreathed branches were primarily used as prizes in the ancient Olympic Games and for other honors. The myrtle branches, in particular, were symbols of Aphrodite, the goddess of love.

Allegory: "A story, poem, or picture that can be interpreted to reveal a hidden meaning, typically a moral or political one" (*Oxford Dictionary*). *Lysistrata* as a whole has been interpreted by most critics as an anti-war allegory. The meaning is not particularly well hidden, as it should be obvious to most readers that the Women's refusal to have intercourse with their husbands and lovers to stop their warring is a pro-peace message. Stories that have many symbolic characters, such as *Animal Farm*, usually have a larger allegorical meaning to the plot as a whole. The allegory here is also about the "proper" role for women to play in deciding if their husbands and sons should enter and potentially die in armed conflicts. The conflict is between the choruses of Men and Women, and they clash in an allegorical War of the Sexes.

Theme: "An idea that recurs in or pervades a work of art or literature" (*Oxford Dictionary*). The theme can be displayed in an object that keeps re-appearing and thus gains additional significance. In this story, fish (141), eels and other sea creatures appear frequently enough so that they probably refer to women's femininity and the power of their sex. The idea that is discussed throughout is the power struggle between men and women, and how the sexes win or lose in different roles.

Form: "Style, design, and arrangement in an artistic work as distinct from its content" (*Oxford Dictionary*). Ancient tragedies and comedies have set the roller coaster plot line that is still dominant in popular formulaic literature. In this section of the reading, the Magistrate's entrance ends the violent clash between Men and Women, only to begin the legal and political debate on the war and the War of the Sexes. After the Magistrate leaves, the women face mutiny from within as some of them attempt to flee back to their husbands, as well as a male spy that has snuck into their midst to be with his wife. Each time a challenge is resolved, a new challenge appears to keep the plot flowing along onto a new roller coaster incline. Critics typically separate literature into genres based on the form this roller coaster plot takes, as well as on other elements of style and design. Ancient Greek, 19th century Russian, and 20th century American plays can be distinguished from each other even without names or dates stamped on the plays through analysis of these elements. Thus, understanding form is a very important step of evaluating and criticizing any work of literature.

Allusion: "An expression designed to call something to mind without mentioning it explicitly; an indirect or passing reference" (*Oxford Dictionary*). There are numerous passing references in *Lysistrata*, such as this one: "I'm sure a Tyranny/ Like that of Hippias" (144). According to *Encyclopedia Britannica*, Hippias was an Athenian tyrant in the century before Aristophanes' time. He was particularly known for suppressing nobles' power and ruling the country on his own, in contrast with previous rulers' tendency to share power with them. Allusions such as this one allowed Aristophanes to briefly make a statement against tyranny by giving a negative example of it, instead of going into the details of how the Women were acting tyrannically. Since allusions are typically written for modern audiences, if you are reading an ancient text such as this one, it's a good idea to look up names that you don't recognize as they are likely to offer clues about the author's intended meaning for the play.

Myth: "A traditional story, especially one concerning the early history of a people or explaining a natural or social phenomenon, and typically involving supernatural beings or events" (*Oxford Dictionary*). Most of the allusions in Aristophanes' work are to mythological figures. For example, the Women sing that one of them was prevented from acquiring a "fat eel" for "Hecate's feast" because of yet another unhelpful decree (147). According to *Britannica*, Hecate is the Greek goddess of magic, spells, or even mythology itself, as she has powers over "heaven, dearth and sea" and can offer blessings that encompass the powers of many other gods.

Religious stories that do not represent a major ongoing modern religious belief are typically labeled as myths. At the time of *Lysistrata's* composition, Aristophanes and his contemporaries viewed Hecate and other alluded to gods and goddesses as religious deities rather than as distant myths. Failure to bring food for a feast in Hecate's honor would be a sin, so this is a strong theological and political argument against decrees.

Staging: "The method of presenting a play or other dramatic performance" (*Oxford Dictionary*). As I mentioned in the previous section, the staging in ancient Greek plays is very sparse. The main stage directions in the middle of the play are: "MAGISTRATE *enters with attendant* SCYTHIANS" (131) and "MAGISTRATE *retires,* LYSISTRATA *returns within*" (144). The names of the main characters are capitalized not only before their dialogues, but also in stage directions such as these. Other than Lysistrata, the Magistrate has one of the longest speaking parts in the play. A Magistrate in this period had broad military, law executing and judicial duties, which reflected a portion of the duties that were carried out by kings before the aristocracy and later the bourgeoisie received a portion of them. The Magistrate shows up just as the conflict between the Women and the Men nears violence as the Men are burning and beating the Women, and the Women are retaliating by showering the men with smelly water. The actions are related in the dialogue more so than in these separate directions, as in when Lysistrata invites the Magistrate to: "Step aboard the boat" (144). The audience is invited to imagine where the actions are taking place, and what the actors are doing from these types of details in the interactions between the characters. The actors might have also acted out some of the directions that Aristophanes and his director/producer gave them orally, but which were not included in the written version of the play. It was uncommon in Aristophanes' time that a play would be performed by outsiders based on a written text after the playwriter's death. In modern times, a playwriter's greatest achievement is for his or her play to be performed based on very specific staging directions by complete strangers hundreds of years after its first production. Thus, even Beckett's absurd and abstract play, *Waiting for Godot*, begins with these directions:

Estragon, sitting on a low mound, is trying to take off his boot. He pulls at it with both hands, panting. He gives up, exhausted rests, tries again. As before… (Act One).

The dialogue and stage directions in this play have more in common with Aristophanes works than with modern realistic play directions and dialogue, which attempt to place viewers into a specific and actual time, place and situation. Chekhov's *Uncle Vanya* begins with:

A garden. A terrace and part of the house are visible. There is a table set for tea under an old poplar in a tree-lined walk. Benches, chairs. A guitar is lying on one of the benches. There is a swing near the table. It is shortly after two on an overcast afternoon. MARINA, *a sluggish, heavyset old woman is sitting at the samovar, knitting a stocking.* ASTROV *is pacing up and down nearby* (Act One).

Statuette of Triple-bodied Hekate

Beckett's intro can be taking place any time from the invention of "boots" to the present. In contrast, Chekhov includes items such as the "samovar," which are specific to Russian culture in the nineteenth and twentieth century. Knitting and the location-specific "poplar" trees also place and date the scene. Beckett's lack of specifics allows the scene to be relatable for a larger number of international readers. Beckett's emphasis is on Estragon's struggle with something that nearly all of us at some point encounter: removing tight shoes.

While one is more specific, and the other more general, both Beckett and Chekhov attempt to attract the reader's sympathy and interest in the story by describing what the characters are doing. In contrast with both of these, Aristophanes only includes stage directions for entries, exits and other bits that include movements on the stage. Actions, such as water being poured and beatings being given, are described in the dialogues.

Ancient Greek theatrical performances included some painted background scenes to help viewers visualize where the play is taking place. In addition to singing, the chorus also danced in the orchestra in front of the main actors.

Aristophanes

Aristophanes started composing comedies at the dawn of the written word, or when papyrus scrolls were first utilized. This was the point that marks the beginning of history, separating the years that followed from the pre-historic period when humans merely drew on walls, without the ability to leave an account of the stories of their lives or imaginings. Aristophanes was preceded by only three historic centuries at the start of which Homer wrote the first surviving western poem, the *Iliad*, somewhere between 760-710 BC. Nearly nothing is known about Homer's biography because there were few literate people around to record it. By Aristophanes' time, historical records were advanced enough for us to know the exact years of his life (446-386 BC) and that he was active in Athens, Greece. His pieces managed to survive through the millennia because he was the most respected and award-winning author of his day, known especially for his biting, political and social comedies. Athenians were primarily exposed to literature at whole-day, multi-day festival competitions in honor of Dionysus, the Greek god of wine and fertility, which were sponsored by the Greek Empire. These were in parallel with sport competitions, such as the ancient Olympic Games that were around since Homer's time, and they had a similar competitive spirit that brought about extraordinary developments in the comic and tragic genres that have not been matched in later periods. The performances were very different from modern theaters. First, a major part of the play were the long songs from the 24-person chorus in comedies. Second, the actors wore masks, called the *terracotta*, that showed either smiling or frowning faces so that those sitting far from the stage in giant oval amphitheaters, such as the Colosseum, could see the intended character type of the actors. Aristophanes was around eighteen when he started competing in the theatre and most of his surviving eleven plays were written during a short span of the Peloponnesian War, in which the great city of Athens was defeated by Sparta, a rival Greek city-state. Aristophanes' plays are colored by this war as well as by the corrupt, imperial political climate that he was artistically battling in. Aristophanes was among the earliest authors to develop the satirical genre as a defense to censorship of the theater. Satire is simply harsh criticism of politics, culture, business and other leaders and culture in various art forms. Even in times of the most repressive leaders, artists such as Aristophanes and Poe have managed to speak up to power by using satire or the mask of the comedic jester.

LYSISTRATA

THE PERSONS OF THE DRAMA:

LYSISTRATA
CALONICE
MYRRHINE
LAMPITO
STRATYLLIS
CHORUS OF WOMEN
MAGISTRATE
CINESIAS
SPARTAN HERALD
ENVOYS
ATHENIANS
PORTER
MARKET IDLERS
CHORUS OF OLD MEN

LYSISTRATA *stands alone with the Propylaea at her back.*

LYSISTRATA
If they were trysting for a Bacchanal,
A feast of Pan or Colias or Genetyllis,
The tambourines would block the rowdy streets,
But now there's not a woman to be seen
Except—ah, yes—this neighbour of mine yonder.
Enter CALONICE.
Good day Calonice.

CALONICE
Good day Lysistrata.
But what has vexed you so? Tell me, child.
What are these black looks for? It doesn't suit you

To knit your eyebrows up glumly like that.

LYSISTRATA
Calonice, it's more than I can bear,
I am hot all over with blushes for our sex.
Men say we're slippery rogues—

CALONICE
And aren't they right?

LYSISTRATA
Yet summoned on the most tremendous business
For deliberation, still they snuggle in bed.

CALONICE
My dear, they'll come. It's hard for women, you know,
To get away. There's so much to do:
Husbands to be patted and put in good tempers,
Servants to be poked out, children washed
Or soothed with lullays or fed with mouthfuls of pap.

LYSISTRATA
But I tell you, here's a far more weighty object.

CALONICE
What is it all about, dear Lysistrata,
That you've called the women hither in a troop?
What kind of an object is it?

LYSISTRATA
A tremendous thing!

CALONICE
And long?

LYSISTRATA
Indeed, it may be very lengthy.

CALONICE
Then why aren't they here?

LYSISTRATA
No man's connected with it;
If that was the case, they'd soon come fluttering along.
No, no. It concerns an object I've felt over
And turned this way and that for sleepless nights.

CALONICE
It must be fine to stand such long attention.

LYSISTRATA
So fine it comes to this—Greece saved by Woman!

CALONICE
By Woman? Wretched thing, I'm sorry for it.

LYSISTRATA
Our country's fate is henceforth in our hands:
To destroy the Peloponnesians root and branch—

CALONICE
What could be nobler!

LYSISTRATA
Wipe out the Boeotians—

CALONICE
Not utterly. Have mercy on the eels![7]

LYSISTRATA
But with regard to Athens, note I'm careful
Not to say any of these nasty things;
Still, thought is free.... But if the women join us
From Peloponnesus and Boeotia, then
Hand in hand we'll rescue Greece.

---

7   The Boeotian eels were esteemed delicacies in Athens.

CALONICE
How could we do
Such a big wise deed? We women who dwell
Quietly adorning ourselves in a back-room
With gowns of lucid gold and gawdy toilets
Of stately silk and dainty little slippers....

LYSISTRATA
These are the very armaments of the rescue.
These crocus-gowns, this outlay of the best myrrh,
Slippers, cosmetics dusting beauty, and robes
With rippling creases of light.

CALONICE
Yes, but how?

LYSISTRATA
No man will lift a lance against another—

CALONICE
I'll run to have my tunic dyed crocus.

LYSISTRATA
Or take a shield—

CALONICE
I'll get a stately gown.

LYSISTRATA
Or unscabbard a sword—

CALONICE
Let me buy a pair of slippers.

LYSISTRATA
Now, tell me, are the women right to lag?

CALONICE
They should have turned birds, they should have grown

wings and flown.

LYSISTRATA
My friend, you'll see that they are true Athenians:
Always too late. Why, there's not a woman
From the shoreward demes arrived, not one from Salamis.

CALONICE
I know for certain they awoke at dawn,
And got their husbands up if not their boat sails.

LYSISTRATA
And I'd have staked my life the Acharnian dames
Would be here first, yet they haven't come either!

CALONICE
Well anyhow there is Theagenes' wife
We can expect—she consulted Hecate.
But look, here are some at last, and more behind them.
See... where are they from?

CALONICE
From Anagyra they come.

LYSISTRATA
Yes, they generally manage to come first.
Enter MYRRHINE.

MYRRHINE
Are we late, Lysistrata?... What is that?
Nothing to say?

LYSISTRATA
I've not much to say for you,
Myrrhine, dawdling on so vast an affair.

MYRRHINE
I couldn't find my girdle in the dark.
But if the affair's so wonderful, tell us, what is it?

LYSISTRATA
No, let us stay a little longer till
The Peloponnesian girls and the girls of Bocotia
Are here to listen.

MYRRHINE
That's the best advice.
Ah, there comes Lampito.
Enter LAMPITO.

LYSISTRATA
Welcome Lampito!
Dear Spartan girl with a delightful face,
Washed with the rosy spring, how fresh you look
In the easy stride of your sleek slenderness,
Why you could strangle a bull!

LAMPITO
I think I could.
It's frae exercise and kicking high behint.[8]

LYSISTRATA
What lovely breasts to own!

LAMPITO
Oo... your fingers
Assess them, ye tickler, wi' such tender chucks
I feel as if I were an altar-victim.

LYSISTRATA
Who is this youngster?

LAMPITO
A Boeotian lady.

---

8   The translator has put the speech of the Spartan characters in Scottish dialect which is related to English about as was the Spartan dialect to the speech of Athens. The Spartans, in their character, anticipated the shrewd, canny, uncouth Scottish highlander of modern times.

LYSISTRATA
There never was much undergrowth in Boeotia,
Such a smooth place, and this girl takes after it.

CALONICE
Yes, I never saw a skin so primly kept.

LYSISTRATA
This girl?

LAMPITO
A sonsie open-looking jinker!
She's a Corinthian.

LYSISTRATA
Yes, isn't she
Very open, in some ways particularly.

LAMPITO
But who's ga'rred this Council o' Women to meet here?

LYSISTRATA
I have.

LAMPITO
Propound then what you want o' us.

MYRRHINE
What is the amazing news you have to tell?

LYSISTRATA
I'll tell you, but first answer one small question.

MYRRHINE
As you like.

LYSISTRATA
Are you not sad your children's fathers
Go endlessly off soldiering afar

In this plodding war? I am willing to wager
There's not one here whose husband is at home.

CALONICE
Mine's been in Thrace, keeping an eye on Eucrates
For five months past.

MYRRHINE
And mine left me for Pylos
Seven months ago at least.

LAMPITO
And as for mine
No sooner has he slipped out frae the line
He straps his shield and he's snickt off again.

LYSISTRATA
And not the slightest glitter of a lover!
And since the Milesians betrayed us, I've not seen
The image of a single upright man
To be a marble consolation to us.
Now will you help me, if I find a means
To stamp the war out.

MYRRHINE
By the two Goddesses, Yes!
I will though I've to pawn this very dress
And drink the barter-money the same day.

CALONICE
And I too though I'm split up like a turbot
And half is hackt off as the price of peace.

LAMPITO
And I too! Why, to get a peep at the shy thing
I'd clamber up to the tip-top o' Taygetus.

LYSISTRATA
Then I'll expose my mighty mystery.

O women, if we would compel the men
To bow to Peace, we must refrain—

MYRRHINE
From what?
O tell us!

LYSISTRATA
Will you truly do it then?

MYRRHINE
We will, we will, if we must die for it.

LYSISTRATA
We must refrain from every depth of love....
Why do you turn your backs? Where are you going?
Why do you bite your lips and shake your heads?
Why are your faces blanched? Why do you weep?
Will you or won't you, or what do you mean?

MYRRHINE
No, I won't do it. Let the war proceed.

CALONICE
No, I won't do it. Let the war proceed.

LYSISTRATA
You too, dear turbot, you that said just now
You didn't mind being split right up in the least?

CALONICE
Anything else? O bid me walk in fire
But do not rob us of that darling joy.
What else is like it, dearest Lysistrata?

LYSISTRATA
And you?

MYRRHINE
O please give me the fire instead.

LYSISTRATA
Lewd to the least drop in the tiniest vein,
Our sex is fitly food for Tragic Poets,
Our whole life's but a pile of kisses and babies.
But, hardy Spartan, if you join with me
All may be righted yet. O help me, help me.

LAMPITO
It's a sair, sair thing to ask of us, by the Twa,
A lass to sleep her lane and never fill
Love's lack except wi' makeshifts... But let it be.
Peace maun be thought of first.

LYSISTRATA
My friend, my friend!
The only one amid this herd of weaklings.

CALONICE
But if—which heaven forbid—we should refrain
As you would have us, how is Peace induced?

LYSISTRATA
By the two Goddesses, now can't you see
All we have to do is idly sit indoors
With smooth roses powdered on our cheeks,
Our bodies burning naked through the folds
Of shining Amorgos' silk, and meet the men
With our dear Venus-plats plucked trim and neat.
Their stirring love will rise up furiously,
They'll beg our arms to open. That's our time!
We'll disregard their knocking, beat them off—
And they will soon be rabid for a Peace.
I'm sure of it.

LAMPITO
Just as Menelaus, they say,

Seeing the bosom of his naked Helen
Flang down the sword.

CALONICE
But we'll be tearful fools
If our husbands take us at our word and leave us.

LYSISTRATA
There's only left then, in Pherecrates' phrase,
To flay a skinned dog—flay more our flayed desires.

CALONICE
Bah, proverbs will never warm a celibate.
But what avail will your scheme be if the men
Drag us for all our kicking on to the couch?

LYSISTRATA
Cling to the doorposts.

CALONICE
But if they should force us?

LYSISTRATA
Yield then, but with a sluggish, cold indifference.
There is no joy to them in sullen mating.
Besides we have other ways to madden them;
They cannot stand up long, and they've no delight
Unless we fit their aim with merry succour.

CALONICE
Well if you must have it so, we'll all agree.

LAMPITO
For us I ha' no doubt. We can persuade
Our men to strike a fair an' decent Peace,
But how will ye pitch out the battle-frenzy
O' the Athenian populace?

LYSISTRATA
I promise you
We'll wither up that curse.

LAMPITO
I don't believe it.
Not while they own ane trireme oared an' rigged,
Or a' those stacks an' stacks an' stacks O' siller.

LYSISTRATA
I've thought the whole thing out till there's no flaw.
We shall surprise the Acropolis today:
That is the duty set the older dames.
While we sit here talking, they are to go
And under pretence of sacrificing, seize it.

LAMPITO
Certie, that's fine; all's working for the best.

LYSISTRATA
Now quickly, Lampito, let us tie ourselves
To this high purpose as tightly as the hemp of words
Can knot together.

LAMPITO
Set out the terms in detail
And we'll a' swear to them.

LYSISTRATA
Of course.... Well then,
Where is our Scythianess? Why are you staring?
First lay the shield, boss downward, on the floor
And bring the victim's inwards.

CAILONICE
But, Lysistrata,
What is this oath that we're to swear?

LYSISTRATA
What oath!
In Aeschylus they take a slaughtered sheep
And swear upon a buckler. Why not we?

CALONICE
O Lysistrata, Peace sworn on a buckler!

LYSISTRATA
What oath would suit us then?

CALONICE
Something burden bearing
Would be our best insignia.... A white horse!
Let's swear upon its entrails.

LYSISTRATA
A horse indeed!

CALONICE
Then what will symbolise us?

LYSISTRATA
This, as I tell you—
First set a great dark bowl upon the ground
And disembowel a skin of Thasian wine,
Then swear that we'll not add a drop of water.

LAMPITO
Ah, what aith could clink pleasanter than that!

LYSISTRATA
Bring me a bowl then and a skin of wine.

CALONICE
My dears, see what a splendid bowl it is;
I'd not say *No* if asked to sip it off.

LYSISTRATA
Put down the bowl. Lay hands, all, on the victim.
Skiey Queen who givest the last word in arguments,
And thee, O Bowl, dear comrade, we beseech:
Accept our oblation and be propitious to us.

CALONICE
What healthy blood, la, how it gushes out!

LAMPITO
An' what a leesome fragrance through the air.

LYSISTRATA
Now, dears, if you will let me, I'll speak first.

CALONICE
Only if you draw the lot, by Aphrodite!

LYSISTRATA
You, Calonice, repeat for the rest
And pledge your arms to the same stern conditions—

LYSISTRATA
To husband or lover I'll not open arms.

CALONICE
To husband or lover I'll not open arms.

LYSISTRATA
Though love and denial may enlarge his charms.

CALONICE
Though love and denial may enlarge his charms.
O, O, my knees are failing me, Lysistrata!

LYSISTRATA
But still at home, ignoring him, I'll stay.

CALONICE
But still at home, ignoring him, I'll stay.

LYSISTRATA
Beautiful, clad in saffron silks all day.

CALONICE
Beautiful, clad in saffron silks all day.

LYSISTRATA
If then he seizes me by dint of force.

CALONICE
If then he seizes me by dint of force.

LYSISTRATA
I'll give him reason for a long remorse.

CALONICE
I'll give him reason for a long remorse.

LYSISTRATA
I'll never lie and stare up at the ceiling.

CALONICE
I'll never lie and stare up at the ceiling.

LYSISTRATA
Nor like a lion on all fours go kneeling.

CALONICE
Nor like a lion on all fours go kneeling.

LYSISTRATA
If I keep faith, then bounteous cups be mine.

CALONICE
If I keep faith, then bounteous cups be mine.

LYSISTRATA
If not, to nauseous water change this wine.

CALONICE
If not, to nauseous water change this wine.

LYSISTRATA
Do you all swear to this?

MYRRHINE
We do, we do.

LYSISTRATA
Then I shall immolate the victim thus.
She drinks.

CALONICE
Here now, share fair, haven't we made a pact?
Let's all quaff down that friendship in our turn.

LAMPITO
Hark, what caterwauling hubbub's that?

LYSISTRATA
As I told you,
The women have appropriated the citadel.
So, Lampito, dash off to your own land
And raise the rebels there. These will serve as hostages,
While we ourselves take our places in the ranks
And drive the bolts right home.

CALONICE
But won't the men
March straight against us?

LYSISTRATA
And what if they do?
No threat shall creak our hinges wide, no torch
Shall light a fear in us; we will come out

To Peace alone.

CALONICE
That's it, by Aphrodite!
As of old let us seem hard and obdurate.

LAMPITO *and some go off; the others go up into the Acropolis.*

Chorus of OLD MEN *enter to attack the captured Acropolis.*
Make room, Draces, move ahead; why your shoulder's chafed, I see,
With lugging uphill these lopped branches of the olive-tree.
How upside-down and wrong-way-round a long life sees things grow.
Ah, Strymodorus, who'd have thought affairs could tangle so?
The women whom at home we fed,
Like witless fools, with fostering bread,
Have impiously come to this—
They've stolen the Acropolis,
With bolts and bars our orders flout
And shut us out.
Come, Philurgus, bustle thither; lay our faggots on the ground,
In neat stacks beleaguering the insurgents all around;
And the vile conspiratresses, plotters of such mischief dire,
Pile and burn them all together in one vast and righteous pyre:
Fling with our own hands Lycon's wife to fry in the thickest fire.
By Demeter, they'll get no brag while I've a vein to beat!
Cleomenes himself was hurtled out in sore defeat.
His stiff-backed Spartan pride was bent.
Out, stripped of all his arms, he went:
A pigmy cloak that would not stretch
To hide his rump (the draggled wretch),
Six sprouting years of beard, the spilth
Of six years' filth.
That was a siege! Our men were ranged in lines of seventeen deep
Before the gates, and never left their posts there, even to sleep.
Shall I not smite the rash presumption then of foes like these,
Detested both of all the gods and of Euripides—
Else, may the Marathon-plain not boast my trophied victories!
Ah, now, there's but a little space
To reach the place!

A deadly climb it is, a tricky road
With all this bumping load:
A pack-ass soon would tire....
How these logs bruise my shoulders! further still
Jog up the hill,
And puff the fire inside,
Or just as we reach the top we'll find it's died.
Ough, phew!
I choke with the smoke.
Lord Heracles, how acrid-hot
Out of the pot
This mad-dog smoke leaps, worrying me
And biting angrily....
'Tis Lemnian fire that smokes,
Or else it would not sting my eyelids thus....
Haste, all of us;
Athene invokes our aid.
Laches, now or never the assault must be made!
Ough, phew!
I choke with the smoke...
Thanked be the gods! The fire peeps up and crackles as it should.
Now why not first slide off our backs these weary loads of wood
And dip a vine-branch in the brazier till it glows, then straight
Hurl it at the battering-ram against the stubborn gate?
If they refuse to draw the bolts in immediate compliance,
We'll set fire to the wood, and smoke will strangle their defiance.
Phew, what a spluttering drench of smoke! Come, now from off my back....
Is there no Samos-general to help me to unpack?
Ah there, that's over! For the last time now it's galled my shoulder.
Flare up thine embers, brazier, and dutifully smoulder,
To kindle a brand, that I the first may strike the citadel.
Aid me, Lady Victory, that a triumph-trophy may tell
How we did anciently this insane audacity quell!

Chorus of WOMEN.
What's that rising yonder? That ruddy glare, that smoky skurry?
O is it something in a blaze? Quick, quick, my comrades, hurry!
Nicodice, helter-skelter!

Or poor Calyce's in flames
And Cratylla's stifled in the welter.
O these dreadful old men
And their dark laws of hate!
There, I'm all of a tremble lest I turn out to be too late.
I could scarcely get near to the spring though I rose before dawn,
What with tattling of tongues and rattling of pitchers in one jostling din
With slaves pushing in!...
Still here at last the water's drawn
And with it eagerly I run
To help those of my friends who stand
In danger of being burned alive.
For I am told a dribbling band
Of greybeards hobble to the field,
Great faggots in each palsied hand,
As if a hot bath to prepare,
And threatening that out they'll drive
These wicked women or soon leave them charring into ashes there.
O Goddess, suffer not, I pray, this harsh deed to be done,
But show us Greece and Athens with their warlike acts repealed!
For this alone, in this thy hold,
Thou Goddess with the helm of gold,
We laid hands on thy sanctuary,
Athene.... Then our ally be
And where they cast their fires of slaughter
Direct our water!

STRATYLLIS (*caught*)
Let me go!

WOMEN
You villainous old men, what's this you do?
No honest man, no pious man, could do such things as you.

MEN
Ah ha, here's something most original, I have no doubt:
A swarm of women sentinels to man the walls without.

WOMEN
So then we scare you, do we? Do we seem a fearful host?
You only see the smallest fraction mustered at this post.

MEN
Ho, Phaedrias, shall we put a stop to all these chattering tricks?
Suppose that now upon their backs we splintered these our sticks?

WOMEN
Let us lay down the pitchers, so our bodies will be free,
In case these lumping fellows try to cause some injury.

MEN
O hit them hard and hit again and hit until they run away,
And perhaps they'll learn, like Bupalus, not to have too much to say.

WOMEN
Come on, then—do it! I won't budge, but like a dog I'll bite
At every little scrap of meat that dangles in my sight.

MEN
Be quiet, or I'll bash you out of any years to come.

WOMEN
Now you just touch Stratyllis with the top-joint of your thumb.

MEN
What vengeance can you take if with my fists your face I beat?

WOMEN
I'll rip you with my teeth and strew your entrails at your feet.

MEN
Now I appreciate Euripides' strange subtlety:
Woman is the most shameless beast of all the beasts that be.

WOMEN
Rhodippe, come, and let's pick up our water-jars once more.

MEN
Ah cursed drab, what have you brought this water for?

WOMEN
What is your fire for then, you smelly corpse? Yourself to burn?

MEN
To build a pyre and make your comrades ready for the urn.

WOMEN
And I've the water to put out your fire immediately.

MEN
What, you put out my fire?

WOMEN
Yes, sirrah, as you soon will see.

MEN
I don't know why I hesitate to roast you with this flame.

WOMEN
If you have any soap, you'll go off cleaner than you came.

MEN
Cleaner, you dirty slut?

WOMEN
A nuptial-bath in which to lie!

MEN
Did you hear that insolence?

WOMEN
I'm a free woman, I.

MEN
I'll make you hold your tongue.

WOMEN
Henceforth you'll serve in no more juries.

MEN
Burn off her hair for her.

WOMEN
Now forward, water, quench their furies!

MEN
O dear, O dear!

WOMEN
So... was it hot?

MEN
Hot!... Enough, O hold.

WOMEN
Watered, perhaps you'll bloom again—why not?

MEN
Brrr, I'm wrinkled up from shivering with cold.

WOMEN
Next time you have fire, you'll warm yourself and leave us to our lot.

MAGISTRATE *enters with attendant* SCYTHIANS.

MAGISTRATE
Have the luxurious rites of the women glittered
Their libertine show, their drumming tapped out crowds,
The Sabazian Mysteries summoned their mob,
Adonis been wept to death on the terraces,
As I could hear the last day in the Assembly?
For Demostratus—let bad luck befoul him—
Was roaring, "We must sail for Sicily,"
While a woman, throwing herself about in a dance
Lopsided with drink, was shrilling out "Adonis,

Woe for Adonis." Then Demostratus shouted,
"We must levy hoplites at Zacynthus,"
And there the woman, up to the ears in wine,
Was screaming "Weep for Adonis" on the house-top,
The scoundrelly politician, that lunatic ox,
Bellowing bad advice through tipsy shrieks:
Such are the follies wantoning in them.

MEN
O if you knew their full effrontery!
All of the insults they've done, besides sousing us
With water from their pots to our public disgrace
For we stand here wringing our clothes like grown-up infants.

MAGISTRATE
By Poseidon, justly done! For in part with us
The blame must lie for dissolute behaviour
And for the pampered appetites they learn.
Thus grows the seedling lust to blossoming:
We go into a shop and say, "Here, goldsmith,
You remember the necklace that you wrought my wife;
Well, the other night in fervour of a dance
Her clasp broke open. Now I'm off for Salamis;
If you've the leisure, would you go tonight
And stick a bolt-pin into her opened clasp."
Another goes to a cobbler; a soldierly fellow,
Always standing up erect, and says to him,
"Cobbler, a sandal-strap of my wife's pinches her,
Hurts her little toe in a place where she's sensitive.
Come at noon and see if you can stretch out wider
This thing that troubles her, loosen its tightness."
And so you view the result. Observe my case—
I, a magistrate, come here to draw
Money to buy oar-blades, and what happens?
The women slam the door full in my face.
But standing still's no use. Bring me a crowbar,
And I'll chastise this their impertinence.
What do you gape at, wretch, with dazzled eyes?
Peering for a tavern, I suppose.

Come, force the gates with crowbars, prise them apart!
I'll prise away myself too.... (LYSISTRATA *appears*.)

LYSISTRATA
Stop this banging.
I'm coming of my own accord.... Why bars?
It is not bars we need but common sense.

MAGISTRATE
Indeed, you slut! Where is the archer now?
Arrest this woman, tie her hands behind.

LYSISTRATA
If he brushes me with a finger, by Artemis,
The public menial, he'll be sorry for it.

MAGISTRATE
Are you afraid? Grab her about the middle.
Two of you then, lay hands on her and end it.

CALONICE
By Pandrosos I, if your hand touches her
I'll spread you out and trample on your guts.

MAGISTRATE
My guts! Where is the other archer gone?
Bind that minx there who talks so prettily.

Notes on Text
First Half

Most critics agree that *Lysistrata* is a cry for peace, and an objection to the Peloponnesian War. Aristophanes depicts the war as devastating, murdering and harvest-devastating disaster. Noting these problems, the women of the fantastic cities depicted gather together and engineer a plan to refuse their husbands and lovers sex until they give up on the war, and agree on peace. Their aim is to save all of Greece, rather than only two warring city-states, so the events are not historically accurate depictions of the Peloponnesian War, but are rather a utopian Greece that Aristophanes imagines. He mentions Athens, Sparta and other cities, but the causes and movements of the war in question are hidden. The women carry this experiment to the happy ending, when their scheme succeeds in frustrating the men into submission.

The play includes two choruses with singing parts: that of the women and that of the old men. There are few stage directions, when compared with modern plays, because the actors did not have many props other than their masks. There was no furniture or room dividers to give a sense of "reality" to the viewers. Instead, everything was exaggerated to stress the dramatic performance.

Vocabulary

"The Birth of Venus" by Sandro Botticelli. 1485.

Menelaus: "in Greek mythology, king of Sparta and younger son of Atreus, king of Mycenae; the abduction of his wife, Helen, led to the Trojan War... After the fall of Troy, Menelaus recovered Helen and brought her home. Menelaus was a prominent figure in the Iliad and the Odyssey, where he was promised a place in Elysium after his death because he was married to a daughter of Zeus" (*Encyclopedia Britannica*).

Aphrodite: "ancient Greek goddess of sexual love and beauty... she was also honoured as a goddess of war, especially at Sparta, Thebes, Cyprus, and other places. However, she was known primarily as a goddess of love and fertility and even occasionally presided over marriage. Although prostitutes considered Aphrodite their patron, her public cult was generally solemn and even austere" (*Encyclopedia Britannica*).

Comments on the Text

"nauseous water" (124): From pre-history through the recent invention of water filtration systems, water was not safe to drink in most cities. There was no plumbing system in this period and the local rivers, lakes and other bodies of water were heavily polluted when they were next to large human habitations. To fix this problem, people primarily drank alcohol because the fermentation process tends to kill bad bacteria, so that it is safe to drink. Thus, people developed a high tolerance to alcohol as they drank it from morning through night, rather than only during times of rest. Wine was so important in Greece that, as I mentioned before, the theatrical festivals were created in honor of Dionysus.

Questions for Discussion

1. One modern critic, H. D. Westlake, began "The *Lysistrata* and the War" thus: "It is notoriously difficult for modern readers to determine precisely what serious advice, if indeed any, Aristophanes intended to convey to his audiences about the war in which they were engaged" (38). He argues that most other critics have been in agreement that *Lysistrata* is an anti-war play, but he attempts to find clues that Aristophanes might have just as likely been making a pro-war statement. Can you find any clues that might support either of these positions? What's the best way to judge an author's intentions?
2. In Greece, sex was a common topic for comedies and satires, where phallic symbols and literal phalluses frequently appeared. Give an example of a sexual bit of dialogue in this section that might have been common when Aristophanes wrote this play, but is typically censored out of modern American fiction, which might have a Protestant ethic. Who might benefit from censoring sex-education out of popular fiction? At the same time, is human sexuality overly exploited in some other modern pop mediums, such as R-rated films, or extreme forms of it in pornography. Is the discussion of

sexuality in Aristophanes in a happy middle-ground between obscenity and instruction?
3. Despite being written thousands of years ago, this play shows women arguing publicly to defend their rights. Similar plays are uncommon even today, as female roles are typically submissive and include fewer lines of dialogue than their male counterparts. The chorus of men objects, "And perhaps they'll learn, like Bupalus, not to have too much to say" (128). Bupalus committed suicide after his satirical caricature of Hipponax backfired. The men are telling the women to refrain from similar politically risky jokes that might endanger their sex lives. Do you see the women in this play as empowered feminists or as victims of sexual and physical abuse that are taking final desperate actions? Give an example, of something the women or a particular woman says that shows power or weakness.
4. Write three possible thesis statements or three possible ideas for the Essay 2 assignment. You might want to brainstorm or freely write about anything in connection with the play first, before recording these polished ideas.

Works Cited

Aristophanes. *Birds: Lysistrata; Assembly-Women; Wealth*. Stephen Halliwell, Ed. Oxford: Oxford University Press, 1997. EBSCOhost. 19 March 2017. Web.

Westlake, H. D. "The *Lysistrata* and the War." *Phoenix*, Vol. 34, No. 1 (Spring, 1980), pp. 38-54. Classical Association of Canada. *JStor*. 19 March 2017. Web.

LYSISTRATA Continued...

MYRRHINE
By Phosphor, if your hand moves out her way
You'd better have a surgeon somewhere handy.

MAGISTRATE
You too! Where is that archer? Take that woman.
I'll put a stop to these surprise-parties.

STRATYLLIS
By the Tauric Artemis, one inch nearer
My fingers, and it's a bald man that'll be yelling.

MAGISTRATE
Tut tut, what's here? Deserted by my archers....
But surely women never can defeat us;
Close up your ranks, my Scythians. Forward at them.

LYSISTRATA
By the Goddesses, you'll find that here await you
Four companies of most pugnacious women
Armed cap-a-pie from the topmost louring curl
To the lowest angry dimple.

MAGISTRATE
On, Scythians, bind them.

LYSISTRATA
On, gallant allies of our high design,
Vendors of grain-eggs-pulse-and-vegetables,
Ye garlic-tavern-keepers of bakeries,
Strike, batter, knock, hit, slap, and scratch our foes,
Be finely imprudent, say what you think of them....
Enough! retire and do not rob the dead.

MAGISTRATE
How basely did my archer-force come off.

LYSISTRATA
Ah, ha, you thought it was a herd of slaves
You had to tackle, and you didn't guess
The thirst for glory ardent in our blood.

MAGISTRATE
By Apollo, I know well the thirst that heats you—
Especially when a wine-skin's close.

MEN
You waste your breath, dear magistrate, I fear, in answering back.
What's the good of argument with such a rampageous pack?
Remember how they washed us down (these very clothes I wore)
With water that looked nasty and that smelt so even more.

WOMEN
What else to do, since you advanced too dangerously nigh.
If you should do the same again, I'll punch you in the eye.
Though I'm a stay-at-home and most a quiet life enjoy,
Polite to all and every (for I'm naturally coy),
Still if you wake a wasps' nest then of wasps you must beware.

MEN
How may this ferocity be tamed? It grows too great to bear.
Let us question them and find if they'll perchance declare
The reason why they strangely dare
To seize on Cranaos' citadel,
This eyrie inaccessible,
This shrine above the precipice,
The Acropolis.
Probe them and find what they mean with this idle talk; listen,
but watch they don't try to deceive.
You'd be neglecting your duty most certainly if now this mystery
unplumbed you leave.

MAGISTRATE
Women there! Tell what I ask you, directly....
Come, without rambling, I wish you to state
What's your rebellious intention in barring up thus on our noses
our own temple-gate.

LYSISTRATA
To take first the treasury out of your management, and so stop the
war through the absence of gold.

MAGISTRATE
Is gold then the cause of the war?

LYSISTRATA
Yes, gold caused it and miseries more, too many to be told.
'Twas for money, and money alone, that Pisander with all of the army
of mob-agitators.
Raised up revolutions. But, as for the future, it won't be worthwhile
to set up to be traitors.
Not an obol they'll get as their loot, not an obol! While we have the
treasure-chest in our command.

MAGISTRATE
What then is that you propose?

LYSISTRATA
Just this—merely to take the exchequer henceforth in hand.

MAGISTRATE
The exchequer!

LYSISTRATA
Yes, why not? Of our capabilities you have had various clear
evidences.
Firstly remember we have always administered soundly the budget of
all home-expenses.

MAGISTRATE
But this matter's different.

LYSISTRATA
How is it different?

MAGISTRATE
Why, it deals chiefly with war-time supplies.

LYSISTRATA
But we abolish war straight by our policy.

MAGISTRATE
What will you do if emergencies arise?

LYSISTRATA
Face them our own way.

MAGISTRATE
What *you* will?

LYSISTRATA
Yes *we* will!

MAGISTRATE
Then there's no help for it; we're all destroyed.

LYSISTRATA
No, willy-nilly you must be safeguarded.

MAGISTRATE
What madness is this?

LYSISTRATA
Why, it seems you're annoyed.
It must be done, that's all.

MAGISTRATE
Such awful oppression never,
O never in the past yet I bore.

LYSISTRATA
You must be saved, sirrah—that's all there is to it.

MAGISTRATE
If we don't want to be saved?

LYSISTRATA
All the more.

MAGISTRATE
Why do you women come prying and meddling in matters of state touching war-time and peace?

LYSISTRATA
That I will tell you.

MAGISTRATE
O tell me or quickly I'll—

LYSISTRATA
Hearken awhile and from threatening cease.

MAGISTRATE
I cannot, I cannot; it's growing too insolent.

WOMEN
Come on; you've far more than we have to dread.

MAGISTRATE
Stop from your croaking, old carrion-crow there....
Continue.

LYSISTRATA
Be calm then and I'll go ahead.
All the long years when the hopeless war dragged along we,
    unassuming,
forgotten in quiet,
Endured without question, endured in our loneliness all your
    incessant child's antics and riot.

Our lips we kept tied, though aching with silence, though well all the while in our silence we knew
How wretchedly everything still was progressing by listening dumbly the day long to you.
For always at home you continued discussing the war and its politics loudly, and we
Sometimes would ask you, our hearts deep with sorrowing though we spoke lightly, though happy to see:
"What's to be inscribed on the side of the Treaty-stone
What, dear, was said in the Assembly today?"
"Mind your own business," he'd answer me growlingly.
"Hold your tongue, woman, or else go away."
And so I would hold it.

WOMEN
I'd not be silent for any man living on earth, no, not I!

MAGISTRATE
Not for a staff?

LYSISTRATA
Well, so I did nothing but sit in the house, feeling dreary, and sigh,
While ever arrived some fresh tale of decisions more foolish by far and presaging disaster.
Then I would say to him, "O my dear husband, why still do they rush on destruction the faster?"
At which he would look at me sideways, exclaiming, "Keep for your web and your shuttle your care,
Or for some hours hence your cheeks will be sore and hot; leave this alone, war is Man's sole affair!"

MAGISTRATE
By Zeus, but a man of fine sense, he.

LYSISTRATA
How sensible?
You dotard, because he at no time had lent
His intractable ears to absorb from our counsel one temperate word of

advice, kindly meant?
But when at the last in the streets we heard shouted (everywhere ringing
the ominous cry)
"Is there no one to help us, no saviour in Athens?" and, "No, there is no one," come back in reply.
At once a convention of all wives through Hellas here for a serious purpose was held,
To determine how husbands might yet back to wisdom despite their reluctance in time be compelled.
Why then delay any longer? It's settled. For the future you'll take up our old occupation.
Now in turn you're to hold tongue, as we did, and listen while we show
the way to recover the nation.

MAGISTRATE
You talk to *us!* Why, you're mad. I'll not stand it.

LYSISTRATA
Cease babbling, you fool; till I end, hold your tongue.

MAGISTRATE
If I should take orders from one who wears veils, may my neck straightaway be deservedly wrung.

LYSISTRATA
O if that keeps pestering you,
I've a veil here for your hair,
I'll fit you out in everything
As is only fair.

CALONICE
Here's a spindle that will do.

MYRRHINE
I'll add a wool-basket too.

LYSISTRATA
Girdled now sit humbly at home,
Munching beans, while you card wool and comb. For war from now on is the Women's affair.

WOMEN
Come then, down pitchers, all,
And on, courageous of heart,
In our comradely venture
Each taking her due part.
I could dance, dance, dance, and be fresher after,
I could dance away numberless suns,
To no weariness let my knees bend.
Earth I could brave with laughter,
Having such wonderful girls here to friend.
O the daring, the gracious, the beautiful ones!
Their courage unswerving and witty
Will rescue our city.
O sprung from the seed of most valiant-wombed grand-mothers, scions of savage and dangerous nettles!
Prepare for the battle, all. Gird up your angers. Our way the wind of sweet victory settles.

LYSISTRATA
O tender Eros and Lady of Cyprus, some flush of beauty I pray you devise
To flash on our bosoms and, O Aphrodite, rosily gleam on our valorous thighs!
Joy will raise up its head through the legions warring and all of the far-serried ranks of mad-love
Bristle the earth to the pillared horizon, pointing in vain to the heavens above.
I think that perhaps then they'll give us our title—
Peace-makers.

MAGISTRATE
What do you mean? Please explain.

LYSISTRATA
First, we'll not see you now flourishing arms about into the Marketing-place clang again.

WOMEN
No, by the Paphian.

LYSISTRATA
Still I can conjure them as past were the herbs stand or crockery's sold
Like Corybants jingling (poor sots) fully armoured, they noisily
    round on their promenade strolled.

MAGISTRATE
And rightly; that's discipline, they—

LYSISTRATA
But what's sillier than to go on an errand of buying a fish
Carrying along an immense Gorgon-buckler instead the usual platter
    or dish?
A phylarch I lately saw, mounted on horse-back, dressed for the part
    with long ringlets and all,
Stow in his helmet the omelet bought steaming from an old woman
    who kept a food-stall.
Nearby a soldier, a Thracian, was shaking wildly his spear like Tereus
    in the play,
To frighten a fig-girl while unseen the ruffian filched from her
    fruit-trays the ripest away.

MAGISTRATE
How, may I ask, will your rule re-establish order and justice in lands
    so tormented?

LYSISTRATA
Nothing is easier.

MAGISTRATE
Out with it speedily—what is this plan that you boast you've
    invented?

LYSISTRATA

If, when yarn we are winding,
It chances to tangle, then, as perchance you may know, through the skein.
This way and that still the spool we keep passing till it is finally clear all again:
So to untangle the War and its errors, ambassadors out on all sides we will send
This way and that, here, there and roundabout—soon you will find that the War has an end.

MAGISTRATE

So with these trivial tricks of the household, domestic analogies of threads, skeins and spools,
You think that you'll solve such a bitter complexity, unwind such political problems, you fools!

LYSISTRATA

Well, first as we wash dirty wool so's to cleanse it, so with a pitiless zeal we will scrub
Through the whole city for all greasy fellows; burrs too, the parasites, off we will rub.
That verminous plague of insensate place-seekers soon between thumb and forefinger we'll crack.
All who inside Athens' walls have their dwelling into one great common basket we'll pack.
Disenfranchised or citizens, allies or aliens, pell-mell the lot of them in we will squeeze.
Till they discover humanity's meaning.... As for disjointed and far colonies,
Them you must never from this time imagine as scattered about just like lost hanks of wool.
Each portion we'll take and wind in to this centre, inward to Athens each loyalty pull,
Till from the vast heap where all's piled together at last can be woven a strong Cloak of State.

MAGISTRATE

How terrible is it to stand here and watch them carding and winding

       at will with our fate,
Witless in war as they are.

LYSISTRATA
What of us then, who ever in vain for our children must weep
Borne but to perish afar and in vain?

MAGISTRATE
Not that, O let that one memory sleep!

LYSISTRATA
Then while we should be companioned still merrily, happy as brides
      may, the livelong night,
Kissing youth by, we are forced to lie single.... But leave for a moment
      our pitiful plight,
It hurts even more to behold the poor maidens helpless wrinkling in
      staler virginity.

MAGISTRATE
Does not a man age?

LYSISTRATA
Not in the same way. Not as a woman grows withered, grows he.
He, when returned from the war, though grey-headed, yet
      if he wishes can choose out a wife.
But she has no solace save peering for omens, wretched and
      lonely the rest of her life.

MAGISTRATE
But the old man will often select—

LYSISTRATA
O why not finish and die?
A bier is easy to buy,
A honey-cake I'll knead you with joy,
This garland will see you are decked.

CALONICE
I've a wreath for you too.

MYRRHINE
I also will fillet you.

LYSISTRATA
What more is lacking? Step aboard the boat.
See, Charon shouts ahoy.
You're keeping him, he wants to shove afloat.

MAGISTRATE
Outrageous insults! Thus my place to flout!
Now to my fellow-magistrates I'll go
And what you've perpetrated on me show.

LYSISTRATA
Why are you blaming us for laying you out?
Assure yourself we'll not forget to make
The third day offering early for your sake.

MAGISTRATE *retires*, LYSISTRATA *returns within.*

OLD MEN
All men who call your loins your own, awake at last, arise
And strip to stand in readiness. For as it seems to me
Some more perilous offensive in their heads they now devise.
I'm sure a Tyranny
Like that of Hippias
In this I detect....
They mean to put us under
Themselves I suspect,
And that Laconians assembling
At Cleisthenes' house have played
A trick-of-war and provoked them
Madly to raid
The Treasury, in which term I include
The Pay for my food.
For is it not preposterous
They should talk this way to us
On a subject such as battle!
And, women as they are, about bronze bucklers dare prattle—

Make alliance with the Spartans—people I for one
Like very hungry wolves would always most sincerely shun....
Some dirty game is up their sleeve,
I believe.
A Tyranny, no doubt... but they won't catch me, that know.
Henceforth on my guard I'll go,
A sword with myrtle-branches wreathed forever in my hand,
And under arms in the Public Place I'll take my watchful stand,
Shoulder to shoulder with Aristogeiton. Now my staff I'll draw
And start at once by knocking
that shocking
Hag upon the jaw.

WOMEN
Your own mother will not know you when you get back to the town.
But first, my friends and allies, let us lay these garments down,
And all ye fellow-citizens, hark to me while I tell
What will aid Athens well.
Just as is right, for I
Have been a sharer
In all the lavish splendour
Of the proud city.
I bore the holy vessels
At seven, then
I pounded barley
At the age of ten,
And clad in yellow robes,
Soon after this,
I was Little Bear to
Brauronian Artemis;
Then neckletted with figs,
Grown tall and pretty,
I was a Basket-bearer,
And so it's obvious I should
Give you advice that I think good,
The very best I can.
It should not prejudice my voice that I'm not born a man,
If I say something advantageous to the present situation.
For I'm taxed too, and as a toll provide men for the nation

While, miserable greybeards, you,
It is true,
Contribute nothing of any importance whatever to our needs;
But the treasure raised against the Medes
You've squandered, and do nothing in return, save that you make
Our lives and persons hazardous by some imbecile mistakes
What can you answer? Now be careful, don't arouse my spite,
Or with my slipper I'll take you napping,
faces slapping
Left and right.

MEN
What villainies they contrive!
Come, let vengeance fall,
You that below the waist are still alive,
Off with your tunics at my call—
Naked, all.
For a man must strip to battle like a man.
No quaking, brave steps taking, careless what's ahead, white shoed,
in the nude, onward bold,
All ye who garrisoned Leipsidrion of old....
Let each one wag
As youthfully as he can,
And if he has the cause at heart
Rise at least a span.
We must take a stand and keep to it,
For if we yield the smallest bit
To their importunity.
Then nowhere from their inroads will be left to us immunity.
But they'll be building ships and soon their navies will attack us,
As Artemisia did, and seek to fight us and to sack us.
And if they mount, the Knights they'll rob
Of a job,
For everyone knows how talented they all are in the saddle,
Having long practised how to straddle;
No matter how they're jogged there up and down, they're never thrown.
Then think of Myron's painting, and each horse-backed Amazon
In combat hand-to-hand with men.... Come, on these women fall,

And in pierced wood-collars let's stick
quick
The necks of one and all.

WOMEN
Don't cross me or I'll loose
The Beast that's kennelled here....
And soon you will be howling for a truce,
Howling out with fear.
But my dear,
Strip also, that women may battle unhindered....
But you, you'll be too sore to eat garlic more, or one black bean,
I really mean, so great's my spleen, to kick you black and blue
With these my dangerous legs.
I'll hatch the lot of you,
If my rage you dash on,
The way the relentless Beetle
Hatched the Eagle's eggs.
Scornfully aside I set
Every silly old-man threat
While Lampito's with me.
Or dear Ismenia, the noble Theban girl. Then let decree
Be hotly piled upon decree; in vain will be your labours,
You futile rogue abominated by your suffering neighbour
To Hecate's feast I yesterday went.
Off I sent
To our neighbours in Boeotia, asking as a gift to me
For them to pack immediately
That darling dainty thing... a good fat eel
I meant of course;
But they refused because some idiotic old decree's in force.
O this strange passion for decrees nothing on earth can check,
Till someone puts a foot out tripping you,
and slipping you
Break your neck.

LYSISTRATA *enters in dismay.*

WOMEN
Dear Mistress of our martial enterprise,
Why do you come with sorrow in your eyes?

LYSISTRATA
O 'tis our naughty femininity,
So weak in one spot, that hath saddened me.
WOMEN
What's this? Please speak.

LYSISTRATA
Poor women, O so weak!

WOMEN
What can it be? Surely your friends may know.

LYSISTRATA
Yea, I must speak it though it hurt me so.

WOMEN
Speak; can we help? Don't stand there mute in need.

LYSISTRATA
I'll blurt it out then—our women's army's mutinied.

WOMEN
O Zeus!

LYSISTRATA
What use is Zeus to our anatomy?
Here is the gaping calamity I meant:
I cannot shut their ravenous appetites
A moment more now. They are all deserting.
The first I caught was sidling through the postern
Close by the Cave of Pan: the next hoisting herself
With rope and pulley down: a third on the point
Of slipping past: while a fourth malcontent, seated
For instant flight to visit Orsilochus
On bird-back, I dragged off by the hair in time....

They are all snatching excuses to sneak home.
Look, there goes one.... Hey, what's the hurry?

1ST WOMAN
I must get home. I've some Milesian wool
Packed wasting away, and moths are pushing through it.

LYSISTRATA
Fine moths indeed, I know. Get back within.

1ST WOMAN
By the Goddesses, I'll return instantly.
I only want to stretch it on my bed.

LYSISTRATA
You shall stretch nothing and go nowhere either.

1ST WOMAN
Must I never use my wool then?

LYSISTRATA
If needs be.

2ND WOMAN
How unfortunate I am! O my poor flax!
It's left at home unstript.

LYSISTRATA
So here's another
That wishes to go home and strip her flax.
Inside again!

2ND WOMAN
No, by the Goddess of Light,
I'll be back as soon as I have flayed it properly.

LYSISTRATA
You'll not flay anything. For if you begin
There'll not be one here but has a patch to be flayed.

3RD WOMAN
O holy Eilithyia, stay this birth
Till I have left the precincts of the place!

LYSISTRATA
What nonsense is this?
3RD WOMAN
I'll drop it any minute.

LYSISTRATA
Yesterday you weren't with child.

3RD WOMAN
But I am today.
O let me find a midwife, Lysistrata.
O quickly!

LYSISTRATA
Now what story is this you tell?
What is this hard lump here?

3RD WOMAN
It's a male child.

LYSISTRATA
By Aphrodite, it isn't. Your belly's hollow,
And it has the feel of metal.... Well, I soon can see.
You hussy, it's Athene's sacred helm,
And you said you were with child.

3RD WOMAN
And so I am.

LYSISTRATA
Then why the helm?

3RD WOMAN
So if the throes should take me
Still in these grounds I could use it like a dove

As a laying-nest in which to drop the child.

LYSISTRATA
More pretexts! You can't hide your clear intent,
And anyway why not wait till the tenth day
Meditating a brazen name for your brass brat?

3RD WOMAN
And I can't sleep a wink. My nerve is gone
Since I saw that snake-sentinel of the shrine.
And all those dreadful owls with their weird hooting!
Though I'm wearied out, I can't close an eye.

LYSISTRATA
You wicked women, cease from juggling lies.
You want your men. But what of them as well?
They toss as sleepless in the lonely night,
I'm sure of it. Hold out awhile, hold out,
But persevere a teeny-weeny longer.
An oracle has promised Victory
If we don't wrangle. Would you hear the words?

WOMEN
Yes, yes, what is it?

LYSISTRATA
Silence then, you chatterboxes.
Here—
Whenas the swallows flocking in one place from the hoopoes
Deny themselves love's gambols any more,
All woes shall then have ending and great Zeus the Thunderer
Shall put above what was below before.

WOMEN
Will the men then always be kept under us?

LYSISTRATA
But if the swallows squabble among themselves and fly away
Out of the temple, refusing to agree,

Then The Most Wanton Birds in all the World
They shall be named for ever. That's his decree.

WOMEN
It's obvious what it means.

LYSISTRATA
Now by all the gods
We must let no agony deter from duty,
Back to your quarters. For we are base indeed,
My friends, if we betray the oracle.
    She goes out.

OLD MEN.
I'd like to remind you of a fable they used to employ,
When I was a little boy:
How once through fear of the marriage-bed a young man,
Melanion by name, to the wilderness ran,
And there on the hills he dwelt.
For hares he wove a net
Which with his dog he set—
Most likely he's there yet.
For he never came back home, so great was the fear he felt.
I loathe the sex as much as he,
And therefore I no less shall be
As chaste as was Melanion.

MEN
Grann'am, do you much mind men?

WOMEN
Onions you won't need, to cry.

MEN
From my foot you shan't escape.

WOMEN
What thick forests I espy.

MEN
So much Myronides' fierce beard
And thundering black back were feared,
That the foe fled when they were shown—
Brave he as Phormion.

WOMEN
Well, I'll relate a rival fable just to show to you
A different point of view:
There was a rough-hewn fellow, Timon, with a face
That glowered as through a thorn-bush in a wild, bleak place.
He too decided on flight,
This very Furies' son,
All the world's ways to shun
And hide from everyone,
Spitting out curses on all knavish men to left and right.
But though he reared this hate for men,
He loved the women even then,
And never thought them enemies.

WOMEN
O your jaw I'd like to break.

MEN
That I fear do you suppose?

WOMEN
Learn what kicks my legs can make.

MEN
Raise them up, and you'll expose—

WOMEN
Nay, you'll see there, I engage,
All is well kept despite my age,
And tended smooth enough to slip
From any adversary's grip.

LYSISTRATA *appears.*

LYSISTRATA
Hollo there, hasten hither to me
Skip fast along.

WOMEN
What is this? Why the noise?

LYSISTRATA
A man, a man! I spy a frenzied man!
He carries Love upon him like a staff.
O Lady of Cyprus, and Cythera, and Paphos,
I beseech you, keep our minds and hands to the oath.

WOMEN
Where is he, whoever he is?

LYSISTRATA
By the Temple of Chloe.

WOMEN
Yes, now I see him, but who can he be?

LYSISTRATA
Look at him. Does anyone recognise his face?

MYRRHINE
I do. He is my husband, Cinesias.

LYSISTRATA
You know how to work. Play with him, lead him on,
Seduce him to the cozening-point—kiss him, kiss him,
Then slip your mouth aside just as he's sure of it,
Ungirdle every caress his mouth feels at
Save that the oath upon the bowl has locked.

MYRRHINE
You can rely on me.

LYSISTRATA
I'll stay here to help
In working up his ardor to its height
Of vain magnificence.... The rest to their quarters.
Enter CINESIAS.
Who is this that stands within our lines?

CINESIAS
I.

LYSISTRATA
A man?

CINESIAS
Too much a man!

LYSISTRATA
Then be off at once.

CINESIAS
Who are you that thus eject me?

LYSISTRATA
Guard for the day.

CINESIAS
By all the gods, then call Myrrhine hither.

LYSISTRATA
So, call Myrrhine hither! Who are you?

CINESIAS
I am her husband Cinesias, son of Anthros.

LYSISTRATA
Welcome, dear friend! That glorious name of yours
Is quite familiar in our ranks. Your wife
Continually has it in her mouth.
She cannot touch an apple or an egg

But she must say, "This to Cinesias!"

CINESIAS
O is that true?

LYSISTRATA
By Aphrodite, it is.
If the conversation strikes on men, your wife
Cuts in with, "All are boobies by Cinesias."

CINESIAS
Then call her here.

LYSISTRATA
And what am I to get?

CINESIAS
This, if you want it.... See, what I have here.
But not to take away.

LYSISTRATA
Then I'll call her.

CINESIAS
Be quick, be quick. All grace is wiped from life
Since she went away. O sad, sad am I
When there I enter on that loneliness,
And wine is unvintaged of the sun's flavour.
And food is tasteless. But I've put on weight.

MYRRHINE (*above*)
I love him O so much! but he won't have it.
Don't call me down to him.

CINESIAS
Sweet little Myrrhine!
What do you mean? Come here.

MYRRHINE
O no I won't.
Why are you calling me? You don't want me.

CINESIAS
Not want you! With this week-old strength of love.

MYRRHINE
Farewell.

CINESIAS
Don't go, please don't go, Myrrhine.
At least you'll hear our child. Call your mother, lad.

CHILD
Mummy... mummy... mummy!

CINESIAS
There now, don't you feel pity for the child?
He's not been fed or washed now for six days.

MYRRHINE
I certainly pity him with so heartless a father.

CINESIAS
Come down, my sweetest, come for the child's sake.

MYRRHINE
A trying life it is to be a mother!
I suppose I'd better go.   *She comes down.*

CINESIAS
How much younger she looks,
How fresher and how prettier! Myrrhine,
Lift up your lovely face, your disdainful face;
And your ankle... let your scorn step out its worst;
It only rubs me to more ardor here.

MYRRHINE (*playing with the child*)
You're as innocent as he's iniquitous.
Let me kiss you, honey-petting, mother's darling.

CINESIAS
How wrong to follow other women's counsel
And let loose all these throbbing voids in yourself
As well as in me. Don't you go throb-throb?

MYRRHINE
Take away your hands.

CINESIAS
Everything in the house
Is being ruined.

MYRRHINE
I don't care at all.

CINESIAS
The roosters are picking all your web to rags.
Do you mind that?

MYRRHINE
Not I.

CINESIAS
What time we've wasted
We might have drenched with Paphian laughter, flung
On Aphrodite's Mysteries. O come here.

MYRRHINE
Not till a treaty finishes the war.

CINESIAS
If you must have it, then we'll get it done.

MYRRHINE
Do it and I'll come home. Till then I am bound.

CINESIAS
Well, can't your oath perhaps be got around?

MYRRHINE
No... no... still I'll not say that I don't love you.

CINESIAS
You love me! Then dear girl, let me also love you.

MYRRHINE
You must be joking. The boy's looking on.

CINESIAS
Here, Manes, take the child home!... There, he's gone.
There's nothing in the way now. Come to the point.

MYRRHINE
Here in the open! In plain sight?

CINESIAS
In Pan's cave.
A splendid place.

MYRRHINE
Where shall I dress my hair again
Before returning to the citadel?

CINESIAS
You can easily primp yourself in the Clepsydra.

MYRRHINE
But how can I break my oath?

CINESIAS
Leave that to me,
I'll take all risk.

MYRRHINE
Well, I'll make you comfortable.

CINESIAS
Don't worry. I'd as soon lie on the grass.

MYRRHINE
No, by Apollo, in spite of all your faults
I won't have you lying on the nasty earth.
(*From here MYRRHINE keeps on going off to fetch things.*)

CINESIAS
Ah, how she loves me.

MYRRHINE
Rest there on the bench,
While I arrange my clothes. O what a nuisance,
I must find some cushions first.

CINESIAS
Why some cushions?
Please don't get them!

MYRRHINE
What? The plain, hard wood?
Never, by Artemis! That would be too vulgar.

CINESIAS
Open your arms!

MYRRHINE
No. Wait a second.

CINESIAS
O....
Then hurry back again.

MYRRHINE
Here the cushions are.
Lie down while I—O dear! But what a shame,
You need more pillows.

CINESIAS
I don't want them, dear.

MYRRHINE
But I do.

CINESIAS
Thwarted affection mine,
They treat you just like Heracles at a feast
With cheats of dainties, O disappointing arms!

MYRRHINE
Raise up your head.

CINESIAS
There, that's everything at last.

MYRRHINE
Yes, all.

CINESIAS
Then run to my arms, you golden girl.

MYRRHINE
I'm loosening my girdle now. But you've not forgotten?
You're not deceiving me about the Treaty?

CINESIAS
No, by my life, I'm not.

MYRRHINE
Why, you've no blanket.

CINESIAS
It's not the silly blanket's warmth but yours I want.

MYRRHINE
Never mind. You'll soon have both. I'll come straight back.

CINESIAS
The woman will choke me with her coverlets.

MYRRHINE
Get up a moment.

CINESIAS
I'm up high enough.

MYRRHINE
Would you like me to perfume you?

CINESIAS
By Apollo, no!

MYRRHINE
By Aphrodite, I'll do it anyway.

CINESIAS
Lord Zeus, may she soon use up all the myrrh.

MYRRHINE
Stretch out your hand. Take it and rub it in.

CINESIAS
Hmm, it's not as fragrant as might be; that is,
Not before it's smeared. It doesn't smell of kisses.

MYRRHINE
How silly I am: I've brought you Rhodian scents.

CINESIAS
It's good enough, leave it, love.

MYRRHINE
You must be jesting.

CINESIAS
Plague rack the man who first compounded scent!

MYRRHINE
Here, take this flask.

CINESIAS
I've a far better one.
Don't tease me, come here, and get nothing more.

MYRRHINE
I'm coming.... I'm just drawing off my shoes....
You're sure you will vote for Peace?

CINESIAS
I'll think about it.
She runs off.
I'm dead: the woman's worn me all away.
She's gone and left me with an anguished pulse.

MEN
Baulked in your amorous delight
How melancholy is your plight.
With sympathy your case I view;
For I am sure it's hard on you.
What human being could sustain
This unforeseen domestic strain,
And not a single trace
Of willing women in the place!

CINESIAS
O Zeus, what throbbing suffering!

MEN
She did it all, the harlot, she
With her atrocious harlotry.

WOMEN
Nay, rather call her darling-sweet.

MEN
What, sweet? She's a rude, wicked thing.

CINESIAS
A wicked thing, as I repeat.
O Zeus, O Zeus,
Canst Thou not suddenly let loose
Some twirling hurricane to tear
Her flapping up along the air
And drop her, when she's whirled around,
Here to the ground
Neatly impaled upon the stake
That's ready upright for her sake.
He goes out.

Enter SPARTAN HERALD.
The MAGISTRATE *comes forward.*

HERALD
What here gabs the Senate an' the Prytanes?
I've fetcht despatches for them.

MAGISTRATE
Are you a man
Or a monstrosity?

HERALD
My scrimp-brained lad,
I'm a herald, as ye see, who hae come frae Sparta
Anent a Peace.

MAGISTRATE
Then why do you hide that lance
That sticks out under your arms?

HERALD
I've brought no lance.

MAGISTRATE
Then why do you turn aside and hold your cloak
So far out from your body? Is your groin swollen
With stress of travelling?

HERALD
By Castor, I'll swear
The man is wud.

MAGISTRATE
Indeed, your cloak is wide,
My rascal fellow.

HERALD
But I tell ye No!
Enow o' fleering!

MAGISTRATE
Well, what is it then?

HERALD
It's my despatch cane.

MAGISTRATE
Of course—a Spartan cane!
But speak right out. I know all this too well.
Are new privations springing up in Sparta?

HERALD
Och, hard as could be: in lofty lusty columns
Our allies stand united. We maun get Pellene.

MAGISTRATE
Whence has this evil come? Is it from Pan?

HERALD
No. Lampito first ran asklent, then the others
Sprinted after her example, and blocked, the hizzies,
Their wames unskaithed against our every fleech.

MAGISTRATE
What did you do?

HERALD
We are broken, and bent double,
Limp like men carrying lanthorns in great winds
About the city. They winna let us even
Wi' lightest neif skim their primsie pretties
Till we've concluded Peace-terms wi' a' Hellas.

MAGISTRATE
So the conspiracy is universal;
This proves it. Then return to Sparta. Bid them
Send envoys with full powers to treat of Peace;
And I will urge the Senate here to choose
Plenipotentiary ambassadors,
As argument adducing this connection.

HERALD
I'm off. Your wisdom none could controvert.
They retire.

MEN
There is no beast, no rush of fire, like woman so untamed.
She calmly goes her way where even panthers would be shamed.

WOMEN
And yet you are fool enough, it seems, to dare to war with me,
When for your faithful ally you might win me easily.

MEN
Never could the hate I feel for womankind grow less.

WOMEN
Then have your will. But I'll take pity on your nakedness.
For I can see just how ridiculous you look, and so
Will help you with your tunic if close up I now may go.

MEN
Well, that, by Zeus, is no scoundrel-deed, I frankly will admit.
I only took them off myself in a scoundrel raging-fit.

WOMEN
Now you look sensible, and that you're men no one could doubt.
If you were but good friends again, I'd take the insect out
That hurts your eye.

MEN
Is that what's wrong? That nasty bitie thing.
Please squeeze it out, and show me what it is that makes this sting.
It's been paining me a long while now.

WOMEN
Well I'll agree to that,
Although you're most unmannerly. O what a giant gnat.
Here, look! It comes from marshy Tricorysus, I can tell.

MEN
O thank you. It was digging out a veritable well.
Now that it's gone, I can't hold back my tears. See how they fall.

WOMEN
I'll wipe them off, bad as you are, and kiss you after all.

MEN
I won't be kissed.

WOMEN
O yes, you will. Your wishes do not matter.

MEN
O botheration take you all! How you cajole and flatter.
A hell it is to live with you; to live without, a hell:
How truly was that said. But come, these enmities let's quell.
You stop from giving orders and I'll stop from doing wrong.
So let's join ranks and seal our bargain with a choric song.

CHORUS.
Athenians, it's not our intention
To sow political dissension
By giving any scandal mention;

But on the contrary to promote good feeling in the state
By word and deed. We've had enough calamities of late.
So let a man or woman but divulge
They need a trifle, say,
Two minas, three or four,
I've purses here that bulge.
There's only one condition made
(Indulge my whim in this I pray)—
When Peace is signed once more,
On no account am I to be repaid.
And I'm making preparation
For a gay select collation
With some youths of reputation.
I've managed to produce some soup and they're slaughtering for me
A sucking-pig: its flesh should taste as tender as could be.
I shall expect you at my house today.
To the baths make an early visit,
And bring your children along;
Don't dawdle on the way.
Ask no one; enter as if the place
Was all your own—yours henceforth is it.
If nothing chances wrong,
The door will then be shut bang in your face.

The SPARTAN AMBASSADORS *approach.*

CHORUS
Here come the Spartan envoys with long, worried beards.
Hail, Spartans how do you fare?
Did anything new arise?

SPARTANS
No need for a clutter o' words. Do ye see our condition?

CHORUS
The situation swells to greater tension.
Something will explode soon.

SPARTANS
It's awfu' truly.
But come, let us wi' the best speed we may
Scribble a Peace.

CHORUS
I notice that our men
Like wrestlers poised for contest, hold their clothes
Out from their bellies. An athlete's malady!
Since exercise alone can bring relief.

ATHENIANS
Can anyone tell us where Lysistrata is?
There is no need to describe our men's condition,
It shows up plainly enough.

CHORUS
It's the same disease.
Do you feel a jerking throbbing in the morning?

ATHENIANS
By Zeus, yes! In these straits, I'm racked all through.
Unless Peace is soon declared, we shall be driven
In the void of women to try Cleisthenes.

CHORUS
Be wise and cover those things with your tunics.
Who knows what kind of person may perceive you?

ATHENIANS
By Zeus, you're right.

SPARTANS
By the Twa Goddesses,
Indeed ye are. Let's put our tunics on.

ATHENIANS
Hail O my fellow-sufferers, hail Spartans.

SPARTANS
O hinnie darling, what a waefu' thing!
If they had seen us wi' our lunging waddies!

ATHENIANS
Tell us then, Spartans, what has brought you here?

SPARTANS
We come to treat o' Peace.

ATHENIANS
Well spoken there!
And we the same. Let us callout Lysistrata
Since she alone can settle the Peace-terms.

SPARTANS
Callout Lysistratus too if ye don't mind.

CHORUS
No indeed. She hears your voices and she comes.
Enter LYSISTRATA
Hail, Wonder of all women! Now you must be in turn
Hard, shifting, clear, deceitful, noble, crafty, sweet, and stern.
The foremost men of Hellas, smitten by your fascination,
Have brought their tangled quarrels here for your sole arbitration.

LYSISTRATA
An easy task if the love's raging home-sickness
Doesn't start trying out how well each other
Will serve instead of us. But I'll know at once
If they do. O where's that girl, Reconciliation?
Bring first before me the Spartan delegates,
And see you lift no rude or violent hands—
None of the churlish ways our husbands used.
But lead them courteously, as women should.
And if they grudge fingers, guide them by other methods,
And introduce them with ready tact. The Athenians
Draw by whatever offers you a grip.
Now, Spartans, stay here facing me. Here you,

Athenians. Both hearken to my words.
I am a woman, but I'm not a fool.
And what of natural intelligence I own
Has been filled out with the remembered precepts
My father and the city-elders taught me.
First I reproach you both sides equally
That when at Pylae and Olympia,
At Pytho and the many other shrines
That I could name, you sprinkle from one cup
The altars common to all Hellenes, yet
You wrack Hellenic cities, bloody Hellas
With deaths of her own sons, while yonder clangs
The gathering menace of barbarians.

ATHENIANS
We cannot hold it in much longer now.

LYSISTRATA
Now unto you, O Spartans, do I speak.
Do you forget how your own countryman,
Pericleidas, once came hither suppliant
Before our altars, pale in his purple robes,
Praying for an army when in Messenia
Danger growled, and the Sea-god made earth quaver.
Then with four thousand hoplites Cimon marched
And saved all Sparta. Yet base ingrates now,
You are ravaging the soil of your preservers.

ATHENIANS
By Zeus, they do great wrong, Lysistrata.

SPARTANS
Great wrong, indeed. O! What a luscious wench!

LYSISTRATA
And now I turn to the Athenians.
Have you forgotten too how once the Spartans
In days when you wore slavish tunics, came
And with their spears broke a Thessalian host

And all the partisans of Hippias?
They alone stood by your shoulder on that day.
They freed you, so that for the slave's short skirt
You should wear the trailing cloak of liberty.

SPARTANS
I've never seen a nobler woman anywhere.

ATHENIANS
Nor I one with such prettily jointing hips.

LYSISTRATA
Now, brethren twined with mutual benefactions,
Can you still war, can you suffer such disgrace?
Why not be friends? What is there to prevent you?

SPARTANS
We're agreed, gin that we get this tempting Mole.

LYSISTRATA
Which one?

SPARTANS
That ane we've wanted to get into,
O for sae lang.... Pylos, of course.

ATHENIANS
By Poseidon,
Never!

LYSISTRATA
Give it up.

ATHENIANS
Then what will we do?
We need that ticklish place united to us—

LYSISTRATA
Ask for some other lurking-hole in return.

ATHENIANS
Then, ah, we'll choose this snug thing here, Echinus,
Shall we call the nestling spot? And this backside haven,
These desirable twin promontories, the Maliac,
And then of course these Megarean Legs.

SPARTANS
Not that, O surely not that, never that.

LYSISTRATA
Agree! Now what are two legs more or less?

ATHENIANS
I want to strip at once and plough my land.

SPARTANS
And mine I want to fertilize at once.

LYSISTRATA
And so you can, when Peace is once declared.
If you mean it, get your allies' heads together
And come to some decision.

ATHENIANS
What allies?
There's no distinction in our politics:
We've risen as one man to this conclusion;
Every ally is jumping-mad to drive it home.

SPARTANS
And ours the same, for sure.

ATHENIANS
The Carystians first!
I'll bet on that.

LYSISTRATA
I agree with all of you.
Now off, and cleanse yourselves for the Acropolis,

For we invite you all in to a supper
From our commissariat baskets. There at table
You will pledge good behaviour and uprightness;
Then each man's wife is his to hustle home.

ATHENIANS
Come, as quickly as possible.

SPARTANS
As quick as ye like.
Lead on.

ATHENIANS
O Zeus, quick, quick, lead quickly on.
They hurry off.

CHORUS
Broidered stuffs on high I'm heaping,
Fashionable cloaks and sweeping
Trains, not even gold gawds keeping.
Take them all, I pray you, take them all (I do not care)
And deck your children—your daughter, if the Basket she's to bear.
Come, everyone of you, come in and take
Of this rich hoard a share.
Nought's tied so skilfully
But you its seal can break
And plunder all you spy inside.
I've laid out all that I can spare,
And therefore you will see
Nothing unless than I you're sharper-eyed.
If lacking corn a man should be
While his slaves clamour hungrily
And his excessive progeny,
Then I've a handful of grain at home which is always to be had,
And to which in fact a more-than-life-size loaf I'd gladly add.

Then let the poor bring with them bag or sack
And take this store of food.
Manes, my man, I'll tell

To help them all to pack
Their wallets full. But O take care.
I had forgotten; don't intrude,
Or terrified you'll yell.
My dog is hungry too, and bites—beware!

Some LOUNGERS *from the Market with torches approach the Banqueting hall. The* PORTER *bars their entrance.*

1ST MARKET-LOUNGER
Open the door.

PORTER
Here move along.

1ST MARKET-LOUNGER
What's this?
You're sitting down. Shall I singe you with my torch?
That's vulgar! O I couldn't do it... yet
If it would gratify the audience,
I'll mortify myself.

2ND MARKET-LOUNGER
And I will too.
We'll both be crude and vulgar, yes we will.

PORTER
Be off at once now or you'll be wailing
Dirges for your hair. Get off at once,
And see you don't disturb the Spartan envoys
Just coming out from the splendid feast they've had.
The banqueters begin to come out.

1ST ATHENIAN
I've never known such a pleasant banquet before,
And what delightful fellows the Spartans are.
When we are warm with wine, how wise we grow.

2ND ATHENIAN
That's only fair, since sober we're such fools:
This is the advice I'd give the Athenians—
See our ambassadors are always drunk.
For when we visit Sparta sober, then
We're on the alert for trickery all the while
So that we miss half of the things they say,
And misinterpret things that were never said,
And then report the muddle back to Athens.
But now we're charmed with each other. They might cap
With the Telamon-catch instead of the Cleitagora,
And we'd applaud and praise them just the same;
We're not too scrupulous in weighing words.

PORTER
Why, here the rascals come again to plague me.
Won't you move on, you sorry loafers there!

MARKET-LOUNGER
Yes, by Zeus, they're already coming out.

SPARTANS
Now hinnie dearest, please tak' up your pipe
That I may try a spring an' sing my best
In honour o' the Athenians an' oursels.

ATHENIANS
Aye, take your pipe. By all the gods, there's nothing
Could glad my heart more than to watch you dance.

SPARTANS
Mnemosyne,
Let thy fire storm these younkers,
O tongue wi' stormy ecstasy
My Muse that knows
Our deeds and theirs, how when at sea
Their navies swooped upon
The Medes at Artemision—
Gods for their courage, did they strike

Wrenching a triumph frae their foes;
While at Thermopylae
Leonidas' army stood: wild-boars they were like
Wild-boars that wi' fierce threat
Their terrible tusks whet;
The sweat ran streaming down each twisted face,
Faen blossoming i' strange petals o' death
Panted frae mortal breath,
The sweat drenched a' their bodies i' that place,
For the hurly-burly o' Persians glittered more
Than the sands on the shore.
Come, Hunting Girl, an' hear my prayer—
You whose arrows whizz in woodlands, come an' bless
This Peace we swear.
Let us be fenced wi' age long amity,
O let this bond stick ever firm through thee
In friendly happiness.
Henceforth no guilefu' perjury be seen!
O hither, hither O
Thou wildwood queen.

LYSISTRATA
Earth is delighted now, peace is the voice of earth.
Spartans, sort out your wives: Athenians, yours.
Let each catch hands with his wife and dance his joy,
Dance out his thanks, be grateful in music,
And promise reformation with his heels.

ATHENIANS
O Dancers, forward. Lead out the Graces,
Call Artemis out;
Then her brother, the Dancer of Skies,
That gracious Apollo.
Invoke with a shout
Dionysus out of whose eyes
Breaks fire on the maenads that follow;
And Zeus with his flares of quick lightning, and call,
Happy Hera, Queen of all,
And all the Daimons summon hither to be

Witnesses of our revelry
And of the noble Peace we have made,
Aphrodite our aid.

Io Paieon, Io, cry—
For victory, leap!
Attained by me, leap!
Euoi Euoi Euai Euai.

SPARTANS
Piper, gie us the music for a new sang.

SPARTANS
Leaving again lovely lofty Taygetus
Hither O Spartan Muse, hither to greet us,
And wi' our choric voice to raise
To Amyclean Apollo praise,
And Tyndareus' gallant sons whose days
Alang Eurotas' banks merrily pass,
An' Athene o' the House o' Brass.
Now the dance begin;
Dance, making swirl your fringe o' woolly skin,
While we join voices
To hymn dear Sparta that rejoices
I' a beautifu' sang,
An' loves to see
Dancers tangled beautifully;
For the girls i' tumbled ranks
Alang Eurotas' banks
Like wanton fillies thrang,
Frolicking there.

An' like Bacchantes shaking the wild air
To comb a giddy laughter through the hair,
Bacchantes that clench thyrsi as they sweep
To the ecstatic leap.
An' Helen, Child o' Leda, come
Thou holy, nimble, gracefu' Queen,
Lead thou the dance, gather thy joyous tresses up i' bands

An' play like a fawn. To madden them, clap thy hands,
And sing praise to the warrior goddess templed i' our lands,
Her o' the House o' Brass.

Second Half
Questions for Discussion

1. Give an example of a dialogue that also describes the actions the actors are carrying out in *Lysistrata*. As I explained above, there are few stage directions in Aristophanes plays, and what the characters are doing is primarily depicted in what they're saying. Are there benefits to this? Use the example you found of actions in a dialogue to explain this.
2. Find an allusion in *Lysistrata* that I have not mentioned in my notes, and explain what this is an allusion to, and its significance.
3. Find something in the reading that has a deeper, symbolic meaning and explain what this symbol means.

Works Cited

Beckett, Samuel. *Waiting for Godot: A Tragicomedy in Two Acts*. New York: Grove/Atlantic, Inc., 2011. Google Books. 23 March 2017. Web.

Chekhov, Anton. *Chekhov: The Essential Plays: The Seagull, Uncle Vanya, Three Sisters & The Cherry Orchard*. New York: Random House Publishing Group, 2003. Google Books. 23 March 2017. Web.

POETRY

The authors covered in this Poetry section are organized chronologically. They start with William Shakespeare and his well-known sonnets. Then, there are a few poems from the Scottish nationalist Sir Walter Scott. Only one poem per poet is presented for the rest to cover a more diverse set of writers and poetic stylistics. All of the poets are American or British. The poems are primarily either about love, or about war, national identity and human rights. The other writers covered are: Lord Byron, Oscar Wilde, Elizabeth Barrett Browning, Robert Browning, Rudyard Kipling, Edgar Allan Poe, Walt Whitman, and Henry W. Longfellow.

Each of the poets has a different poetic style and structure. So, each poet's section begins with a biographical summary, followed by some context to their poetry. Definitions and explanations are given for the terms and concepts that define each type of poem. For example, in William Shakespeare's section, definitions and discussion is offered on terms such as: quatrain, couplet, iambic pentameter, stress, and repeating rhythm. Each individual poem is contextualized, summarized and otherwise dissected. All of the poems in the readings part of the book are fully explored here. In the middle of this section, the "6-Page Research Paper Assignment" is provided. It asks students to utilize one of the focal literary theories discussed earlier to closely analyze any one of the works covered in the readings section. This essay asks for outside research and full in-text and bibliographic citations of secondary sources.

Poetic Terms

This section serves to explain the terms and concepts related to poetry in more depth than the shorter definitions and explanations offered next to each of the poets and their unique poems. These general poetic terms apply to most poems rather than narrowly defining a specific author's style. The term "style" itself is likely to be too vague for students to comprehend and discuss in their own essays without the definition provided. Other concepts like tone or voice might seem self-explanatory, but only with their close inspection can poetry gain new dimensions of meaning and feeling. Also covered are imagery, language, figures of speech and sound.

Style: The concept of poetic style is a bit less solidified than terms like allusion or imagery. A given critic might look closely for linguistic stylistic elements, while another might look more broadly for patterns in style. One of the frequently quoted scholarly books on this topic is Donald Davie's *Purity of Diction in English Verse*. He explains that due to the easy access modern writers have to styles of all cultures and across all of history, they can choose which of these styles they imitate. Before this availability, writers had to mimic the style that was popular in their place and time. If a writer does not mimic some specific style or does not develop a consistent style of their own, their work is not likely to be digestible to readers, who might interpret it as being chaotic or lacking in identifiable stylistic patterns. Here is how he puts it: "These styles the modern artist has learnt to appreciate independent of the different cultures of which they were the flowers; and he can choose among them at will, seeking the one he shall use as a model. I think this is largely true, though the artist is still determined by his society to some extent. Yeats must have found in the Irish culture of his time some points of contact with the noble culture of Japan, or the courtly culture of Spenser" (Davie 9). Later in the book, he explains that style can be categorized into "the **three styles of verse** (the lofty, the mean, the base) are equally closely in touch with spoken usage. The **lofty** style uses the speech of the court; the **mean** style, the speech of merchants and yeomanry; the **base** style, the speech of menial trades and the peasantry" (Davie 58). Obviously, breaking down style into economic classes is problematic nowadays as there are some highly educated farmers, and some barely literate billionaires. But, books are still broken down into highbrow and lowbrow literature, with the lowbrow fiction intended for less literate and poorer readers, who are more numerous. Thus, this fiction is called "popular" fiction or fiction for the majority of the populace.

Tone: can be humorous, understated, ironical, tragic, reserved, detached, and the like. Each genre of fiction has a particular tone common to it. Satires have humorous tones, while tragedies take on a tragic tone. Historical fiction is informative, while romance fiction is sentimental. The tone is the attitude the author or narrator shows towards the narrative or characters being depicted. With a different tone, a character can jump from being the hero to being the villain. Thus, if murderous or adulterous behavior is glorified in tone, the murderer is an anti-hero, while if these actions are colored with a negative tone, the murderer is a villain in need of suppression or punishment from the moral authority of the author.

Language: The term "language" seems to be an obvious one that refers to the English language in general, but this is not the meaning that "language" has in the context of poetry. Here is Davie's explanation: "Presumably, if a bad diction is the result of selecting from the language at random, according to the whim of fashion, then good diction comes from making a selection from the language on reasonable principles and for a reasonable purpose." Thus, there is a spectrum of language, ranging from random choices from the words available in the dictionary to very formulaic language that puts words (not only in grammatical), but also stylistically, phonetically, and logically prescribed patterns that are prized by critics in a given field. This is how formulaic films and books are frequently prized above more spontaneous and innovative books because the presence of a consistent formula allows critics to say a book is good because it meets the requirements of the formula. Davie goes on: "All poets when they write have one purpose. They want to create an effect upon the mind of the reader. These effects are various, and the poets dispute about which effects are legitimate and worth-while. When the poets and critics are very sure about what effects are legitimate, then they can construct a very elaborate structure of poetic diction, as it were departmentalized, according to the different effects which the poet may legitimately seek to produce…" In the section on Shakespeare, I explained how Shakespeare wrote a set of love sonnets that have a connected narrative and theme behind them because this exact formula was popular in the decade that preceded his publication. He did not write predominantly sonnets because poems happened to come to him in that form, but rather through following the prescribed rules of what readers and critics wanted at the time. Shakespeare's sonnets don't only have a repeating rhythm and rhyme structure, but also repeat some of the same, fashionable vocabulary. Davie then explains that in contrast with hyper-formulaic writers such as Shakespeare, there is another camp of writers with a "slack" view towards language that implies that "every poem in its kind is as good as every other poem in another kind." Shakespeare's sonnets would fall into the category of "dogmatic purism, which says, 'This good poem is written in this way. Therefore all good poems must be written in this way'" (5-7). As a critic of literature, you have to be aware if the literature you are criticizing falls into the "slack" or the purist categories, so that you can judge the work by the appropriate measuring stick. Thus, you should not judge a free or an unrhymed poem for this lack, and you should judge harshly an attempt at a pure sonnet that fails to rhyme a couple of lines that are supposed to rhyme.

Voice: The voice is different from the tone because it combines it with language and with the presence of a narrator (be it the author or a fictional character who is speaking). The style the voice is using can be defined by the chosen diction, thus "pure" diction creates an "impersonal and timeless" voice (128). Davie later makes a distinction between three different types of "voice," which are listed in order from least to most advanced (according to some scholars): "impersonal (= 'undistinguished'), through the personal (= 'distinctive'), to the impersonal ([=] 'a disembodied voice')" (161). There are two occurrences of "impersonal" in this string. Davie is arguing that very structured poetry employs "poetic diction," which needs a touch of personal or "distinctive" voice, which also needs to then be edited to seem to come out of "inspiration" rather than from a studious writing process. Thus, a distinctive poetic voice is needed to elevate poetry from a structured writing exercise to an emotional and inspired art that touches readers' emotions. Davie also stresses the difference between the poet's and the speaker's voices. Writers can obtain detachment and can express views different from their own by strengthening the illusion of separation by crafting a voice for the speaker that is very different from the poet's "natural" voice. "To make poetry out of moral commonplace, a poet has to make it clear that he speaks not in his own voice (that would be impertinent) but as the spokesman of a social tradition." Davie explains that this was why Horatian imitated Pope and Juvenal imitated Johnson, to touch on ingrained styles of voice that readers respected and admired (191).

Imagery: Davie only touches on "imagery" to point out that there is more to it than the visual images a poem offers. *Encyclopedia Britannica* also stresses that "poetic imagery" is composed of both "sensory and figurative language." The term "imagery" comes from the simple examination of "images," but the symbolic meaning of these images is frequently more important in the compressed poetic form. There are only so many words a poet can use per line and symbolic meanings help to give a richer inner life to the poem.

Figures of Speech: Davie does not dwell on this term because it is colloquial or used in casual conversations about literature, rather than by serious critics, who might instead use terms such as "symbolism" or "metaphor" rather than using the broad concept of "figures of speech." According to *Encyclopedia Britannica*, a **metaphor** is a type of figurative language that compares two things without using "like" or "as," where as a **simile** makes a comparison with the help of "like" or "as." **Personification** is another figure of speech, and it attributes personal qualities to an inanimate object. All sorts of other things can be figurative, including irony and repetition. All of these different artistic formulas deviate from the "literal statement or common usage," by embellishing "written and spoken language." Poetry would not be possible without figurative language because it would just be a very simple narration of an event or a description of a character without the hidden clues and meanings that inspire readers to keep re-reading and finding new interpretations of a very short, but condensed poem.

Sound: Poetry can sound pleasing or grinding and distressing to the ear. This is accomplished by using soft or hard sounding words to help set the intended tone through this background element. A poem can be musical and melodic, or it can be jumpy and comprised of many consonants and disruptive sounds. The sound of the ocean is an example of a pleasing sound, while the banging of drums in a hard rock song is its opposite.

William Shakespeare

William Shakespeare is a leading playwriter and director from the peak of the Elizabethan age. He was briefly forgotten after his death, before he was resurrected as one of its all-time best poets and playwriters. His sonnets are a great introduction to the passions, jealousies and violence that he detailed in his plays.

He was born in Stratford-upon-Avon in 1564. He married at eighteen to Anne Hathaway; early marriages were common in this period. They had three children in the following years. His son died young, and only his daughters survived. Shakespeare wrote some of his early plays as a traveling actor with small theater companies.

The Globe Theatre in Southwark, where Shakespeare made a name for himself, was only built in 1599. It was uniquely popular and cheap enough for the poor to afford viewing a show. Shakespeare's *Julius Caesar* (about the assassination of a tyrant by his friend Brutus and other politicians) was performed at the Globe in its first year of operation. The plays were preserved because they were printed and reprinted in collections. Shakespeare died three years after the Globe Theatre was destroyed in a fire and had to be re-built in 1616.

Most of Shakespeare's known sonnets (154 of them) were published by Thomas Thorpe in 1609, at the peak of his triumph. He started writing them at least a decade earlier, when there was a "vogue for sonnet sequences that told the story of a tormented love affair, with lofty mystical and symbolic overtones," but which had gone out of "fashion" by 1609. There is a repeating formula to this set of poems: "the same simple rhyme scheme and standard division into three four-line quatrains and a final couplet," into which "he packed an entire universe of love, lust and longing" ("Shakespeare's Super Sonnets"). We are reading some of the poems from this collection in this class.

A **quatrain** is a stanza, typically with every other line rhyming. The **couplet** is two lines at the end of the poem that rhyme and echo each other in meter. The meter across these poems is the **iambic pentameter**, which has five metrical feet. Each foot begins with an unstressed syllable and then a stressed syllable. The syllable that's **stressed** is the one that is given more emphasis when a poem is read aloud. Typically, prepositions and articles are never stressed, unless they are italicized for emphasis. Pronouns are almost always stressed. The first syllable in a long word is more likely to be stressed. The iambic pentameter is infrequently perfect in meter, but if most of the syllables follow this pattern this creates a **repeating rhythm** that gives it musicality.

IT WAS A LOVER AND HIS LASS

It was a lover and his lass
  With a hey, and a ho, and a hey-nonino!
That o'er the green cornfield did pass,
In the spring time, the only pretty ring time,
When birds do sing hey ding a ding:
  Sweet lovers love the Spring.
Between the acres of the rye
These pretty country folks would lie:
This carol they began that hour,
How that life was but a flower:
And therefore take the present time
  With a hey, and a ho, and a hey-nonino!
For love is crownéd with the prime
In spring time, the only pretty ring time,
When birds do sing, hey ding a ding;
  Sweet lovers love the Spring.

***

How like a winter hath my absence been
From Thee, the pleasure of the fleeting year!
What freezings have I felt, what dark days seen,

What old December's bareness everywhere!

And yet this time removed was summer's time:
The teeming autumn, big with rich increase,
Bearing the wanton burden of the prime
Like widow'd wombs after their lords' decease:

Yet this abundant issue seem'd to me
But hope of orphans, and unfather'd fruit;
For summer and his pleasures wait on thee,
And, thou away, the very birds are mute;

Or if they sing, 'tis with so dull a cheer,
That leaves look pale, dreading the winter's near.

TO HIS LOVE

Shall I compare thee to a summer's day?
Thou art more lovely and more temperate:
Rough winds do shake the darling buds of May,
And summer's lease hath all too short a date:

Sometime too hot the eye of heaven shines,
And often is his gold complexion dimm'd,
And every fair from fair sometime declines,
By chance, or nature's changing course, untrimm'd.

But thy eternal summer shall not fade,
Nor lose possession of that fair thou owest;
Nor shall death brag thou wanderest in his shade,
When in eternal lines to time thou growest.

So long as men can breathe, or eyes can see,
So long lives this, and this gives life to thee.

***

When in the chronicle of wasted time
I see descriptions of the fairest wights,
And beauty making beautiful old rhyme
In praise of ladies dead, and lovely knights;

Then in the blazon of sweet beauty's best
Of hand, of foot, of lip, of eye, of brow,
I see their antique pen would have exprest
Ev'n such a beauty as you master now.

So all their praises are but prophecies
Of this our time, all, you prefiguring;
And for they look'd but with divining eyes,
They had not skill enough your worth to sing:

For we, which now behold these present days,
Have eyes to wonder, but lack tongues to praise.

TRUE LOVE

Let me not to the marriage of true minds
Admit impediments. Love is not love
Which alters when it alteration finds,
Or bends with the remover to remove—

O no! it is an ever-fixéd mark
That looks on tempests and is never shaken;
It is the star to every wandering bark
Whose worth's unknown, although his height be taken.

Love's not Time's fool, though rosy lips and cheeks
Within his bending sickle's compass come;
Love alters not with his brief hours and weeks,
But bears it out ev'n to the edge of doom—

If this be error and upon me proved,
I never writ, nor no man ever loved.

END OF THE CIVIL WAR.
FROM *KING RICHARD III.*, ACT I. SC. I.

Now is the winter of our discontent
Made glorious summer by this sun of York,
And all the clouds that lowered upon our house
In the deep bosom of the ocean buried.
Now are our brows bound with victorious wreaths;
Our bruisèd arms hung up for monuments;
Our stern alarums changed to merry meetings,
Our dreadful marches to delightful measures.
Grim-visaged War hath smoothed his wrinkled front.
And now, instead of mounting barbed steeds
To fright the souls of fearful adversaries,
He capers nimbly in a lady's chamber,
To the lascivious pleasing of a lute.

IT WAS A LOVER AND HIS LASS

This first poem breaks with the sonnet pattern in its first half, as it has a four-line stanza at the end instead of a couplet, but its second half is a conventionally structured sonnet. The first part also stands out as a very light sing-songy sonnet that celebrates the Spring and youthful love with an equally youthful and carefree poetic style. The second part includes fewer repetitions (i.e.: "ding a ding"), and its otherwise more complex and dark to reflect the winter or old age of love. The author is addressing a young man in this poem, and this youth is the main friend or possibly lover that Shakespeare is attempting to educate about love across the collection.

TO HIS LOVE

This famous sonnet begins with a contemplation on the nature of metaphors. Love poems typically compare love interests to objects, creatures, or other things. Shakespeare objects that such comparisons fail to express the loveliness of his particular love interest. The second half includes a reference that also appears at the center of *Don Quixote* to chivalry tales: "And beauty making beautiful old rhyme/ In praise of ladies dead, and lovely knights." Like Cervantes, Shakespeare also criticizes the chivalry romances as being inadequate to depict the reality and beauty of the world: "They had not skill enough your worth to sing."

TRUE LOVE

This poem is frequently quoted as an almost cliché statement about love's unchanging nature. The change in question is old age, as it was in the first poem in this set. The relationship between age and love is a major concern for Shakespeare. Much of the sentimental sadness in these sonnets comes from the tension of slipping time, age, ugliness and their opposites. The final couplet, as usual, explains the central point of the poem with conviction. In this final couplet, Shakespeare insists that love is unchanging or it cannot be real.

END OF THE CIVIL WAR.: FROM KING RICHARD III., ACT I. SC. I.

This last poem is from the first scene of Shakespeare's play, *King Richard III*, so it does not follow the same poetic structure as the sonnets. There are some somewhat rhyming endings but there are no full rhymes anywhere, and the metric length is inconsistent within the lines. As the name suggests, this poem celebrates the end of the Civil War, and warriors coming back home to perhaps find love and to be glorified as heroes.

Sir Walter Scott

The following brief biography of Sir Walter Scott is from my published book, *The History of British and American Author-Publishers*.

Sir Walter Scott started his career by apprenticing to his father, Walter Scott WS, who hired him during bread riots when it was difficult to find other helpers, despite the lameness

Sir Walter Scott by Sir William Allan

the young Scott developed in a childhood illness. Scott succeeded in this challenge and was then hired as a copying clerk for Scott Senior's Chalmers and Scott law firm in Edinburgh in 1786, speed copying court documents because he was paid "threepence a page," which, if we believe the accounts that he occasionally copied 120 pages in a day, earning 30s, is a very high rate for a fifteen-year-old apprentice (Sutherland, *Life* 28-31). Scott was then offered a partnership in the firm in 1790 despite his father's criticism of his drinking, fiddling, and wondering around the countryside with shady friends. Scott refused the partnership because his father had stayed a Writer to the Signet across the bulk of his career and never left the middle class by running his law firm. Instead, the young Scott insisted on finishing his studies to become an advocate, burying himself in his studies between 1789 and 1792 (41). Scott qualified as an advocate in July of 1792. One of Scott's notable early cases was his defense of a delinquent clergyman, M'Naught before the General Assembly of the Kirk in May 1793. The trial caused hilarity among Scott's youthful lawyer comrades because Scott stumbled in miniscule points, failing to make a convincing oration, and his friends hollered and were thrown out from the proceedings because they were rolling with laughter at being guilty of all of the crimes M'Naught was being accused of: "habitual drunkenness, singing of lewd and profane songs, dancing and toying at a penny-wedding with a 'sweetie wife'" as well as a crime they were not a party to, "promoting irregular marriages as a justice of the peace" (48). In his first three years of practicing law as an advocate Scott made £23, £55, and £84, defending mostly petty crimes and one murderer. In these years, Scott seemingly took an anti-Jacobite stand, but he did it in a way that proved more rebellious than the mob he swore to squash. In one incident in April of 1794, Scott and his advocate friends "attended the Edinburgh Theatre armed with staves to ensure the singing of the National Anthem was not interrupted or mocked. A brawl broke out with some democratically inclined Irish medical students. Heads were broken (Scott boasted that he split three himself). Scott and his friends were arrested, and bound over to keep the peace" (Sutherland, *Life* 50).

One of these patriotic friends was James Ballantyne who founded his own printing press in Kelso, Scotland, where they were residing, a couple of years after this incident in 1796. Scott met James and John Ballantyne back in grammar school. Scott might have gone permanently unpublished if Ballantyne had not started this venture, thus making Scott feel as if he had a friend supporting his publications, rather than a censor that might reject or unjustly chop up his creations. Publishing with a friend is frequently similar to publishing with your own press in the ease of access to acceptance. Scott's early publications were extensions of his academic pursuits, as he published translations from German, and a collection of Scottish ballads. Sometime later, he started publishing poetry with Ballantyne. It took James Ballantyne a decade to build up his publishing business enough for one of his Scott releases, *The Lay of the Last Minstrel*, to become a best-seller in 1805, so it was no spontaneous publishing success. The Ballantyne Publishing Company gave root to many writers and editors in the Ballantyne family. It predominantly published works edited or written by Sir Walter Scott, who financed a portion of the venture. One of the other Ballantynes to spring out of this family was Robert Michael Ballantyne, who was born in the year when a UK-wide banking crisis left the Ballantyne printing business with £130,000 in debt, equivalent to $13,400,000 today. This enormous sum also shows the volume of business Ballantyne was doing before its collapse, and how potentially profitable the publishing ventures were, if only the investing environment had remained stable. The young R. M. Ballantyne went to Canada to work in fur trading at sixteen, and only returned to Scotland in 1847 after his father's death. He released his first book on the following year, *Hudson's Bay: or, Life in the Wilds of North America*, probably sponsoring it with money from his inheritance. In his first years back in Scotland, he worked for Messrs Constable, a publisher in Edinburgh that was previously affiliated with Archibald Constable. He went on to publish over a hundred young adult titles.

Back in 1799, Scott Senior died, leaving the young Scott an estate to untangle. In the same year, Walter was appointed Sheriff-Depute of Selkirkshire for £250 annually. The appointment came with the help of his mentor, Henry Dundas. He only assisted Scott's rise because Scott had expressed anti-Jacobite and anti-sedition views that are uncharacteristic when compared with the ideas Scott expressed later in his career, when he was secure in his legal post, and no longer needed to court favors from the conservative establishment. He held the same post of sheriff of Roxburgh, Berwick and Selkirk from this point until his death, with the only change being a raise to £300, thus eliminating any need for further groveling and patronages. The bulk of the busy work was done by a Sheriff Substitute, similarly to modern American law clerks but with authority to rule over sessions in the judge's absence in undefended cases (the vast majority). Scott only "dealt personally" with 112, mostly minor, law suits over his 33 years in office. This left Scott with plenty of time for his literary hobby, while he lived in Edinburgh and Abbotsford, mailing in his written judgements based on case materials he received from the Substitute via the mail (Sutherland, *Life* 71-2). Scott served as the Principal Clerk of Session, administering the Supreme Courts of Scotland between 1806 and 1811, when David Hume, his old law school professor, took over the position. The Clerkship started paying £1,300 annually until the end of Scott's life in 1812, making his employment income £1,600 annually across his peak publishing years. Scott held this post in addition to his judgeship, upon a special petition to maintain both jobs simultaneously despite their geographical disagreements. Another immediate challenge Scott faced upon his appointment to the clerkship was the fall of the Tory government, and the triumph of the Whigs in that election, which meant he had to defend his job to the other side and the fact that he managed this signifies that he had to be very close to the middle for the Whigs not to have raised an objection to his appointment (109).

During a period when Scott attempted to "rest" after the success of *Marmion*, in 1809, he was in a small group that took over the patent of the Edinburgh Theater, paying out the previous owners, the Jackson family, while buying a share and becoming its trustee and legal representative. The Theater had early successes with Shakespearean productions, but Scott always had an ambition to bring new, innovative artistic masterpieces to its stage. He attempted to sell his own *The House of Aspen*, but failed to convince the other members of the board in the strength of his playwriting. Scott's search for a national Scottish theatrical masterpiece landed him on Joanna Baillie, a Scot that spent her youth in London and had stayed with the Scott's when the idea for the Theater took root with Scott. He might have solicited a tale about a Highland feud from her, thus bringing about the nationalist, *The Family Legend*, a precursor to Scott's own hyper-Scottish-nationalist Waverley novels, which also glorified the Highlands, clan leadership, and the dying Scottish culture. Despite Scott's promotion of this play to the chieftains of the clans and others that the play promoted, it only played for fourteen nights in January of 1810. Scott put in a great deal of effort into the promotion of the Theater after this point, but never really saw a return on his artistic or financial investments, as it gradually declined first under Henry Siddons and after his death in 1815 under his widow's management until 1830, when it finally failed (Sutherland, *Life* 132-4)…

I continue this biography in my book. The bulk of Scott's poetic publications occurred before this point, so I think this should suffice to explain his character and motivations.

TO A LOCK OF HAIR

    Thy hue, dear pledge, is pure and bright
    As in that well-remember'd night
    When first thy mystic braid was wove,
    And first my Agnes whisper'd love.

      Since then how often hast thou prest
    The torrid zone of this wild breast,

Whose wrath and hate have sworn to dwell
With the first sin that peopled hell;
A breast whose blood's a troubled ocean,
Each throb the earthquake's wild commotion!
O if such clime thou canst endure
Yet keep thy hue unstain'd and pure,
What conquest o'er each erring thought
Of that fierce realm had Agnes wrought!
I had not wander'd far and wide
With such an angel for my guide;
Nor heaven nor earth could then reprove me
If she had lived, and lived to love me.

Not then this world's wild joys had been
To me one savage hunting scene,
My sole delight the headlong race,
And frantic hurry of the chase;
To start, pursue, and bring to bay,
Rush in, drag down, and rend my prey,
Then—from the carcass turn away!
Mine ireful mood had sweetness tamed,
And soothed each wound which pride inflamed:—
Yes, God and man might now approve me
If thou hadst lived, and lived to love me!

THE OUTLAW

O Brignall banks are wild and fair,
 And Greta woods are green,
And you may gather garlands there
 Would grace a summer-queen.
And as I rode by Dalton-Hall
 Beneath the turrets high,
A Maiden on the castle-wall
 Was singing merrily:
"O, Brignall banks are fresh and fair,

And Greta woods are green;
I'd rather rove with Edmund there
  Than reign our English queen."

"If, Maiden, thou wouldst wend with me,
  To leave both tower and town,
Thou first must guess what life lead we
  That dwell by dale and down.
And if thou canst that riddle read,
  As read full well you may,
Then to the greenwood shalt thou speed
  As blithe as Queen of May."
Yet sung she "Brignall banks are fair,
  And Greta woods are green;
I'd rather rove with Edmund there
  Than reign our English queen.

"I read you by your bugle-horn
  And by your palfrey good,
I read you for a ranger sworn
  To keep the King's greenwood."
"A Ranger, Lady, winds his horn,
  And 'tis at peep of light;
His blast is heard at merry morn,
  And mine at dead of night."
Yet sung she, "Brignall banks are fair,
  And Greta woods are gay;
I would I were with Edmund there
  To reign his Queen of May!

"With burnish'd brand and musketoon
  So gallantly you come,
I read you for a bold Dragoon,
  That lists the tuck of drum."
"I list no more the tuck of drum,
  No more the trumpet hear;
But when the beetle sounds his hum
  My comrades take the spear.
And O! though Brignall banks be fair,

And Greta woods be gay,
Yet mickle must the maiden dare,
   Would reign my Queen of May!

"Maiden! a nameless life I lead,
   A nameless death I'll die;
The fiend whose lantern lights the mead
   Were better mate than I!
And when I'm with my comrades met
   Beneath the greenwood bough,
What once we were we all forget,
   Nor think what we are now.

   Chorus.

Yet Brignall banks are fresh and fair,
   And Greta woods are green,
And you may gather flowers there
   Would grace a summer-queen.

SCOTLAND.
FROM "THE LAY OF THE LAST MINSTREL", CANTO VI

O Caledonia! stern and wild,
Meet nurse for a poetic child!
Land of brown heath and shaggy wood,
Land of the mountain and the flood,
Land of my sires! what mortal hand
Can e'er untie the filial band
That knits me to thy rugged strand?
Still, as I view each well-known scene,
Think what is now, and what hath been,
Seems, as to me, of all bereft,
Sole friends thy woods and streams were left;
And thus I love them better still,

Even in extremity of ill.
By Yarrow's stream still let me stray,
Though none should guide my feeble way;
Still feel the breeze down Ettrick break,
Although it chilled my withered cheek;
Still lay my head by Teviot stone,
Though there, forgotten and alone,
The bard may draw his parting groan.

BEAL' AN DHUINE
(1411)
FROM "THE LADY OF THE LAKE", CANTO VI

There is no breeze upon the fern,
  No ripple on the lake,
Upon her eyrie nods the erne,
  The deer has sought the brake;
The small birds will not sing aloud,
  The springing trout lies still,
So darkly glooms yon thunder-cloud,
That swathes, as with a purple shroud,
  Benledi's distant hill.
Is it the thunder's solemn sound
  That mutters deep and dread,
Or echoes from the groaning ground
  The warrior's measured tread?
Is it the lightning's quivering glance
  That on the thicket streams,
Or do they flash on spear and lance
  The sun's retiring beams?
I see the dagger crest of Mar,
  I see the Moray's silver star
Wave o'er the cloud of Saxon war,
  That up the lake comes winding far!
To hero bound for battle strife,
  Or bard of martial lay,

'Twere worth ten years of peaceful life,
  One glance at their array!
Their light-armed archers far and near
  Surveyed the tangled ground,
Their centre ranks, with pike and spear,
  A twilight forest frowned,
Their barbèd horsemen, in the rear,
  The stern battalia crowned.
No cymbal clashed, no clarion rang,
  Still were the pipe and drum;
Save heavy tread, and armor's clang,
  The sullen march was dumb.
There breathed no wind their crests to shake,
  Or wave their flags abroad;
Scarce the frail aspen seemed to quake,
  That shadowed o'er their road.
Their vaward scouts no tidings bring,
  Can rouse no lurking foe,
Nor spy a trace of living thing,
  Save when they stirred the roe;
The host moves like a deep sea wave,
Where rise no rocks its pride to brave,
  High swelling, dark, and slow.
The lake is passed, and now they gain
A narrow and a broken plain,
Before the Trosach's rugged jaws;
And here the horse and spearmen pause,
While, to explore the dangerous glen,
Dive through the pass the archer men.
At once there rose so wild a yell
Within that dark and narrow dell.
As all the fiends, from heaven that fell,
Had pealed the banner cry of hell!
Forth from the pass in tumult driven,
Like chaff before the winds of heaven,
  The archery appear:
For life! for life! their flight they ply—
And shriek, and shout, and battle-cry,
And plaids and bonnets waving high,

And broadswords flashing to the sky,
  Are maddening in the rear.
Onward they drive, in dreadful race,
  Pursuers and pursued;
Before that tide of flight and chase,
How shall it keep its rooted place,
  The spearmen's twilight wood?
—"Down, down," cried Mar, "your lances down!
  Bear back both friend and foe!"
Like reeds before the tempest's frown,
That serried grove of lances brown
  At once lay levelled low;
And closely shouldering side to side,
The bristling ranks the onset bide.—
"We'll quell the savage mountaineer,
  As their Tinchel[9] cows the game;
They come as fleet as forest deer,
  We'll drive them back as tame."
Bearing before them, in their course,
The relics of the archer force,
Like wave with crest of sparkling foam,
Right onward did Clan-Alpine come.
Above the tide, each broadsword bright
Was brandishing like beam of light,
  Each targe was dark below;
And with the ocean's mighty swing,
When heaving to the tempest's wing,
  They hurled them on the foe.
I heard the lance's shivering crash,
As when the whirlwind rends the ash;
I heard the broadsword's deadly clang,
As if a hundred anvils rang!
But Moray wheeled his rearward flank—
Of horsemen on Clan-Alpine's flank—
  "My bannerman, advance!
I see," he cried, "their columns shake.
Now, gallants! for your ladies' sake,
  Upon them with the lance!"

---

9   A circle of sportsmen, surrounding the deer.

The horsemen dashed among the rout,
  As deer break through the broom;
Their steeds are stout, their swords are out,
  They soon make lightsome room.
Clan-Alpine's best are backward borne—
  Where, where was Roderick then?
One blast upon his bugle-horn
  Were worth a thousand men!
And refluent through the pass of fear
  The battle's tide was poured;
Vanished the Saxon's struggling spear,
  Vanished the mountain sword.
As Bracklinn's chasm, so black and steep,
  Receives her roaring linn,
As the dark caverns of the deep
  Suck the wild whirlpool in,
So did the deep and darksome pass
  Devour the battle's mingled mass;
None linger now upon the plain,
Save those who ne'er shall fight again.

TO A LOCK OF HAIR

Scott uses abbreviations and some Scottish words in his poetry to give them a Scottish, national character. As Mark Twain and other American writers insert contractions to signify the strong southern accent, Scott uses abbreviations, as in "well-remember'd" and "o'er" (over) to show a strong Scottish Highlands accent. Scott was a fan of Scottish tales and oral traditions and worked to distinguish the Scottish from the English character or identity. As in Shakespeare's couplets (but not in the rest of his sonnets), this poem has rhyming lines next to each other, stressing these repetitions. This poem expresses dire, sentimental longing for a deceased lover.

THE OUTLAW

Poetry is frequently centered on repetitions, but songs are more so. Thus, this is more of a song than a poem because of the number of identical, or nearly so, last two lines in two sets of stanzas (as if these are choruses). This poem is also deliberately difficult to comprehend because it's a riddle. Scott frequently uses subversive or convoluted language and structures to convey a rebellious message. In this case, there are some radical references to reigning as the English queen being inferior to being with a love interest in the Scottish countryside. The repetition of "English" cannot be accidental, as the United Kingdom was still new at this point, and England was only one of the kingdoms in this union (one of the others being Scotland). To understand the riddles and suggested meanings, you'd have to look up all of the allusions and uncommon words that appear throughout.

SCOTLAND: FROM "THE LAY OF THE LAST MINSTREL," CANTO VI.

The *Lay of the Last Minstrel* is a long narrative poem of Scott's, which was an early success before he started writing novels. This poem as a whole, and this section in particular are a nationalist message in support of the superiority of Scotland in contrast with its rivals. Instead of the usual nationalist propaganda, Scott stresses the problems Scotland has been facing and admits that one of the best things left to it is its "woods." The final lines proved to be prophetic, as Scott was traveling abroad and came back despite not feeling well to die in Scotland, as it was clearly calling to him to issue his "parting groan." This poem is a great example of the positive side of nationalist pride and promotion.

BEAL' AN DHUINE (1411): FROM "THE LADY OF THE LAKE," CANTO VI.

The *Lady of the Lake* was another famous narrative poem of Scott's. This is a better example of the structure of a narrative poem than the other works from Scott because you can see a story with a plotline being told by the narrator. The presence of a plot and progression of events distinguishes epic or other narrative poems from all other types of poetry, which is typically very brief, or a stanza or two long. In this work, the story is about a war march, love and war being the subject of much of narrative fiction. The tone in the description of the war is tragic, rather than congratulatory towards the victors, as was Shakespeare's "End of the Civil War."

Questions for Discussion

1. What does the consistent structure of Shakespeare's sonnets achieve? Why do you think Shakespeare used the same rhyme scheme and meter, with only a few deviations? How does this structure make you feel, or does it have a strong impact on you (as a popular song might with a repeating catchy chorus)?
2. Name the worst cliché comparison you've heard or read in love stories or poems that might be similar to those Shakespeare criticizes in "To His Love"?
3. In Shakespeare's time divorce was illegal. He abandoned his wife to start his acting and writing career. He had various young lovers (possibly of both genders). With this in mind, what do you think about Shakespeare's declaration that love does not alter with age?
4. Pick the most difficult and confusing line out of Scott's poems and look up in online dictionaries, encyclopedias or other sources what it means. Explain what you discovered in detail. Did this search help you to appreciate Scott's subversive or hidden radical messages?

Works Cited

"Shakespeare's Super Sonnets." *Independent*. London, England. 20 May 2009. p. 2. General OneFile: Gale. Web. 9 April 2017.

Sutherland, John. *The Life of Walter Scott*. Oxford: Blackwell Publishers Ltd., 1998.

Lord George Gordon, 6th Baron Byron

Lord Byron by Henry Pierce Bone, 1837

The following section of Lord Byron's biography is taken out of a chapter from my forthcoming book on author-publishers.

Lord Byron took his hereditary peer seat in the House of Lords immediately upon coming of age at twenty in 1808, taking over the seat Lord Carlisle, his guardian, was holding for him. Before taking this seat, Byron was asked to prove his legitimacy by producing his grandfather, the Admiral's, marriage certificate to his grandmother, a task that his solicitor charged him £158 for at a time when Byron was in debt and had to borrow money from his mother to settle this and other claims (Moore 100-1). As a result, when Byron arrived in the House of Lords, he was in a bad humor, and must have felt that the leadership of the House was hostile towards him or they would not have asked him to prove a matter of honor like his legitimacy, a topic that he had previously proved via less formal means. Thus, Byron was not well received in the House because he immediately took seats with the opposition, criticized his fellow politicians in his writing, and otherwise showed his distaste, so much so that after taking the seat and attending eight meetings, he went on an extensive trip abroad (Gilmour 174-6). Thus, Byron's passionate maiden speech in support of the Luddites was the first time in four years when he overcame his shyness to speak before the House. In his speech against making frame-breaking a capital offence, Byron argued on behalf of "these men, as I have seen them, meagre with famine, sullen with despair, careless of a life, - which your lordships are perhaps about to value at something less than the price of a stocking-frame…" (Hansard XXI, 964-72). Lord Byron explained his opposition to the strict handling of the rioters more directly in a letter to the man he was trying to convince on the other side of the debate, the leader of the Moderate Whigs, Lord Holland: "My own motive for opposing the bill is founded on its palpable injustice, and its certain inefficacy. I have seen the state of these miserable men, and it is a disgrace to civilized country. Their excesses may be condemned, but cannot be a subject of wonder. The effect of the present bill would be to drive them into actual rebellion… P.S.—I am a little apprehensive that your Lordship will think me too lenient towards these men, & *half a framebreaker myself*" (Prothero, 25 February 1812, ii, 103). Byron was faced with overwhelming opposition, and failed to protect the rioters, as twenty-seven of them were hanged (Gilmour 328). Still, this is a great example of just how the future King George IV might have heard Byron's direct pro-rebel sentiments, and then overseen Byron's financial success on the notoriety of this open attack. In general, if the King was given rights to his crown by God, then an attack on organized religion was also an attack on the source of a monarch's power. Byron must have gone beyond even these radical statements in his autobiography to some height of sedition that even John Murray could not tolerate, which prompted him to collaborate with associates in the burning of Byron's memoirs to protect his posthumous reputation.

Byron did not anticipate the cold shoulder he received from other Lords in response to his rhetoric. After a year of trying to make a difference with his House speeches, he became disgruntled and on March 26, 1813 he wrote to Augusta Leigh, "…my parliamentary schemes are not much to my taste—I spoke twice last Session - & was told it was well enough—but I hate the thing altogether - & have no intention to 'strut another hour' on that stage" (Byron, *Byron's Letters*, Vol. 3, 32). Then, on November 14, 1813 he wrote in his *Journal* that he "declined presenting the Debtor's Petition, being sick of parliamentary mummeries" (Byron, *Byron's Letters*, Vol. 3, 206). In the following year, his disgust intensified still further into a pro-anarchy position, and he wrote on January 16, 1814 in his *Journal* that he has "an utter detestation of all existing governments" (Byron, *Byron's Letters*, Vol. 3, 242). By 1821, he became a revolutionary, writing in his *Ravenna Journal* on January 13, "The king-times are fast finishing. There will be blood shed like water, and tears like mist; but the people will conquer in the end" (Byron, *Byron's Letters*, Vol. 8, 26). This track of thought led him to focus on a "liberated" and "free Italy!!!" in particular (Byron, *Byron's Letters*, Vol. 8, 47). Since he lived in Italy at the time, it was natural for him to fixate on this area in the last years of his life. He could not have made such revolutionary statements in the House, as they would have been sedition and punishable by death; so, the further he marched towards an anti-totalitarian position, the closer he came to openly joining the peoples' revolutions.

Byron came in direct contact with the future King, and then Prince Regent George IV in June of that same year when he made his first pro-rebel speech in the House of Lords, 1812. Byron was presented to the Prince Regent at a party at Carlton House by either Lady Caroline Lamb, or, more likely according to Doris Langley Moore, Lady Oxford. Byron had a volatile relationship with Lady Lamb after their passionate affair, including Byron's rejected proposal to one of her cousins, so much so that he wrote to James Wedderburn Webster from the Piccadilly Terrace on September 4, 1815 that "she is a villainous intriguante… mad & malignant—capable of all & every mischief… there is an indefatigable & active spirit of meanness & destruction about her… keep her from all that you value" (Byron, *Selected* 112). Lady Oxford, the Countess "was forty… but had retained her beauty and seductiveness" and had a "classical education" and Byron had a lengthy affair with her in 1812. "Lady Oxford was an intimate friend of Caroline of Brunswick, the Regent's discarded consort" (Moore 199). During their meeting at the party, "the Prince had been so agreeable and so pleasing in his conversation that Byron decided to pay his respects at Court." Byron ordered an uncharacteristically expensive "green coat" and other components of an outfit to match the latest fashions for £52, and for the first time had his hairdresser "powder his hair—still requisite for Court attendance." Just when Byron finished the strenuous and expensive task of getting in "full regalia," he received a notice that the levee was being put off till a later date. Instead of waiting to use this outfit at the next Court visitation, Byron realized how embarrassed he was that his liberal friends might discover that he was planning on paying homage at Court, and he never again attempted visiting the Prince Regent and later King George IV, and this slight must have contributed to the later tensions between George IV and Byron (Moore 195).

ALL FOR LOVE

O talk not to me of a name great in story;
The days of our youth are the days of our glory;
And the myrtle and ivy of sweet two-and-twenty
Are worth all your laurels, though ever so plenty.

What are garlands and crowns to the brow that is wrinkled?
'Tis but as a dead flower with May-dew besprinkled:
Then away with all such from the head that is hoary—
What care I for the wreaths that can only give glory?

O Fame!—if I e'er took delight in thy praises,
'Twas less for the sake of thy high-sounding phrases,
Than to see the bright eyes of the dear one discover
She thought that I was not unworthy to love her.

There chiefly I sought thee, there only I found thee;
Her glance was the best of the rays that surround thee;
When it sparkled o'er aught that was bright in my story,
I knew it was love, and I felt it was glory.

Considering Byron's background as a politician and radical writer, this is one of his lighter non-political love poems. It conveys a similar message to Shakespeare's poems about age and love, as well as the tension between love and war or ambitious political attainments. The lines have a song-like quality because they are exact rhymes and the rhyming lines are next to each other.

Oscar Wilde

Wilde and Alfred Douglas, 1893

Oscar Wilde was an Irish-born playwright, who gained popularity in London. His mother was an outspoken Irish nationalist. Most of Wilde's plays, such as *The Importance of Being Earnest*, were apolitical, displaying interpersonal, aristocratic and upper class struggles over power in love and upwards mobility. Aside from writing some essays about socialism, Wilde's most radical fictional work was *The Picture of Dorian Gray* (1890), which featured homosexual suggestions beyond the friendships the leading men in the story engage in. Around five years after this release, Wilde filed a case against Lord Alfred Douglas' father, to which he retaliated by launching an anti-obscenity case against Wilde for his "…involvement with the handsome young Lord Alfred Douglas, their association with various male prostitutes and blackmailers." Young, the writer of this essay, calls the father, "the mad Marquess of Queensbury," and explains that the Marquess was mad because his other son had potentially committed suicide after having a similar affair with the man who was a leading politician in the UK in this period. Wilde made an "ill-advised attempt to defend himself in the courts," claiming that he had not performed homosexual acts because there was no penetration. However, because it could be proven that other things happened between Wilde and these shady men, he received a "savage punishment by the British legal system" in the form of years of labor camp imprisonment, which permanently damaged his health (Young).

Given this background, the "Ave Imperatrix" poem takes on a radical shade. The title means "Hail Empress" in Latin. Rudyard Kipling published a poem with the same name, but with an exclamation mark after it, "Ave Imperatrix!" after an attempted assassination on

Queen Victoria in 1882, a year after Wilde's publication in 1881. But, Kipling's poem accuses the radical who attempted to kill the Empress of "madness" and expresses support for her cause. Wilde's poem has a more ambiguous message, to which Kipling might have been responding with his patriotic declaration. For example, Wilde questions: "England! What shall men say of thee," suggesting that they will not say any good things about the Empress (Queen). Wilde accuses England of having "bloody feet" from its attempt to control and subdue a "wide empire." He stresses that an empire is won with the death of youths and innocents across the world: "For every inch of ground a son?" He uses exact rhymes in every other line, but the musicality assists the political message instead of being the center of the work.

AVE IMPERATRIX

Set in this stormy Northern sea,
   Queen of these restless fields of tide,
England! what shall men say of thee,
   Before whose feet the worlds divide?
The earth, a brittle globe of glass,
   Lies in the hollow of thy hand,
And through its heart of crystal pass,
   Like shadows through a twilight land,
The spears of crimson-suited war,
   The long white-crested waves of fight,
And all the deadly fires which are
   The torches of the lords of Night.
The yellow leopards, strained and lean,
   The treacherous Russian knows so well,
With gaping blackened jaws are seen
   To leap through hail of screaming shell.
The strong sea-lion of England's wars
   Hath left his sapphire cave of sea,
To battle with the storm that mars
   The star of England's chivalry.
The brazen-throated clarion blows

Across the Pathan's reedy fen,
And the high steeps of Indian snows
  Shake to the tread of armèd men.
And many an Afghan chief, who lies
  Beneath his cool pomegranate-trees,
Clutches his sword in fierce surmise
  When on the mountain-side he sees
The fleet-foot Marri scout, who comes
  To tell how he hath heard afar
The measured roll of English drums
  Beat at the gates of Kandahar.
For southern wind and east wind meet
  Where, girt and crowned by sword and fire,
England with bare and bloody feet
  Climbs the steep road of wide empire.
O lonely Himalayan height,
  Gray pillar of the Indian sky,
Where saw'st thou last in clanging fight
  Our wingèd dogs of Victory?
The almond groves of Samarcand,
  Bokhara, where red lilies blow,
And Oxus, by whose yellow sand
  The grave white-turbaned merchants go;
And on from thence to Ispahan,
  The gilded garden of the sun,
Whence the long dusty caravan
  Brings cedar and vermilion;
And that dread city of Cabool
  Set at the mountain's scarpèd feet,
Whose marble tanks are ever full
  With water for the noonday heat,
Where through the narrow straight Bazaar
  A little maid Circasian
Is led, a present from the Czar
  Unto some old and bearded khan,—
Here have our wild war-eagles flown,
  And flapped wide wings in fiery flight;
But the sad dove, that sits alone
  In England—she hath no delight.

In vain the laughing girl will lean
  To greet her love with love-lit eyes:
Down in some treacherous black ravine,
  Clutching his flag, the dead boy lies.
And many a moon and sun will see
  The lingering wistful children wait
To climb upon their father's knee;
  And in each house made desolate
Pale women who have lost their lord
  Will kiss the relics of the slain—
Some tarnished epaulette—some sword—
  Poor toys to soothe such anguished pain.
For not in quiet English fields
  Are these, our brothers, lain to rest,
Where we might deck their broken shields
  With all the flowers the dead love best.
For some are by the Delhi walls,
  And many in the Afghan land,
And many where the Ganges falls
  Through seven mouths of shifting sand.
And some in Russian waters lie,
  And others in the seas which are
The portals to the East, or by
  The wind-swept heights of Trafalgar.
O wandering graves! O restless sleep!
  O silence of the sunless day!
O still ravine! O stormy deep!
  Give up your prey! Give up your prey!
And those whose wounds are never healed,
  Whose weary race is never won,
O Cromwell's England! must thou yield
  For every inch of ground a son?
Go! crown with thorns thy gold-crowned head,
  Change thy glad song to song of pain;
Wind and wild wave have got thy dead,
  And will not yield them back again.
Wave and wild wind and foreign shore
  Possess the flower of English land—
Lips that thy lips shall kiss no more,

Hands that shall never clasp thy hand.
What profit now that we have bound
  The whole round world with nets of gold,
If hidden in our heart is found
  The care that groweth never old?
What profit that our galleys ride,
  Pine-forest like, on every main?
Ruin and wreck are at our side,
  Grim warders of the House of pain.
Where are the brave, the strong, the fleet?
  Where is our English chivalry?
Wild grasses are their burial-sheet,
  And sobbing waves their threnody.
O loved ones lying far away,
  What word of love can dead lips send?
O wasted dust! O senseless clay!
  Is this the end? is this the end?
Peace, peace! we wrong the noble dead
  To vex their solemn slumber so;
Though, childless, and with thorn-crowned head,
  Up the steep road must England go,
Yet when this fiery web is spun,
  Her watchmen shall descry from far
The young Republic like a sun
  Rise from these crimson seas of war.

Elizabeth Barrett Browning

Elizabeth Barrett and Robert Browning by Thomas B. Read, 1853

This poem stands out because of the length of the lines, which are nearly twice as long as those of the other poems we are studying. The long lines allow for a more flowing narrative style that relates a full story, instead of chopping lines short to fit with a rhyme. There are exact rhymes on neighboring lines but because there are so many words between them, they are not too forced. This poem's message is puzzling, as a beautifully dressed woman goes up to random soldiers in a hospital and weeps for them. Dorothy Mermin's explanation helps to put it in perspective:

> "A Court Lady" refers to the fashion among patriotic Milanese ladies of visiting military hospitals in formal dress and open carriages… This is a commentary both on the proper behavior of great ladies and on the romantic aura that Florence Nightingale's almost mythic popularity had given to the idea of women as nurses, especially for soldiers. Barrett Browning's experience of the sickroom and her exalted notion of women's proper work immunized her against the Nightingale glamor—it was only, she thought, a reaffirmation of the old assumption that woman's highest function is

to bind men's wounds… (Mermin 232).

In other words, Browning is criticizing the pointlessness of such beatific weeping or caring for the wounded soldiers. She might have championed a female doctor practicing medicine, but she thought that sentimental care without intellectual engagement was demeaning for women.

A COURT LADY

Her hair was tawny with gold, her eyes with purple were dark,
Her cheeks' pale opal burnt with a red and restless spark.

Never was lady of Milan nobler in name and in race;
Never was lady of Italy fairer to see in the face.

Never was lady on earth more true as woman and wife,
Larger in judgment and instinct, prouder in manners and life.

She stood in the early morning, and said to her maidens, "Bring
That silken robe made ready to wear at the court of the king.

"Bring me the clasps of diamonds, lucid, clear of the mote,
Clasp me the large at the waist, and clasp me the small at the throat.

"Diamonds to fasten the hair, and diamonds to fasten the sleeves,
Laces to drop from their rays, like a powder of snow from the eaves."

Gorgeous she entered the sunlight which gathered her up in a flame,
While straight, in her open carriage, she to the hospital came.

In she went at the door, and gazing, from end to end,
"Many and low are the pallets, but each is the place of a friend."

Up she passed through the wards, and stood at a young man's bed:
Bloody the band on his brow, and livid the droop of his head.

"Art thou a Lombard, my brother? Happy art thou!" she cried,
And smiled like Italy on him: he dreamed in her face and died.
Pale with his passing soul, she went on still to a second:
He was a grave, hard man, whose years by dungeons were reckoned.

Wounds in his body were sore, wounds in his life were sorer.
"Art thou a Romagnole?" Her eyes drove lightnings before her.

"Austrian and priest had joined to double and tighten the cord
Able to bind thee, O strong one,—free by the stroke of a sword.

"Now be grave for the rest of us, using the life overcast
To ripen our wine of the present (too new) in glooms of the past."

Down she stepped to a pallet where lay a face like a girl's,
Young, pathetic with dying,—a deep black hole in the curls.

"Art thou from Tuscany, brother? and seest thou, dreaming in pain,
Thy mother stand in the piazza, searching the list of the slain?"

Kind as a mother herself, she touched his cheeks with her hands:
"Blessèd is she who has borne thee, although she should weep as she
            stands."

On she passed to a Frenchman, his arm carried off by a ball:
Kneeling,… "O more than my brother! how shall I thank thee for all?

"Each of the heroes round us has fought for his land and line,
But *thou* hast fought for a stranger, in hate of a wrong not thine.

"Happy are all free peoples, too strong to be dispossessed;
But blessèd are those among nations who dare to be strong for the
rest!"

Ever she passed on her way, and came to a couch where pined
One with a face from Venetia, white with a hope out of mind.

Long she stood and gazed, and twice she tried at the name,

But two great crystal tears were all that faltered and came.

Only a tear for Venice?—she turned as in passion and loss,
And stooped to his forehead and kissed it, as if she were kissing the cross.

Faint with that strain of heart, she moved on then to another,
Stern and strong in his death. "And dost thou suffer, my brother?"

Holding his hands in hers—"Out of the Piedmont lion
Cometh the sweetness of freedom! sweetest to live or to die on."

Holding his cold, rough hands—"Well, O, well have ye done
In noble, noble Piedmont, who would not be noble alone."

Back he fell while she spoke. She rose to her feet with a spring—
"That was a Piedmontese! and this is the Court of the King."

Robert Browning

Richard S. Kennedy and Donald S. Hair's *The Dramatic Imagination of Robert Browning* offers great explanations of this poem and other monodramas that Browning composed. They object to earlier critics that labeled Browning's poems as "**dramatic monologues**" because the single focus of these poems is not always a **solitary character**, but can also be the "story that is told, or the presence of a listener," thus making the term "**monodrama**" more fitting. The "mono" prefix means "one," and Browning does not simply employ speeches by a single character, but occasionally focuses on a single event or audience (these making the three main elements of any **drama**) (87). This particular poem, originally called, "Camp (French)," (1842) is used here as an example of a "***Dramatic Narrative***," or "*Dramatic Romance.*" The story related is of a messenger boy riding up with bad news to Napoleon, only to be brutally shot on his journey. This narrative is enhanced by the voice of the **narrator**, who glorifies and honors the boy's sacrifice, thus making the "narrative" portion of this work its primary element (88-9). This narrator stresses his presence by inserting a "we" in the opening line. There are two main characters the narrator describes, Napoleon and the boy, but it's the sympathy for the self-declared "dead" youth coming from the speaker that gives the narrative emotional power.

Browning's poetry has dramatic elements because this was a genre that he also dabbled in, writing several plays. Browning dedicated the bulk of his life to writing, rather than following a practical profession like his father, who became a clerk at the Bank of England. He only moved away from his family's home to secretly marry Elizabeth Barrett (Browning) in his thirties, in 1846. He moved with her to Florence, Italy. After her death in 1861, he kept writing in London.

INCIDENT OF THE FRENCH CAMP

You know we French stormed Ratisbon:
  A mile or so away,
On a little mound, Napoleon
  Stood on our storming-day;
With neck out-thrust, you fancy how,
  Legs wide, arms locked behind,
As if to balance the prone brow,
  Oppressive with its mind.

Just as perhaps he mused, "My plans
  That soar, to earth may fall,
Let once my army-leader Lannes
  Waver at yonder wall,"
Out 'twixt the battery-smokes there flew
  A rider, bound on bound
Full-galloping; nor bridle drew
  Until he reached the mound.

Then off there flung in smiling joy,
  And held himself erect
By just his horse's mane, a boy:
  You hardly could suspect
(So tight he kept his lips compressed,
  Scarce any blood came through),
You looked twice ere you saw his breast
  Was all but shot in two.

"Well," cried he, "Emperor, by God's grace
  We've got you Ratisbon!
The marshal's in the market-place,
  And you'll be there anon
To see your flag-bird flap his vans
  Where I, to heart's desire,
Perched him!" The chief's eye flashed; his plans

Soared up again like fire.

The chief's eye flashed; but presently
  Softened itself, as sheathes
A film the mother-eagle's eye
  When her bruised eaglet breathes:
"You're wounded!" "Nay," his soldier's pride
  Touched to the quick, he said:
"I'm killed, sire!" And, his chief beside,
  Smiling, the boy fell dead.

Rudyard Kipling

Rudyard Kipling by John Collier, 1891

Rudyard Kipling was born in Bombay, India in 1865. His father was a London artist, who moved to India. This poem was published in 1892 in the *Scots Observer*, a year after Kipling became famous for the publication of his short stories in top magazines as well as his novels. Kipling started his writing career as a reporter. His best-known novels are *The Jungle Book* (1894) and *Kim* (1901). These books describe minority cultures in a way that can be exploratory or racist, depending on your perspective.

Harry Ricketts described this poem, in *Rudyard Kipling: A Life*, as an example of Kipling's "**soldier ballads**" (187), also known as the "**Barrack-Room Ballads**" (162). This striking poem depicts "a regimental hanging," and might have been meant to be "set to music" (163). The "Barrack" in the above classifications helps to explain the strange reference to "young recruits" wanting "their beer to-day,/ After hangin' Danny Deever…" (202). This poem was meant to be sung by soldiers as a ballad during heavy drinking in their off-hours. The whiteness and other characteristic flaws that Files-on-Parade notices might be the results of earlier drunkenness, as there are several other references to beer throughout. Thus, this is one of the less serious poems about war, while simultaneously depicting a pretty graphic hanging. I mentioned the relationship between poetry and songs before, and this is an example of long lines with many repetitions that are characteristic of the loose songs meant for casual drinking occasions. While bar-singing is uncommon in the West today, it was a very common bonding element to drinking across the prior centuries. Just like pop music today, a writer like Kipling could gain popularity by writing ballad poetry for such occasions.

DANNY DEEVER

"What are the bugles blowin' for?" said Files-on-Parade.
"To turn you out, to turn you out," the Color-Sergeant said.
"What makes you look so white, so white?" said Files-on-Parade.
"I'm dreadin' what I've got to watch," the Color-Sergeant said.
For they're hangin' Danny Deever, you can hear the Dead March play,
    The regiment's in 'ollow square—they're hangin' him to-day;
    They've taken of his buttons off an' cut his stripes away,
    An' they're hangin' Danny Deever in the mornin'.
"What makes the rear-rank breathe so 'ard?" said Files-on-Parade.
"It's bitter cold, it's bitter cold," the Color-Sergeant said.
"What makes that front-rank man fall down?" says Files-on-Parade.
"A touch o' sun, a touch o' sun," the Color-Sergeant said.
    They are hangin' Danny Deever, they are marchin' of 'im round,
    They 'ave 'alted Danny Deever by 'is coffin on the ground;
    An' 'e'll swing in 'arf a minute for a sneakin' shootin' hound—
    O they're hangin' Danny Deever in the mornin'!
"Is cot was right—'and cot to mine," said Files-on-Parade.
"'E's sleepin' out an' far to-night," the Color-Sergeant said.
"I've drunk 'is beer a score o' times," said Files-on-Parade.
"'E's drinkin' bitter beer alone," the Color-Sergeant said.
    They are hangin' Danny Deever, you must mark 'im to 'is place,
    For 'e shot a comrade sleepin'—you must look 'im in the face;
    Nine 'undred of 'is county an' the regiment's disgrace,
    While they're hangin' Danny Deever in the mornin'.
"What's that so black agin the sun?" said Files-on-Parade.

"It's Danny fightin' 'ard for life," the Color-Sergeant said.
"What's that that whimpers over'ead?" said Files-on-Parade.
"It's Danny's soul that's passin' now," the Color-Sergeant said.
For they're done with Danny Deever, you can 'ear the quickstep play,
   The regiment's in column, an' they're marchin' us away;
   Ho! the young recruits are shakin', an' they'll want their beer to-day,
   After hangin' Danny Deever in the mornin'.

Questions for Discussion

1. What do you think about Wilde's radical poem against the wars that England has fought to maintain its Empire? Do you think this and other radical writings were the cause of the trial against him rather than simply a conspiracy against homosexuals to keep a top politician's own affair with Alfred's brother secret? Do you see evidence in this poem that Wilde is arguing against the Empire? Is it treasonous for a citizen to argue against a war for world dominance by the Empire he or she lives in?
2. What do you think about Dorothy Mermin's interpretation of Browning's "A Court Lady"? Give an example from the poem with a tone or vocabulary that is criticizing what this court lady is doing.
3. Re-read the description of Napoleon in the opening lines of "Incident of the French Camp." What does this description suggest about the narrator's feelings or perception of Napoleon in contrast with the young boy who's shot in two? Give examples.
4. Study "Danny Deever" closely. What does "beer" have to do with the hanging of Danny Deever? Why are the two intertwined here?
5. List three brief possible ideas for the Research Paper.

Works Cited

Fisher, Trevor. "The Mysteries of Oscar Wilde." *History Today*, vol. 50, no. 12, 2000, p. 18. *General OneFile*. Web. 10 April 2017.

Kennedy, Richard S. and Donald S. Hair. *The Dramatic Imagination of Robert Browning: A Literary Life*. Columbia: University of Missouri Press, 2007.

Mermin, Dorothy. *Elizabeth Barrett Browning: The Origins of a New Poetry*. Chicago: University of Chicago Press, 1989.

Ricketts, Harry. *Rudyard Kipling: A Life*. New York: Basic Books, 2001.

Young, Ian. "Who framed Oscar Wilde?" The Gay & Lesbian Review, vol. 7, no. 3, 2000, p. 24. *General OneFile*. Web. 10 April 2017.

Edgar Allan Poe

Poe was born in 1809, and was twenty-six when he married his cousin, Virginia, who was only thirteen. She developed consumption six years into the marriage and died in 1847. He failed to court a new wife, and died under mysterious circumstances that might have been an election-fraud-related homicide, or a suicide by consuming too much alcohol or drugs and exposure to the elements. Here is a portion of my biographical sketch on Poe from the author-publisher book I am developing.

Poe's first editorial job started in August of 1835 part-time for the *Southern Literary Messenger*, a periodical run by Thomas Willis White in Richmond. It became full-time in November of that year. While Poe was the *de facto* editor-in-chief, the December 1835 issue introduced him with, "the paper is now under the conduct of the Proprietor, assisted by a gentleman of distinguished literary talents…" This notice sounds like it was written by Poe himself, as the note adds, "we hope to be pardoned for singling out the name of M. EDGAR A. POE," flattering him as possessing "imagination, and… humorous, delicate satire." Then it explains that "decorum" forbids them from "specifying other names," with the hope that "'by their fruits ye shall know them" (White, "Publisher's Notice" 1). If Poe was writing the bulk of the articles in this paper, there were no "other names" he could have named but his own, and if this note is written in a satirical light, then he expresses a hope that readers will recognize the extent of his contributions. Thus, Poe did not merely proofread this periodical, but also composed the bulk of it at this early stage of his career. From this point of view, it is a lot easier to see why Poe was so frustrated with the proprietors of these magazines that paid him a tiny portion of the profits while he was doing the bulk of the work, and had to disguise his authorship behind unsigned articles. "Having started out as a printer," White "had no training in writing, editing, or marketing and advertising" needed to have penned the content himself (Hutchisson 47). Poe left this periodical at the end of 1836, and ran a retirement notice in the January 1837 issue. The January 1838, Vol. IV, No. 1 issue of

Southern has an introduction called, "The New Year," which while it is verbose, fails to catch the reader's attention and to paint concrete pictures as the one that Poe wrote or edited does. The prose in 1838 is less dense and includes many repetitions, wherein the author cycles around a point without clearly articulating it. Here is an example from the middle of the second paragraph: "Some useful and elegant talent has been called into exercise, nay, it may be said, has been created; since such is the power of exercise over the faculties, that to afford an attractive field for their exertion is in a great degree to create them" (White, "The New Year" 1). What is this sentence trying to communicate? Why would exertion "create" "talent"? Something is missing from this sentence, and yet something also needs to be deleted. If an editor does so much editing that the linguistic density of a work changes, he might as well have written it. Poe explained his perception towards White and his employment for *Southern* in a letter from Philadelphia, addressed to his cousin William Poe on August 14, 1840: "…The drudgery was excessive; the salary was contemptible… my best energies were wasted in the service of an illiterate and vulgar, although well-meaning man, who had neither the capacity to appreciate my labors, nor the will to reward them." Poe began this paragraph by saying that he is attaching the "Prospectus of my contemplated Magazine" (Poe, *Completed* 55). The Magazine Poe is soliciting money for from his cousin is *The Penn*. Poe's insistence that White was "illiterate" should be taken at face-value, as Poe seldom exaggerated in his reviews.

ANNABEL LEE

> It was many and many a year ago,
> In a kingdom by the sea,
> That a maiden lived, whom you may know
> By the name of Annabel Lee;
> And this maiden she lived with no other thought
> Than to love, and be loved by me.
> I was a child and she was a child,
> In this kingdom by the sea;
> But we loved with a love that was more than love,

I and my Annabel Lee,—
With a love that the winged seraphs of heaven
Coveted her and me.
And this was the reason that long ago,
In this kingdom by the sea,
A wind blew out of a cloud, chilling
My beautiful Annabel Lee;
So that her high-born kinsmen came,
And bore her away from me,
To shut her up in a sepulchre,
In this kingdom by the sea.
The angels, not so happy in heaven,
Went envying her and me.
Yes! that was the reason (as all men know)
In this kingdom by the sea,
That the wind came out of the cloud by night,
Chilling and killing my Annabel Lee.
But our love it was stronger by far than the love
Of those who were older than we,
Of many far wiser than we;
And neither the angels in heaven above,
Nor the demons down under the sea,
Can ever dissever my soul from the soul
Of the beautiful Annabel Lee.
For the moon never beams without bringing me dreams
Of the beautiful Annabel Lee,
And the stars never rise but I feel the bright eyes
Of the beautiful Annabel Lee.
And so, all the night-tide I lie down by the side
Of my darling, my darling, my life, and my bride,
In her sepulchre there by the sea,
In her tomb by the sounding sea.

This poem starts like a romance novel with an idyllic love between two youths. Then, it turns into a tragedy of two star-crossed lovers, as a simple chilly wind strikes down Annabel Lee and puts her into a "sepulcher," or "a place of burial" (*Merriam-Webster*). Meanwhile, the style of the poem is melodic and repetitive, lulling the reader into seeing it like a fantastic dream. When the narrator is left alone, he feels that he has been wronged by the angels that were jealous of their youthful love. The ending suggests that the lover misses her so much that he is suicidal and lies down next to her in the tomb, or is considering drowning in the sea. This poem was written shortly before and published shortly after Poe's death in 1849.

Walt Whitman

This is the most random, digressive and rambling poem we are reading. This poem was published in 1856 as "Liberty Poem for Asia, Africa, Europe, America, Australia, Cuba, and The Archipelagoes of the Sea" in the second edition of *Leaves of Grass*. In the *Critical Companion to Walt Whitman*, Charles M. Oliver summarizes this poem as "a plea to rebels throughout the world to fight for liberty" with revolutionary or violent means (216). The title of the well-known poetry collection in which this work appears suggests natural imagery and a transcendental style. Instead, this is a very politicized cry for armed resistance in the face of tyranny. Oliver writes in the introduction on Whitman that this collection set a precedent and inspired the ongoing free verse movement, which expresses a meaning without worrying about the strict rules of poetic meter and rhyme that dominated poetry prior to this turn (3). If this move was an evolution or a devolution is up to a reader's perspective, but whenever a writer causes a major shift in literary tastes, he or she becomes required reading for students of literary history.

TO A FOILED REVOLTER OR REVOLTRESS

1.

Courage! my brother or my sister!
Keep on! Liberty is to be subserved, whatever occurs;
That is nothing that is quelled by one or two failures, or any number of
  failures,
Or by the indifference or ingratitude of the people, or by any
  unfaithfulness,
Or the show of the tushes of power, soldiers, cannon, penal statutes.

2.

What we believe in waits latent for ever through all the continents,
and all the islands and archipelagoes of the sea.
What we believe in invites no one, promises nothing, sits in calmness
and light, is positive and composed, knows no discouragement,
Waiting patiently, waiting its time.

3.

The battle rages with many a loud alarm, and frequent advance and
retreat,
The infidel triumphs—or supposes he triumphs,
The prison, scaffold, garrote, handcuffs, iron necklace and anklet,
lead-balls, do their work,
The named and unnamed heroes pass to other spheres,
The great speakers and writers are exiled—they lie sick in distant
lands,
The cause is asleep—the strongest throats are still, choked
with their own blood,
The young men drop their eyelashes toward the ground when they
meet;
But, for all this, Liberty has not gone out of the place, nor the infidel
 entered into possession.
When Liberty goes out of a place, it is not the first to go, nor the
second
 or third to go,
It waits for all the rest to go—it is the last.
When there are no more memories of heroes and martyrs,
And when all life and all the souls of men and women are discharged
from
 any part of the earth,
Then only shall Liberty be discharged from that part of the earth,
And the infidel and the tyrant come into possession.

4.

Then courage! revolter! revoltress!
For till all ceases neither must you cease.

5.

I do not know what you are for, (I do not know what I am for myself, nor
    what anything is for,)
But I will search carefully for it even in being foiled,
In defeat, poverty, imprisonment—for they too are great.
Did we think victory great?
So it is—But now it seems to me, when it cannot be helped, that defeat is
    great,
And that death and dismay are great.

Henry W. Longfellow

There are five lines in the first stanza that begin with the word "with" until the last of these is, "With their frequent repetitions," obviously stressing the repetition of these with's. All but one of the lines in this stanza also ends with the letter "s." But the only rhyme in these lines is between three "-tions" endings: traditions, repetitions and reverberations. Thus, this is an example of a poem that breaks from nineteenth century and earlier western poetic traditions and proposes other types of musical repetitions and patterns in their place. In between the first-person narration, Hiawatha sings a song about this beautiful countryside. The poem is written in trochaic tetrameter, and it creates a strong sing-songy rhythm. The native words Longfellow uses are from the Dakota Sioux Ojibwe legends, and have English translations that reflect different natural objects, places and the like. Longfellow does not fully understand the oral tradition he is mimicking, so this poem can be slightly insulting to Native Americans who do not want to see their heritage imitated without proper respect for the finer elements of their culture. One hint that Longfellow might not be sympathetic is when he calls them "savage" (211). After the introduction, the story becomes a song of "peace," as the Master of Life delivers a call for the tribes to bury their "clubs" and to unite.

THE SONG OF HIAWATHA

Introduction

Should you ask me, whence these stories?
Whence these legends and traditions,
With the odors of the forest
With the dew and damp of meadows,

With the curling smoke of wigwams,
With the rushing of great rivers,
With their frequent repetitions,
And their wild reverberations
As of thunder in the mountains?

I should answer, I should tell you,
"From the forests and the prairies,
From the great lakes of the Northland,
From the land of the Ojibways,
From the land of the Dacotahs,
From the mountains, moors, and fen-lands
Where the heron, the Shuh-shuh-gah,
Feeds among the reeds and rushes.
I repeat them as I heard them
From the lips of Nawadaha,
The musician, the sweet singer."

Should you ask where Nawadaha
Found these songs so wild and wayward,
Found these legends and traditions,
I should answer, I should tell you,
"In the birds'-nests of the forest,
In the lodges of the beaver,
In the hoofprint of the bison,
In the eyry of the eagle!

"All the wild-fowl sang them to him,
In the moorlands and the fen-lands,
In the melancholy marshes;
Chetowaik, the plover, sang them,
Mahng, the loon, the wild-goose, Wawa,
The blue heron, the Shuh-shuh-gah,
And the grouse, the Mushkodasa!"

If still further you should ask me,
Saying, "Who was Nawadaha?
Tell us of this Nawadaha,"
I should answer your inquiries

Straightway in such words as follow.

"In the vale of Tawasentha,
In the green and silent valley,
By the pleasant water-courses,
Dwelt the singer Nawadaha.
Round about the Indian village
Spread the meadows and the corn-fields,
And beyond them stood the forest,
Stood the groves of singing pine-trees,
Green in Summer, white in Winter,
Ever sighing, ever singing.

"And the pleasant water-courses,
You could trace them through the valley,
By the rushing in the Spring-time,
By the alders in the Summer,
By the white fog in the Autumn,
By the black line in the Winter;
And beside them dwelt the singer,
In the vale of Tawasentha,
In the green and silent valley.

"There he sang of Hiawatha,
Sang the Song of Hiawatha,
Sang his wondrous birth and being,
How he prayed and how he fasted,
How he lived, and toiled, and suffered,
That the tribes of men might prosper,
That he might advance his people!"

Ye who love the haunts of Nature,
Love the sunshine of the meadow,
Love the shadow of the forest,
Love the wind among the branches,
And the rain-shower and the snow-storm,
And the rushing of great rivers
Through their palisades of pine-trees,
And the thunder in the mountains,

Whose innumerable echoes
Flap like eagles in their eyries;—
Listen to these wild traditions,
To this Song of Hiawatha!

Ye who love a nation's legends,
Love the ballads of a people,
That like voices from afar off
Call to us to pause and listen,
Speak in tones so plain and childlike,
Scarcely can the ear distinguish
Whether they are sung or spoken;—
Listen to this Indian Legend,
To this Song of Hiawatha!

Ye whose hearts are fresh and simple,
Who have faith in God and Nature,
Who believe that in all ages
Every human heart is human,
That in even savage bosoms
There are longings, yearnings, strivings
For the good they comprehend not,
That the feeble hands and helpless,
Groping blindly in the darkness,
Touch God's right hand in that darkness
And are lifted up and strengthened;—
Listen to this simple story,
To this Song of Hiawatha!

Ye, who sometimes, in your rambles
Through the green lanes of the country,
Where the tangled barberry-bushes
Hang their tufts of crimson berries
Over stone walls gray with mosses,
Pause by some neglected graveyard,
For a while to muse, and ponder
On a half-effaced inscription,
Written with little skill of song-craft,
Homely phrases, but each letter

Full of hope and yet of heart-break,
Full of all the tender pathos
Of the Here and the Hereafter;
Stay and read this rude inscription,
Read this Song of Hiawatha!

I

The Peace-Pipe

On the Mountains of the Prairie,
On the great Red Pipe-stone Quarry,
Gitche Manito, the mighty,
He the Master of Life, descending,
On the red crags of the quarry
Stood erect, and called the nations,
Called the tribes of men together.

From his footprints flowed a river,
Leaped into the light of morning,
O'er the precipice plunging downward
Gleamed like Ishkoodah, the comet.
And the Spirit, stooping earthward,
With his finger on the meadow
Traced a winding pathway for it,
Saying to it, "Run in this way!"

From the red stone of the quarry
With his hand he broke a fragment,
Moulded it into a pipe-head,
Shaped and fashioned it with figures;
From the margin of the river
Took a long reed for a pipe-stem,
With its dark green leaves upon it;
Filled the pipe with bark of willow,
With the bark of the red willow;

Breathed upon the neighboring forest,
Made its great boughs chafe together,
Till in flame they burst and kindled;
And erect upon the mountains,
Gitche Manito, the mighty,
Smoked the calumet, the Peace-Pipe,
As a signal to the nations.

And the smoke rose slowly, slowly,
Through the tranquil air of morning,
First a single line of darkness,
Then a denser, bluer vapor,
Then a snow-white cloud unfolding,
Like the tree-tops of the forest,
Ever rising, rising, rising,
Till it touched the top of heaven,
Till it broke against the heaven,
And rolled outward all around it.

From the Vale of Tawasentha,
From the Valley of Wyoming,
From the groves of Tuscaloosa,
From the far-off Rocky Mountains,
From the Northern lakes and rivers
All the tribes beheld the signal,
Saw the distant smoke ascending,
The Pukwana of the Peace-Pipe.

And the Prophets of the nations
Said: "Behold it, the Pukwana!
By the signal of the Peace-Pipe,
Bending like a wand of willow,
Waving like a hand that beckons,
Gitche Manito, the mighty,
Calls the tribes of men together,
Calls the warriors to his council!"

Down the rivers, o'er the prairies,
Came the warriors of the nations,

Came the Delawares and Mohawks,
Came the Choctaws and Camanches,
Came the Shoshonies and Blackfeet,
Came the Pawnees and Omahas,

Came the Mandans and Dacotahs,
Came the Hurons and Ojibways,
All the warriors drawn together
By the signal of the Peace-Pipe,
To the Mountains of the Prairie,
To the great Red Pipe-stone Quarry,

And they stood there on the meadow,
With their weapons and their war-gear,
Painted like the leaves of Autumn,
Painted like the sky of morning,
Wildly glaring at each other;
In their faces stern defiance,
In their hearts the feuds of ages,
The hereditary hatred,
The ancestral thirst of vengeance.

Gitche Manito, the mighty,
The creator of the nations,
Looked upon them with compassion,
With paternal love and pity;
Looked upon their wrath and wrangling
But as quarrels among children,
But as feuds and fights of children!

Over them he stretched his right hand,
To subdue their stubborn natures,
To allay their thirst and fever,
By the shadow of his right hand;
Spake to them with voice majestic
As the sound of far-off waters,
Falling into deep abysses,
Warning, chiding, spake in this wise:

"O my children! my poor children!
Listen to the words of wisdom,
Listen to the words of warning,
From the lips of the Great Spirit,
From the Master of Life, who made you!

"I have given you lands to hunt in,
I have given you streams to fish in,
I have given you bear and bison,
I have given you roe and reindeer,
I have given you brant and beaver,
Filled the marshes full of wild-fowl,
Filled the rivers full of fishes:
Why then are you not contented?
Why then will you hunt each other?

"I am weary of your quarrels,
Weary of your wars and bloodshed,
Weary of your prayers for vengeance,
Of your wranglings and dissensions;
All your strength is in your union,
All your danger is in discord;
Therefore be at peace henceforward,
And as brothers live together.

"I will send a Prophet to you,
A Deliverer of the nations,
Who shall guide you and shall teach you,
Who shall toil and suffer with you.
If you listen to his counsels,
You will multiply and prosper;
If his warnings pass unheeded,
You will fade away and perish!

"Bathe now in the stream before you,
Wash the war-paint from your faces,
Wash the blood-stains from your fingers,
Bury your war-clubs and your weapons,
Break the red stone from this quarry,

Mould and make it into Peace-Pipes,
Take the reeds that grow beside you,
Deck them with your brightest feathers,
Smoke the calumet together,
And as brothers live henceforward!"

Then upon the ground the warriors
Threw their cloaks and shirts of deer-skin,
Threw their weapons and their war-gear,
Leaped into the rushing river,
Washed the war-paint from their faces.
Clear above them flowed the water,
Clear and limpid from the footprints
Of the Master of Life descending;
Dark below them flowed the water,
Soiled and stained with streaks of crimson,
As if blood were mingled with it!

From the river came the warriors,
Clean and washed from all their war-paint;
On the banks their clubs they buried,
Buried all their warlike weapons.
Gitche Manito, the mighty,
The Great Spirit, the creator,
Smiled upon his helpless children!

And in silence all the warriors
Broke the red stone of the quarry,
Smoothed and formed it into Peace-Pipes,
Broke the long reeds by the river,
Decked them with their brightest feathers,
And departed each one homeward,
While the Master of Life, ascending,
Through the opening of cloud-curtains,
Through the doorways of the heaven,
Vanished from before their faces,
In the smoke that rolled around him,
The Pukwana of the Peace-Pipe!

Questions for Discussion

1. Do you think Longfellow's poem is disrespectful towards the Sioux traditions, or do you think it glorifies Native American heritage in a positive way? Give examples, to support your position.
2. To which of the three categories of style (lofty, mean or base) do each of the poems in this section belong?
3. Davie talks about the break from categorizing the quality of poetry thusly: "This good poem is written in this way. Therefore all good poems must be written in this way." Do you agree that good poetry should follow traditional patterns of rhythm and rhyme? Did you like one of the poems in this section that demonstrates either a poem that follows traditional rules or breaks with them? Explain your choice.
4. After answering these questions, also participate in the Research Paper Revision Workshop.

Works Cited

Davie, Donald. *Purity of Diction in English Verse*. London: Chatto and Windus, 1952. *Archive.org*. Web. 17 April 2017.

Hutchisson, James M. *Poe*. Jackson: University Press of Mississippi, 2005.

Oliver, Charles M. *Critical Companion to Walt Whitman: A Literary Reference to His Life and Work*. New York: Infobase Publishing, 2005.

Poe, Edgar Allan. *The Complete Works of Edgar Allan Poe, Volume 17: Poe and His Friends: Letters Relating to Poe*. James Albert Harrison, Ed. New York: Thomas Y. Crowell & Company, 1902. Web.

White, Thomas Willis. "The New Year." *Southern Literary Messenger: Devoted to Every Department of Literature and the Fine Arts*. Vol. IV, No. 1. Richmond: January 1838. Making of America Journal Articles. Web.

White, Thomas Willis. "Publisher's Notice." *Southern Literary Messenger: Devoted to Every Department of Literature and the Fine Arts*. Vol. II, No. 1. Richmond: December 1835. T. W. White, 1836. Web.

Assignments

Comparison/Contrast Essay 1

Write a four-page essay that compares (shows similarities) or contrasts (shows differences) between two of the fictional short stories or novel segments that we will be reading in the first couple of months of the semester. I am assuming that your essay will be double-spaced, Times New Roman, 12pt font when I ask for it to be exactly four-pages long. It should not be shorter or longer so that everybody performs a similar amount of work, and so that you will have enough time to edit your work. You cannot write this essay about any works that are not in our Syllabus or that we will not be covering closely in this class. This rule is in place so that you will have some context on the stories you write about. Your grade will be based on the following components:

Critical comparisons or contrasts drawn that show connections you made between the two (20%)
Presence of two brief narratives that summarize the plotlines related in the two stories, preferably with a focus on the parts of the plots that show similarities or differences between them (10%)
Proper in-text citations, quotes and paraphrasing from the two primary sources (20%)
Presence of a central coherent argument (10%)
Clear writing style free of grammatical, spelling and other errors (30%)
Participation in the Editing Workshop (10%)

Revision Workshop

10% of your essays' grade will come from your active participation in Editing Workshops. The credit is not for improving your essay based on your fellow students' comments, but rather for helping your fellow students improve their work, and for sharing your essays with them in this workshop.

Attach your essay to a Discussion Reply in the Essay 1 Workshop Thread (which will not have the usual questions regarding the reading). Then download an essay another student has posted. You have to respond to at least one other student's papers. Who you respond to might depend on who posts early in the week, and who has not had any replies after posting late in the week. More than one student can respond to the same essay. Once you have your partner's Essay, closely read it. Point out any proofreading corrections you notice that are needed (you can turn on Track Changes for this and attach the proofread version of the essay to your reply). Also, point out any problems with Essay 1's requirements not being met. Does it compare or contrast two of the stories we read this semester? Does it include a coherent and clear argument? Does it offer evidence to support this argument in the form of quotes or paraphrases of the stories? Does it offer a unified argument without unrelated digressions? If you notice problems with any of these or other aspects of the essay, include these comments in your response to his or her posted essay. Once you receive comments on your work, closely read the comments from your partner, and make any necessary corrections to the essay. Feel free to respond to the comments, especially if you disagree with any of the corrections.

After you finish making the necessary corrections, submit Essay 1 by the date specified in the syllabus.

Close Reading of *Lysistrata* Essay 2

Write a four-page essay that executes a close reading of *Lysistrata*. You should focus the essay on one of the theatrical terms that we will be discussing in this section: symbolism, allegory, theme, form, allusion, myth, or staging. If you focus on symbolism or allusion, this should help you to narrow the topic and to form a single coherent argument. Avoid using online sources such as Wikipedia as you write this essay. Instead of finding surface summaries of what happens in the play, do your best to explain the hidden meanings in the details of the dialogues. You might also want to develop your answers to the questions I'm asking in this section into essays. For example, feminism and anti-war protest topics can lead an argument in many interesting directions. Your grade will be comprised of the following elements:

- Closely examine *Lysistrata*, showing your understanding of its deeper meanings (20%)
- Paraphrase the plotline of the play, focusing on the details that are relevant to your central argument (10%)
- Properly use in-text citations, quotes, and paraphrasing from the primary source (20%)
- Create a single, strong central argument (10%)
- Use a clear writing style, free of grammatical, spelling and other errors (30%)
- Participate in the Editing Workshop by posting your essay and offering proofreading/ editing advice to one of your fellow students (10%)

6-Page Research Paper Assignment

This 6-page Research Paper should employ one of the literary theories described in the "Types of Criticism" section of your reading. The three main theoretical branches we examined were: Feminist, Structuralist, and Political or Economic Criticism. If you are going to take a feminist perspective, you should examine a gender-related subject (femininity, masculinity, power between the sexes etc.) in one of the works we've read this semester. If you take the structuralist approach, you would examine the plot, character-types, or other elements or literary terms we've gone over. For the political or economic criticism, you would evaluate the message a work is communicating from these perspectives. Choose only a single poem, novel, short story or play so that you can narrow your subject. The "research" element means that you have to find at least 3 scholarly, secondary sources related to your subject or the work in question to help you evaluate it. You should find these sources through the UTRGV library system, rather than googling for them. This will help you avoid Wikipedia, reviews and various other untrustworthy sources. The essay should not be a set of unconnected ideas, but rather has to be a single coherent argument that employs a literary theory to convince the reader of your take on a given literary work. Don't replicate an earlier essay to avoid self-plagiarism, and so that you can develop a topic that is particularly fitting for a research paper rather than a contrast or close analysis paper. The Research Paper is 20% of your class grade.

Your grade for the Research Paper is composed of the following requirements:

> Form a strong, coherent argument about a single literary work (10%)
> Use one of the three discussed criticism types: feminism, structuralism, or political/ economic (10%)
> Paraphrase the plotline of the story, focusing on the details that are relevant to your central argument (10%)

Properly use in-text citations and quotes from the primary source and secondary sources (20%)

Works Cited page with 3 trustworthy, secondary sources (10%)

Use a clear writing style, free of grammatical, spelling and other errors (30%)

Participate in the Editing Workshop by posting your essay and offering proofreading/ editing advice to one of your fellow students (10%)

Research Paper Revision Workshop

10% of your Research Paper's grade will come from your active participation in this editing workshop. The credit is not for improving your essay based on your fellow students' comments, but rather for helping your fellow students improve their work, and for sharing your essays with them in this workshop. You have to respond to at least one other student's papers. Closely read the requirements for the Research Paper: give advice on how your fellow student's paper might not be fully meeting these requirements, and give general comments on how it might be improved. Follow the same rules as with the previous editing workshops.

OTHER ANAPHORA LITERARY PRESS TITLES

The History of British and American Author-Publishers
By: Anna Faktorovich

Notes for Further Research
By: Molly Kirschner

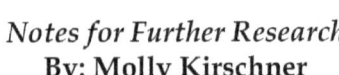

The Encyclopedic Philosophy of Michel Serres
By: Keith Moser

The Visit
By: Michael G. Casey

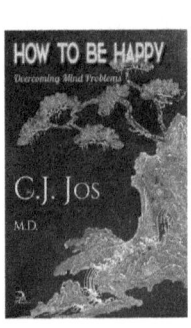

How to Be Happy
By: C. J. Jos

A Dying Breed
By: Scott Duff

Love in the Cretaceous
By: Howard W. Robertson

The Second of Seven
By: Jeremie Guy

www.ingramcontent.com/pod-product-compliance
Lightning Source LLC
Chambersburg PA
CBHW031135160426
43193CB00008B/144